FIFTH EDITION

1

GRAMMAR *in* CONTEXT

Teacher's Edition

The cover photo shows the Leonard P. Zakim Bunker Hill Bridge over the Charles River in Boston, Massachusetts.

HEINLE
CENGAGE Learning

Australia • Brazil • Japan • Korea • Mexico • Singapore • Spain • United Kingdom • United States

HEINLE
CENGAGE Learning™

Grammar in Context 1, Fifth Edition
Teacher's Edition

Publisher: Sherrise Roehr

Acquisitions Editor: Tom Jefferies

Development Editor: Sarah Sandoski

Associate Development Editor: Cécile Engeln

Director of Global Marketing: Ian Martin

Director of U.S. Marketing: Jim McDonough

Product Marketing Manager: Katie Kelley

Marketing Manager: Caitlin Driscoll

Content Project Manager: Andrea Bobotas

Senior Print Buyer: Susan Spencer

Contributing Writers: Sarah J. Brown and
    Hilary Grant

Project Manager: Chrystie Hopkins

Production Services: Nesbitt Graphics, Inc.

Interior Design: Nesbitt Graphics, Inc.

Cover Design: Muse Group, Inc.

Library of Congress Control Number: 2009936997

ISBN 13: 978-1-4240-7900-1

ISBN 10: 1-4240-7900-4

Heinle

20 Channel Center Street

Boston, Massachusetts 02210

USA

Cengage Learning is a leading provider of customized learning solutions with office locations around the globe, including Singapore, the United Kingdom, Australia, Mexico, Brazil, and Japan. Locate our local office at **international.cengage.com/region**

Cengage Learning products are represented in Canada by Nelson Education, Ltd.

Visit Heinle online at **elt.heinle.com**

Visit our corporate Web site at **www.cengage.com**

Printed in the United States of America.
1 2 3 4 5 6 7 8 9 10 — 13 12 11 10 09

Contents

Grammar in Context 1, Fifth Edition

Welcome to
Grammar in Context
TEACHER'S EDITION!

Grammar in Context, Fifth Edition, contains a rich variety of material, making it easy to customize to any program's needs. The new *Teacher's Edition* includes extra resources to make planning your syllabus and preparing lessons easier than ever before.

NEW! Pacing guides for every activity provide a timing framework useful for lesson planning.

NEW! Ten easy solutions for customizing *Grammar in Context, Fifth Edition*, to meet yours and your students' needs (see page v).

NEW! Presentation Ideas suggest alternative ways of presenting select grammar charts.

NEW! Practice Ideas include ways to adapt grammar exercises to target specific skills: reading, writing, listening, and speaking.

NEW! Online Lesson Planner saves you time by planning lessons online. This new tool provides instructors with complete, customizable lesson plans using the pacing guide from the *Teacher's Edition*. Go to elt.heinle.com/technology.

NEW! "Fast Track" option (highlighted by this icon: ⭐) identifies essential readings, charts, and exercises for courses that don't have the time to present and practice the full range of readings, grammar charts, and exercises available in *Grammar in Context, Fifth Edition*. Teaching these essential items gives students a basic understanding and practice of the most important grammar in each unit. Additional material can be used in the following ways:

- Struggling students can understand core grammar by doing extra practice exercises.

- Stronger students can be challenged by studying additional grammar charts and Expansion activities.

- Additional exercises may be used for students who have completed the in-class assignments ahead of other students.

Ten Tips for
Customizing *Grammar in Context, Fifth Edition*, to fit your program:

1. Work within your curriculum.

Let your curriculum guide you on what to cover from this rich, comprehensive series. For example, in book 3, if your program doesn't expect students to learn about *nonrestrictive clauses* at this level, a teacher could skip the chart about *nonrestrictive clauses*. It may be enough to teach *contrary-of-fact clauses* in the present without getting into the past or mixed tenses. The Online Lesson Planner allows you to move, edit, and add to lessons to meet your program needs. These lesson plans can be done by individual teachers or shared across the program.

2. Do the Test/Review section at the start of each lesson.

One way to find out how much practice your students need is to give them the Test/Review section at the beginning of the lesson. If you find that most of your students can do this with relatively few errors, then you can skip the lesson altogether or focus only on the sticking points.

3. Assign the readings as homework.

All the readings are important in introducing the grammar in context and should not be skipped. To save class time, however, the readings can be done at home. The reading level is low enough that classroom instruction on how to read should not be necessary. The reading is not meant to challenge and improve one's reading skills; it is meant to illustrate the grammar in a stimulating context. In class, the teacher can ask questions about the reading or the vocabulary within to ensure that students read and understood the assignment. There can be a short discussion on the Before You Read questions, too, if time permits.

4. Set time limits for each fill-in-the blank exercise.

Set a maximum time limit for each exercise. Suggested times are given in the *Teacher's Edition*. Once the time limit has expired, ask students to put down their pens and move on to the next exercise. Students can complete the rest of the exercise at home.

5. Assign audio-based exercises for lab time.

Many exercises contain audio tracks (indicated with a listening icon ◀))). These exercises can take time to set up and run, so you may wish to assign these for lab credits or homework. You may also decide to only do one of these per class to add variety.

6. Use one of the "About You" exercises per class.

These exercises are fun to do; if you find your students' attention waning, you can insert one of these activities per lesson. If your students attend another class for speech and conversation, these exercises may be skipped.

7. Use Expansion Activities if there is time.

The Expansion Activities at the end are fun, but time is limited. If you do have extra time at the end of the lesson, choose the activity that seems the most enjoyable. Students are likely to remember the lesson better if there is a fun element.

8. Assign exercises for extra credit.

Students can go beyond the basic curriculum and do more of the exercises at home for extra credit.

9. Let students check answers at home.

Print the answer key for each unit from the Heinle Web site (elt.heinle.com/grammarincontext). Give the answer key at the start of each unit so that students can check their answers at home. Set aside ten minutes every week to do a quick troubleshooting of particular grammar points.

10. Use the *Teacher's Edition*.

Each level of the student book has an accompanying *Teacher's Edition*, which gives page-by-page teaching suggestions on how to present and teach each grammar point and corresponding exercises. The *Teacher's Edition* also identifies fast-track material to help you quickly identify essential material when you're pressed for time and have to prioritize what to cover.

Lesson 1

Lesson Overview

GRAMMAR

Ask: *What tense will we study in this lesson?* (present tense of the verb *be*) *What else will we study?* (prepositions of place and *this, that, these, those*) *Do you know any prepositions of place?* (*on, between, behind*, etc.) Have students give examples. Write the examples on the board.

CONTEXT

1. Activate students' prior knowledge. Ask: *What will we learn about in this lesson?* (college life) If students are college students, ask: *What is college life like in the United States?* If students are not in college, ask: *What do you think college life is like in the United States?*

2. Have students share their knowledge and personal experiences.

Presentation Ideas

The topic for this lesson can be enhanced with the following ideas:

1. College catalogues and brochures
2. Posters from colleges
3. Your college yearbook or any college yearbook

Talk about your own college experience. Tell students what you studied, where you studied, what you liked about your college, and anything else that might interest them. Show students your yearbook. Encourage them to ask you questions about your experiences.

Let groups look through college catalogues and brochures you brought along to class.

Say: *Compare these programs with colleges and universities in your native countries. What's the same? What's different?*
Have each group make two lists and share them with the whole class.

Community College Life in the United States READING

1. Have students look at the photo. Ask: *Who are the people?* (students) *What are they doing?* (They're in class. They're listening to the teacher.)

2. Have students look at the title of the reading. Ask: *What is the reading about? How do you know?* Have students make predictions.

3. Preteach any vocabulary words your students may not know, such as *tuition, attention, convenient, semester,* and *child-care center*.

Reading Glossary

attention: care
child-care center: school-like place where parents pay to have small children cared for while the parents work
convenient: easy and comfortable to do or get to
semester: half of the school year
tuition: the cost of attending an educational institution

BEFORE YOU READ

5-10 mins

1. Have students circle T for true or F for false and then discuss the questions in pairs.

2. Ask for a few volunteers to share their answers with the class.

Reading

CD 1
TR 01

15-20 mins

1. Have students read the text silently. Tell them to pay special attention to the verb *be—am, is,* and *are*. Then play the audio and have students read along silently.

2. Check students' comprehension. Ask questions such as: *Is a community college usually bigger or smaller than a university?* (smaller) *Why is Truman College so convenient?* (It is near city transportation. It has evening and weekend classes. It has a child-care center.) *How long is the summer semester?* (eight weeks)

3. Have students read the student composition, "About Me," silently. Tell them to pay special attention to the verb *be—am, is,* and *are.* Then play the audio and have students read along.

4. Check students' comprehension. Ask questions such as: *What is Rolando Lopez's major?* (engineering) *When are his classes?* (at night and on Saturdays) *Why does he like it at Truman College?* (The teachers are friendly and helpful. The students are interesting.)

Context Note

At present, there are 1,075 community colleges in the U.S. More than 5.5 million students are enrolled in degree programs at community colleges.

1.1 Present-Tense Forms of *Be*

🕐 5-10 mins

1. Have students cover up grammar chart **1.1** on page 3. Write several subjects from the readings on the board in a column in no particular order. For example, write: *Truman, I, Rolando, it, they, classes,* etc. Activate students' prior knowledge. Ask students if they know what form of the verb *be* goes with each subject. If students have difficulty with this task, have students find the subjects in the reading and ask them to match them to the correct form of the verb *be.* Write them on the board. For example, write: *classes are.*

2. Have students look at grammar chart **1.1**. Review the example sentences in the chart.

EXERCISE 1

ANSWERS: 1. am; **2.** is; **3.** are; **4.** is; **5.** are; **6.** are; **7.** are; **8.** is; **9.** is

🕐 5-10 mins

1. Tell students that this exercise is about Rolando Lopez, the student who wrote the composition about Truman College. Have students read the direction line. Ask: *What words do we use here?* (*is, are, am*) Go over the example in the book. Then do #1 with the class. Ask: *What form of* be *goes here?* (*am*)

2. Have students complete the rest of Exercise 1 individually. Then have them check their answers in pairs. Remind them to review grammar chart 1.1 on page 3 if necessary. Monitor pair work. Check the answers as a class.

Presentation Idea

1. Have students come to the board and write the verbs next to the subjects.

2. Have more advanced students explain grammar chart **1.1**.

1.2 Uses of *Be*

🕐 10-15 mins

1. Copy the first four explanations from grammar chart **1.2** on page 4 onto the board. Have students cover up grammar chart **1.2** in their books. Ask students to find an example sentence from the readings for the four explanations from the grammar chart. Then have volunteers write sentences from the chart on the board.

2. Have students look at grammar chart **1.2**. Say: *Compare our chart with the chart in the book.*

3. Review the example sentences in the grammar chart, including the examples for age, weather, and time.

4. Go around the room and ask students about their age, the weather, and the time.

EXERCISE 2

Answers will vary.

10-15 mins

1. Have students read the direction line. Go over the example in the book.

2. Have students complete Exercise 2 individually. Remind them to review grammar chart **1.2** on page 4 if necessary. Then check the answers as a class.

Practice Idea: Speaking

Have students make new sentences based on the sentences in Exercise 2. Say: *Change the information in each sentence to make a new sentence. Then give the new sentences to your partner to complete orally. For example:*

Boston is a _____.

Brazil is a _____.

South America is _____.

Monitor pair work. Give help as needed.

1.3 Word Order with *Be*

5-10 mins

1. Have students cover up grammar chart **1.3** on page 5. Elicit the rule for word order with *be*. Say: *Look at the reading on page 2. What comes first? The verb? The subject? The complement?* (subject first, verb second, complement third) Ask them to find sentences to illustrate. Write the sentences on the board.

2. Have students look at grammar chart **1.3**. Review the example sentences in the chart.

EXERCISE 3

ANSWERS: 1. I am a student. **2.** My parents are in Guatemala. **3.** Tuition at a four-year college is high. (OR Tuition is high at a four-year college.) **4.** My college is convenient for me. **5.** My teacher is 40 years old. **6.** My teacher is from New York. **7.** The summer semester is eight weeks long. **8.** Rolando is married. **9.** It is cold in the winter.

10-15 mins

1. Have students read the direction line. Ask: *What is the word order with be?* (subject first, verb second, complement third) Model the

exercise. Go over the example in the book. Then do #1 with the class. Ask a volunteer to give an answer.

2. Have students complete the rest of Exercise 3 individually. Then have them compare their answers in pairs. Remind them to review grammar chart **1.3** on page 5 if necessary. Finally, check the answers as class.

Presentation Idea

Write five mixed-up sentences from the reading on the board. Tell students they have two minutes to put them in the correct order. Then elicit the rule for sentence order.

Practice Idea: Writing

Divide the class into two teams. Give each team ten mixed-up sentences (with subject + *be* + complement) on small pieces of paper. Say: *You must put the words in the correct order and write the sentences on the board. The first team to finish is the winner.*

1.4 The Subject

10-15 mins

1. Ask students to underline every subject in the first two paragraphs in the reading on page 2.

2. Activate students' prior knowledge. Say: *Find an example of a pronoun as a subject.* Then ask students to circle all the subject pronouns in the reading on page 2. Provide an example if necessary.

3. Now have students double-underline the plural subjects. (Note: If possible, check answers with the class using an overhead projector.)

4. Have students look at grammar chart **1.4**. Review the example sentences in the grammar chart. Review all of the subject pronouns. Explain that *you* is both singular and plural. Give examples. Say: *You are all my students.* Indicate this with a sweeping gesture that includes the whole class. Then point to one student in particular and say: *[Student name], you are my student.*

ANSWERS: 1. We; 2. It; 3. It; 4. They; 5. I; 6. It; 7. They; 8. It; 9. They; 10. She; 11. We

5-10 mins

1. Have students read the direction line. Ask: *What words go in the blanks?* (pronouns) Go over the example in the book. Then do #1 with the class. Ask a volunteer to give an answer. Point out the map of Central America.

2. Have students complete the rest of Exercise 4 individually. Have them compare their answers in pairs. Remind them to review grammar chart **1.4** on page 6 if necessary. Finally, check the answers as a class.

Practice Idea: Writing

Have students write an e-mail to a friend about their English class. Tell them to use the relevant sentences in Exercise 4 as a guide. Say: *Make the information in the sentences true for you.* With students' help, write the start of an e-mail on the board as an example. When students are finished, have them exchange e-mails with a partner and read each other's. Encourage them to help each other with any corrections.

Journal Entry (by Maya Levina)
READING

1. Have students look at the photo. Ask: *Who are the people?* (students, a teacher) *What are they doing?* (They're in class. They're having a discussion.)

2. Have students look at the title of the reading. Ask: *What do you think the reading is going to be about? Why?* Have students use the title and photo to make predictions about the reading.

3. Preteach any vocabulary words your students may not know, such as *territory, rows,* and *speech.*

Reading Glossary

row: a line of things, people, pictures, etc., placed front to back or side by side
speech: the expression of thoughts with spoken words
territory: an area of land not totally self-governing or considered a state or province by a central government

BEFORE YOU READ

5-10 mins

1. Have students circle T for true or F for false and then discuss the questions in pairs.

2. Ask for a few volunteers to share their answers with the class.

Reading

CD 1
TR 02

10-15 mins

1. Have students read the text silently. Tell them to pay special attention to the contractions with *am, is,* and *are.* Then play the audio and have students read along silently.

2. Check students' comprehension. Ask questions such as: *Are all the students the same age in Maya's class?* (no) *Where are the students from?* (all over the world) *Are the classrooms comfortable?* (yes)

Presentation Ideas

The topic for this lesson can be enhanced with the following ideas:

1. A map of the world or a globe

2. Photos of different kinds of classroom setups from formal to very informal

Practice Idea: Listening

To practice listening skills, have students first listen to the audio alone. Ask a few comprehension questions such as: *What are Maya's classrooms like?* (big and comfortable, small desks) *How much does education cost in Maya's country?* (education is free) *How much does education cost in the U.S.?* (education is expensive) Repeat the audio if necessary. Then have students open their books and read along as they listen to the audio.

1.5 Contractions with *Be*

10-15 mins

1. Have students cover up grammar chart **1.5** on page 8. Ask students to find examples of contractions from the reading. Write them on the board. For example, write: *he's, we're, teacher's, what's.*

2. Have volunteers explain each contraction. Ask: *How do we make the contraction* he's? (he is = take out the first letter of *is* and add an apostrophe)

3. Have students look at grammar chart **1.5**. Review the example sentences in the grammar chart. Demonstrate what American speech would sound like if there were no contractions. To illustrate, enunciate each word very carefully.

4. Have students go back to the reading on page 7 to circle words that are not contracted (e.g., *college is, students are, language is*). Write the examples that the students give you on the board. Point out that we do not make contractions with *is* if the noun ends in *s, z, g, sh,* or *ch* sounds. Model the pronunciation of each of the sounds. Also point out that we don't make contractions with plural nouns and *are*.

Practice Idea: Speaking

In groups, have students take turns reading parts of the paragraph out loud—first without contractions, then with contractions. Circulate to observe group work. Give help as needed.

Context Note

Education is free in the United States from kindergarten through high school. Some school districts also offer free preschool for three- and four-year-olds, but that isn't very common. College and university programs can be very expensive. State-run universities charge lower fees to state residents, but even state institutions can be expensive. Expensive private colleges can cost as much as $35,000 a year!

EXERCISE 5

Answers: 1. 's / are; **2.** is / are; **3.** are / 're; **4.** 's / 's; **5.** is / 's; **6.** 's / 's; **7.** are / 're; **8.** 's / 's

⏱ 5-10 mins

1. Tell students that the information in the exercise is based on the journal entry they just read. Have students read the direction line. Ask: *Do all sentences have contractions?* (no) Go over the example in the book.

2. Have students complete the rest of Exercise 5 individually. Check the answers as a class.

3. Assess students' performance. If necessary, review grammar chart **1.5** on page 8.

 EXERCISE 6
CD 1
TR 03

Answers: 1. I; **2.** 's; **3.** 's; **4.** is; **5.** He's; **6.** is; **7.** It's; **8.** are; **9.** 're; **10.** are; **11.** 's; **12.** She's; **13.** are; **14.** 're; **15.** is; **16.** 're; **17.** You're; **18.** 'm

---

⏱ 10-15 mins

1. Tell students that this exercise is about a student from Truman College. Have students read the direction line. Ask: *Do all sentences have contractions?* (no) Go over the example in the book. Then do #1 with the class. Ask a volunteer to give an answer. Remind students that sometimes the verb is missing, sometimes the subject is missing, and sometimes both the subject and the verb are missing.

2. Have students complete Exercise 6 individually. Remind them to review grammar chart **1.5** on page 8 if necessary. Then play audio and check answers as a class.

Practice Idea: Listening

To provide practice with listening skills, have students close their books and listen to the audio. Repeat the audio as needed. Ask comprehension questions such as: *What is the student's teacher's name?* (Charles Madison) *How many students come from Asia?* (5) Then have students open their books and complete Exercise 6.

Practice Idea: Writing

Have students write a paragraph about their English class. Tell students to use Exercise 6 as a model. Instruct students not to use contractions. Then have students exchange paragraphs with a partner. The partner should correct the paragraph, inserting contractions where they should be used.

1.6 *Be* with Descriptions

10-15 mins
1. Have students cover up grammar chart **1.6** on page 9. Ask volunteers to describe the school, the classroom they're in, and their classmates. As they talk, write down adjectives they use on the board. If they need help, prompt: *Is the classroom big or small? Is the school expensive? Are your classmates married?* Ask students if they know what the words you've written on the board are called. (adjectives)

2. Remind students that in English adjectives are not plural.

3. Have students look at grammar chart **1.6**. Review the example sentences in the grammar chart. Point out that adjectives can have many different kinds of endings.

EXERCISE 7

Answers will vary.

10-15 mins
1. Have students read the direction line. Go over the examples. Ask volunteers to model the example. Do #1 with the class.

2. Have students complete Exercise 7 individually. Have students compare their answers in pairs. Remind them to review grammar chart **1.6** on page 9 if necessary. Then check answers as a class.

Presentation Idea

Have students circle adjectives in the readings. Elicit the rules for adjectives. Ask: *What do adjectives do?* (describe nouns) *Do adjectives have a plural form?* (no) *What kind of endings do adjectives have?* (some have *-ed* and *-ing* endings)

EXERCISE 8

Answers will vary.

10-15 mins
1. Have students read the direction line. Go over the examples in the book. Have volunteers model the examples.

2. Have students complete the exercise in pairs. Remind them to review grammar chart **1.6** on page 9 if necessary. Check the answers as a class.

1.7 *Be* with Definitions

10-15 mins
1. Have students cover up grammar chart **1.7** on page 11. Instruct students to look at you. Point to yourself and say: *I am …* Elicit the answer from the students (a teacher). Now say: *You are …* Elicit the response from the students (students). Write both sentences on the board. Again, point to yourself and say: *I am an American.* Point to another student (preferably one from another country) and say: *You are …*

2. Have students look at grammar chart **1.7**. Review the example sentences in the chart.

3. Remind students to use *an* before a vowel sound. Also, tell students that saying or *an* is like saying *one,* so plural nouns do not use *a/an.*

EXERCISE 9

Answers will vary.

10-15 mins
1. Tell students that this exercise is to practice writing definitions. Have students read the direction line. Go over the example in the book. Have a volunteer model the example. Do #1 with the class.

2. Have students complete the exercise individually. Remind them to review grammar chart **1.7** on page 11 if necessary. Check the answers as a class.

EXERCISE 10

Answers will vary.

5-10 mins
1. Have students read the direction line. Ask: *What do we use in front of a vowel sound?* (an) Go over the examples in the book.

2. Have students complete the exercise individually. Remind students to review grammar chart **1.7** on page 11 if necessary. Check the answers as a class.

EXERCISE 11

ANSWERS: **1.** is a; **2.** 's an; **3.** 's an; **4.** are; **5.** 're an; **6.** are

5-10 mins
1. Have students read the direction line. Ask: *What will you put in the blanks?* (am, is, are, a, or an) *Will all sentences have* a *or* an? (no)

Remind students that they should also use contractions wherever possible. Go over the examples in the book.

2. Have students complete the exercise individually. Then have students exchange papers to check answers or check the answers as a class.

3. If necessary, review grammar charts **1.1** on page 3, **1.5** on page 8, and **1.7** on page 11.

EXERCISE 12

Answers will vary.

1. Have students read the direction line. Ask: *What will you put in the blanks?* (a subject, *a*, or *an*) *Will all sentences have* a *or* an? (no) *Which sounds don't have* a *or* an? (plural nouns) Go over the examples in the book. Have a volunteer model the example.

2. Have students complete the exercise in pairs. Monitor pair work. Give help as needed.

3. If necessary, review grammar charts **1.4** on page 6 and **1.7** on page 11.

EXERCISE 13

Answers will vary.

1. Tell students that this exercise is about the U.S. Have students read the direction line. Ask: *What will you put in the blanks?* (a subject, the verb *be*) Go over the examples. Have volunteers model the examples.

2. Have students complete the exercise in pairs. Monitor pair work. Give help as needed.

3. If necessary, review grammar charts **1.4** on page 6 and **1.7** on page 11.

1.8 Prepositions of Place

1. Have students cover up grammar chart **1.8** on pages 13–14. Activate students' prior knowledge. Ask: *What prepositions do you know?* As students call them out, write them on the board.

2. Then ask students to demonstrate the prepositions. First model an example. (Point to the book on the desk.) Say: *On. My book is on the desk.*

3. Have students look at grammar chart **1.8**. Review the examples in the grammar chart. Point out the illustrations that show the meanings of the prepositions. As you go down the chart, demonstrate the prepositions yourself or have volunteers demonstrate them.

EXERCISE 14

Answers will vary.

1. Tell students that this exercise is about their classroom and their school. Have students read the direction line. Go over the example with the students. (Put your dictionary in your book bag to demonstrate.) Have a volunteer model #1.

2. Have students complete the exercise individually. Remind them to review grammar chart **1.8** on pages 13–14 if necessary. Have students check answers in pairs or check answers as a class.

Practice Ideas: Writing and Reading

1. Divide students into groups. At the front of the room, create an interesting still life with fruit and other objects. Say: *Describe this still life using prepositions.* Circulate to observe group work. Give help when needed. Have a volunteer from each group read the description. Then have the groups compare.

2. Divide students into groups. Line up a number of interesting objects on a table in front of the classroom. Ask the groups to design a still life using prepositions. Say: *Don't draw a picture. Just describe it using prepositions.* Have groups exchange descriptions and take turns trying to build the other groups' still life. The group that builds the most accurate still life wins.

1.9 Negative Statements with *Be*

1. Have students cover up grammar chart **1.9**. Elicit a negative statement with *be.* Turn to a student who is not married and say, for example: *Jenny is married.* Help Jenny or another student say: *I'm not married* or *She's not married.* Offer more examples to elicit a negative response (e.g., *You're tired; You're late; He's Japanese*). Write the negative sentences on the board.

2. Have students look at grammar chart **1.9**. Review the example sentences in the chart.

3. Explain to students that there are two ways to make contractions. Say: *You can use both contractions. Both are common.* Ask volunteers to demonstrate how to make a negative contraction on the board. Review how to make both contractions with the students. *You're not*—remove the first letter in the verb *be* and replace with an apostrophe. *You aren't*—remove the *o* from *not* and replace with an apostrophe.

4. Point out that there is only one way to contract *I am not—I'm not.*

EXERCISE 15

ANSWERS: 1. We're not (OR We aren't); **2.** It's not (OR It isn't); **3.** I'm not; **4.** They're not (OR They aren't); **5.** You're not (OR You aren't); **6.** We're not (OR We aren't)

1. Tell students that this exercise is for practicing the negative with *be.* Have students read the direction line. Go over the examples in the book.

2. Have students complete the exercise individually. Remind them to review grammar chart **1.9** on page 15 if necessary. Check the answers as a class.

EXERCISE 16

Answers will vary.

1. Tell students that this exercise is about the class. Have students read the direction line. Ask: *What do we put in the blanks?* (*be* in the affirmative or negative) Remind students to use both forms of contractions. Go over the example sentences in the book.

2. Have students complete the exercise individually. Remind them to review grammar chart **1.9** on page 15 if necessary. Then have students compare answers with a partner.

EXERCISE 17

Answers will vary.

1. Tell students that this exercise is about their opinions. Have students read the direction line. Then have a volunteer model #1.

2. Have students complete the rest of the exercise individually. Remind them to review grammar chart **1.9** on page 15 if necessary.

3. Put students into groups to discuss their responses. Monitor group work. Give help when needed. Have some students share their answers.

Practice Idea: Writing and Speaking

Have groups report their groups' opinions to the class. Compile all the information on the board for a survey of the whole class. Discuss the results.

EXERCISE 18

Answers will vary.

10-15 mins

1. Tell students that this exercise is about their native countries. Have students read the direction line. Ask: *What do we put in the blanks?* (*be* in the affirmative or negative) Remind students to use both forms of contractions. Go over the example sentences in the book.

2. Have students complete the exercise individually. Then have students compare answers with a partner. If time allows, have students share a few answers in class.

3. If necessary, review grammar chart **1.9** on page 15.

Practice Idea: Writing and Speaking

If possible, pair students from different countries. Ask each partner to do the same exercise for their partner's country. Have them write their guesses in their notebooks. Then have partners compare their answers. Monitor pair work. Give help as needed.

EXERCISE 19

ANSWERS: 1. They aren't states. (OR They're not states.) **2.** I'm not from Mexico. **3.** Guatemala's not a big country. (OR Guatemala isn't a big country.) **4.** We're not in the library. (OR We aren't in the library.) **5.** You're not a math teacher. (OR You aren't a math teacher.) **6.** Miami's not in Illinois. (OR Miami isn't in Illinois.) **7.** July and August aren't cold months in Chicago.

10-15 mins

1. Have students read the direction line. Ask: *What kind of statements will we write?* (negative statements) Remind students to use both forms of contractions. Go over the example in the book.

2. Have students complete the exercise individually. Remind them to review grammar chart **1.9** on page 15 if necessary. Then check answers as a class.

Practice Idea: Writing

Have students create an exercise like Exercise 19. Instruct students to change the names of the places. Then have students exchange exercises with a partner. After completing the exercises, partners compare answers. Monitor pair work. Give help as needed.

EXERCISE 20

Answers will vary.

10-15 mins

1. Tell students that this exercise is about their class. Have students read the direction line. Ask: *What do we put in the blanks?* (*be* in the affirmative or negative) Remind students to use both forms of contractions. Go over the example in the book.

2. Have students complete the exercise individually. Then have students compare answers with a partner.

3. If necessary, review grammar charts **1.1** on page 3 and **1.9** on page 15.

Conversation About College

READING

1. Have students look at the photo. Ask: *Who is in the photo?* (a man, a student) *What is he doing?* (He's using the computer. He's listening to something.)

2. Have students look at the title of the reading. Ask: *What is the reading about? How do you know?* Have students make predictions.

3. Preteach any vocabulary words your students may not know, such as *sleepy* or *nervous*.

Reading Glossary

nervous: worried about a future event
sleepy: needing sleep, tired

BEFORE YOU READ

5-10 mins

1. Have students discuss the questions in pairs.

2. Ask for a few volunteers to share their answers with the class.

Reading

CD 1
TR 04

⏱ 10-15 mins

1. Have students read the text silently. Tell them to pay special attention to questions. Then play the audio and have students read along silently.

2. Check students' comprehension. Ask questions such as: *Is Ali up late?* (no) *Why is Mohammad nervous?* (He has a test tomorrow.) *How old is the Korean man in Mohammad's class?* (75)

> ## Practice Idea: Listening
>
> Have students first listen to the audio alone. Ask a few comprehension questions such as: *Why is Mohammad nervous about his test?* (because his class is very hard) *Why are Mohammad's parents worried about him?* (because they think there is so much freedom in the U.S.) Repeat the audio if necessary. Then have students open their books and read along as they listen to the audio.

Context Note

In 2003, three programmers in Estonia created software called Skype that allows users to make free phone calls over the Internet. Today, Skype has millions of users worldwide.

1.10 *Be* in *Yes/No* Questions and Short Answers

⏱ 10-15 mins

1. Have students cover up grammar chart **1.10** on page 20. Ask students to find *yes/no* questions in the reading. Write examples on the board. (*Are you at home? Are you serious?*)

2. Have students look at grammar chart **1.10**. Review the example sentences in the grammar chart.

3. Explain to students that in a question you put the verb—*am, is, are*—before the subject.

4. Point out that *yes/no* questions are usually answered with a short answer, such as *Yes, it is.* Or *No, it isn't.* Affirmative short answers are not contracted. (*Yes, it is.*) Negative short answers are usually contracted. (*No, it isn't; No it's not.*)

5. Direct students' attention to the Pronunciation Note. Demonstrate the rising intonation of *yes/no* questions. Lead students in a choral practice of the intonation. Write one or two questions on the board with arrows to show the rising intonation.

EXERCISE 21

ANSWERS: 1. No, he isn't. (OR No, he's not.) **2.** Yes, they are. **3.** Yes, they are. **4.** No, it isn't. (OR No, it's not.) **5.** Yes, he is. **6.** No, they're not. (OR No, they aren't.) **7.** No, he isn't.

⏱ 10-15 mins

1. Tell students that this exercise is about Ali and Mohammad from the last reading. Have students read the direction line. Ask: *What kind of sentences will we write?* (short answers) Go over the example in the book.

2. Have students complete the exercise individually. Remind students to review grammar chart **1.10** on page 20 if necessary. Check answers as a class.

> ## Practice Idea: Speaking
>
> Put students in pairs. Ask students to look at Exercise 17 on page 16. Say: *Ask your partner yes/no questions. For example: Is English easy for you? Take turns asking and answering.*

EXERCISE 22

Answers will vary.

⏱ 10-15 mins

1. Tell students that you will ask them some questions. Have students read the direction line. Say: *If you answer in the negative, please give me more information.* Go over the example in the book. Model the example with a student.

2. Ask several different students each question.

3. If necessary, review grammar chart **1.10** on page 20.

> ## Practice Ideas: Speaking
>
> 1. Use this exercise as an oral assessment. Ask individual students the questions in a quiet setting.
>
> 2. Have students ask and answer questions 1–5 from Exercise 22 in pairs. Instruct students to write three more questions to ask their partners. Monitor pair work. Give help as needed.

EXERCISE 23

Answers. 1. Is it near public transportation? **2.** Is the cafeteria on this floor? **3.** Is it open now? **4.** Is the library in this building? **5.** Is it closed now? **6.** Is this course free? **7.** Are the textbooks free? **8.** Is the teacher strict? **9.** Is this room clean? **10.** Is it big?

1. Tell students that this exercise is about their school and class. Have students read the direction line. Ask: *What kind of questions are we going to ask?* (yes/no questions) Go over the example in the book. Model the example with a volunteer. Then have two volunteers model #1.

2. Have students complete the exercise in pairs. Students take turns asking and answering questions. Monitor pair work. Check for correct intonation of questions. Give help as needed.

3. If necessary, review grammar chart **1.10** on page 20.

Practice Idea: Speaking

Create two rings of students. Have half of the students stand in an outer ring around the classroom. Have the other half stand in an inner ring, facing the outer ring. Instruct students to ask and answer the questions from Exercise 23 and/or Exercise 24. Call out *turn* every minute or so. Students in the inner ring should move one space clockwise. Students now ask and answer questions with their new partners. Make sure students look up at each other when they're speaking.

EXERCISE 24

ANSWERS: 1. Is a high school education free? **2.** Are college books free? **3.** Is medical care free? **4.** Are doctors rich? **5.** Are jeans popular? **6.** Are houses expensive? **7.** Are people friendly? **8.** Are Japanese cars popular? **9.** Are fast-food restaurants popular? **10.** Are movie tickets cheap?

1. Have students read the direction line. Ask: *What kind of questions are we going to ask?* (yes/no questions) Go over the example in the book. Model the example with a volunteer. Then have two volunteers model #1.

2. Have students complete the exercise in pairs, taking turns asking and answering questions. Monitor pair work. Check for correct intonation of questions. Give help as needed.

3. If necessary, review grammar chart **1.10** on page 20.

1.11 *Wh-* Questions with *Be*

1. Have students cover up grammar chart **1.11** on pages 21–22. Activate students' prior knowledge. Say: *What* wh- *questions do you know?* (e.g., *What's your name? Where are you from?*) Write students' examples on the board. Then ask students to find *wh-* questions in the reading on pages 18–19. Write examples on the board. (*How are you? Where are you now?*)

2. Have students look at grammar chart **1.11**. Review the example sentences in the chart. Explain that *wh-* questions ask for information. In contrast, *yes/no* questions ask only for a *yes* or *no* response.

3. Explain the Language Notes. Write the contractions for *wh-* words and *is* on the board. Explain that there is no contraction for *which is* and that there is no written contraction for *wh-* words and *are*, but that it's acceptable in informal speech. Then ask students to find contractions with *wh-* words in the reading on pages 18–19. Write the examples on the board.

4. Model the pronunciation of *wh-* questions in the chart. Be sure to exaggerate a falling intonation. Lead the class in a choral practice of the *wh-* question intonation. Write one or two questions on the board with arrows to show the falling intonation.

Presentation Idea

Activate students' prior knowledge. Say: *What* wh- *questions do you know?* (e.g., *What's your name? Where are you from?*) Write students' examples on the board. Have students cover up the questions column in grammar chart **1.11**. Ask volunteers to create questions from the answers in the chart (e.g., *Who is your teacher?*) Write examples on the board.

EXERCISE 25

ANSWERS: 1. What's; **2.** Who's; **3.** When's; **4.** Where are; **5.** Where's; **6.** Why are; **7.** What's

⏱ 5-10 mins

1. Have students read the direction line. Ask: *What do we write in the blanks?* (question words and the verb *be*) Remind students to use contractions wherever possible. Go over the example in the book. Have a volunteer do #1.

2. Have students complete the exercise individually. Remind students to review grammar chart **1.11** on pages 21–22 if necessary. Check the answers as a class.

Practice Idea: Speaking

Have students practice asking and answering the questions from Exercise 25 with a partner. Say: *Answer the questions with your own information.*

EXERCISE 26

ANSWERS: 1. b; **2.** a; **3.** b; **4.** c; **5.** c; **6.** b; **7.** b; **8.** c; **9.** a

⏱ 5-10 mins

1. Tell students that this exercise tests their knowledge of the U.S. Have students read the direction line. Say: *If you need to, you can use the map of the U.S. in Appendix K.* Point out the features of the map (e.g., state abbreviations, capital cities, time zones).

2. Have students complete the exercise in pairs. Then have pairs compare answers with other pairs. Monitor pair work. Give help as needed.

Practice Idea: Writing and Reading

Have students create a similar exercise with information from their own native countries. Have students exchange exercises with a partner.

1.12 Comparing Statements and Questions with *Be*

⏱ 5-10 mins

1. Have students cover up grammar chart **1.12** on page 24. On the board, write: *Mom and Dad are out.* Ask: *What is the subject of this statement?*

(Mom and Dad) Then write: *Are they at the store?* Ask: *What is the subject of this question?* (they) Write: *No, they aren't.* Ask: *What is the subject of the answer?* (they) Then write: *Where are they?* Ask: *What is the subject of this question?* (they)

2. Now have students look at grammar chart **1.12**. Point out that in questions, the verb comes before the subject. In information questions, question words always come at the beginning of the sentence.

3. Point out that negative statements and questions work the same way. The verb comes before the subject. Question words go at the beginning of a sentence.

EXERCISE 27

ANSWERS: 1. are they worried? **2.** aren't you sleepy? **3.** 's your teacher? **4.** are your classes? **5.** 's his name? **6.** isn't it on? **7.** is she?

⏱ 10-15 mins

1. Have students read the direction line. Ask: *What are we going to write in the blanks?* (a verb and a subject and a complement if necessary) Go over the example.

2. Have students complete the exercise individually. Then have students compare answers in pairs. Check answers as a class.

3. If necessary, review grammar chart **1.12** on page 24.

Practice Idea: Speaking

Have students write three new statements. Students should say their statement to a partner; then, the partner should reply with a question. Then they should switch roles. Monitor pair work. Give help as needed.

1.13 Questions with *What* and *How*

⏱ 10-15 mins

1. Have students cover up grammar chart **1.13** on page 25. Activate students' prior knowledge. Say: *Think of all the kinds of questions you can make with* what. Write examples from the students on the board. If students have trouble thinking of examples, give them hints. For example, point at a book and ask: *What*

questions can you ask about that book? (What color? What kind?) Do the same thing with *how*. Or point at a student and say: *What questions can you ask about Suzy? (How old? How tall?)*

2. On the board, summarize all of the *what* and *how* questions students came up with (*What time? What color? What day?*).

3. Have students look at grammar chart **1.13**, and have them compare their lists on the board with the lists in the grammar chart. Review the examples. Point out that *what* can ask for a description. Review the nouns that can be followed by *what* (nationality, day, time, etc.). Do the same with *how*. Point out that *how* is used to ask for descriptions and to ask about the weather. Review the adjectives and adverbs that can follow *how* (old, tall, long, etc.).

4. Go over the Usage Notes. Remind students that Americans use inches, feet, miles, etc., to measure length and distance. Ask a student: *How tall are you?* If a student doesn't know his/her height in feet and inches, offer to measure him/her. Demonstrate the typical way Americans say their height: *I'm 5 foot 8* (i.e., *not* 5 feet 8). Other students might want to know their height in inches. Have students measure each other's height.

5. Mention that asking *How are you?* is often another way of saying *hello*.

Presentation Idea

Have students cover up grammar chart **1.13**. Write the statements from the grammar chart on the board (e.g., *She's American, It's Friday, It's 4:15*) and have students try to guess the question word and/or question for the statement.

EXERCISE 28

ANSWERS: **1.** time is; **2.** kind of, is; **3.** kind of, are; **4.** color is; **5.** old is your son; **6.** tall is your brother; **7.** old are you; **8.** much is that car; **9.** long is the movie

⏱ 10–15 mins

1. Have students read the direction line. Go over the example in the book. Do #1 as a class.

2. Have students complete the exercise individually. Remind them to review grammar chart **1.13**

on page 25 if necessary. Then check the answers as a class.

EXERCISE 29

Answers will vary.

⏱ 15–20 mins

1. Tell students that this exercise is about them and their native countries. Have students read the direction line. Say: *Complete the statements with your own information.* Go over the example. Model the example with a volunteer.

2. Have students complete the statements individually. Then have students ask and answer questions in pairs. If possible, put students from different countries in pairs. Monitor pair work. Give help as needed.

3. If necessary, review grammar chart **1.13** on page 25.

Practice Idea: Speaking

Create two rings of students. Have half of the students stand in an outer ring around the classroom. Have the other half stand in an inner ring, facing the outer ring. Instruct students to ask and answer the questions from Exercise 29. Call out *turn* every minute or so. Students in the inner ring should move one space clockwise. Students now ask and answer with their new partners. Say: *Ask questions in random order.* Make sure students look up at each other when they're speaking.

🔊 EXERCISE 30

CD 1
TR 05

ANSWERS: **1.** Is this; **2.** aren't you; **3.** long is; **4.** 's your English class; **5.** are they; **6.** Is your teacher; **7.** is it; **8.** are you

⏱ 10–15 mins

1. Tell students that in this exercise Cindy and Maria talk about their classes. Have students read the direction line. Go over the example.

2. Have students complete the exercise individually. Check answers as a class.

3. Then have students practice the conversation. Monitor pair work. Give help as needed.

4. If necessary, review grammar chart **1.13** on page 25.

Practice Idea: Listening

To provide practice with listening skills, have students close their books and listen to the audio. Say: *You will hear a phone conversation between Cindy and Maria.* Repeat the audio as needed. Ask comprehension questions such as: *Where is Maria right now?* (at school) *Is she in class?* (no) *What is she doing?* (taking a break) Then have students open their books and complete Exercise 30.

Practice Idea: Speaking

Have students create a new conversation for Cindy and Maria. Cindy and Maria are going to get together on Sunday afternoon. Maria is going to ask questions about Cindy's class on Saturday. Have volunteers do a role-play in front of the class.

In the School Cafeteria READING

1. Have students look at the illustration. Ask: *Who are the people?* (students) *What are they doing?* (They're getting lunch in the cafeteria.)

2. Have students look at the title of the reading. Ask: *What is the reading about? How do you know? Have students make predictions.*

3. Preteach any vocabulary words your students may not know, such as *vending machine* and *chopsticks.*

Reading Glossary

chopsticks: two thin sticks used to take hold of food and put it in the mouth

vending machine: a machine that gives packaged food, soft drinks, or other items after coins are placed in it

BEFORE YOU READ

1. Have students discuss the questions in pairs.

2. Ask for a few volunteers to share their answers with the class.

  Reading

CD 1
TR 06

10-15 mins

1. Have students read the text silently. Point out that this is a conversation between an American student and his Chinese roommate. Tell students to pay special attention to *this, that, these,* and *those.* Then play the audio and have students read along silently.

2. Check students' comprehension. Ask questions such as: *Is there a cafeteria for teachers?* (yes) *What kind of food do they have in the cafeteria?* (Mexican, Italian, and Chinese) *Does the cafeteria have chopsticks?* (no)

Practice Idea: Listening

To practice listening skills, have students first listen to the audio alone. Ask a few comprehension questions such as: *What kind of food are tacos?* (Mexican) *What kind of food is pizza?* (Italian) *What kind of food is chop suey?* (the American student says it is Chinese, but the Chinese student is sure that it isn't) Repeat the audio if necessary. Then have students open their books and read along as they listen to the audio.

1.14 *This, That, These, Those*

5-10 mins

1. Have students cover up grammar chart **1.14** on page 29. Activate students' prior knowledge. Ask volunteers to demonstrate *this, that, these,* and *those.* Write their examples on the board. Say: This, that, these, *and* those *are used to identify nouns.*

2. Have students look at grammar chart **1.14**. Review the example sentences in the grammar chart. Demonstrate the adjectives again—exaggerating distances. Point out that once you identify a noun—you can use a pronoun in the second sentence.

3. Direct students to the Language Note. Explain that *that is* can be contracted to *that's.* Point out that you cannot contract *this, these,* or *those.*

4. Explain that you use *this, that, these,* and *those* in front of nouns to indicate specific nouns.

EXERCISE 31

Answers: 1. These are; **2.** This is; **3.** Those are; **4.** Those are; **5.** This is; **6.** These are; **7.** That is (OR That's); **8.** That is (OR That's)

5–10 mins

1. Tell students that in this exercise they are showing a new student the school cafeteria. Have students read the direction line. Ask: *What do we put in the blanks?* (*this, that, these,* or *those* and a verb) Remind students to use contractions where they can. Go over the example.

2. Have students complete the exercise individually. Remind them to review grammar chart **1.14** on page 29 if necessary. Check answers as a class.

Presentation Idea

Have students go through the reading to find one example of *this, that, these,* or *those.* Ask volunteers to explain the usage.

Practice Idea: Speaking

Have students do a role-play. One partner is a new student and the other partner is showing him or her around. Say: *You can create a dialog about any place in the school: this classroom, the computer or language lab, the gym,* etc. Monitor pair work. Give help as needed. Have volunteers perform in front of the class.

Summary of Lesson 1

20–30 mins

1. **Uses of *Be*** Review the uses of *be.* Say: *Go to the reading on page 2. Find a sentence for each use of* be. If necessary, have students review:

   1.2 Uses of *Be* (p. 4)
   1.6 *Be* with Descriptions (p. 9)
   1.7 *Be* with Definitions (p. 11)
   1.8 Prepositions of Place (pp. 13–14)

2. **Subject Pronouns** Have students close their books. Instruct students to write a sentence for each subject pronoun. If necessary, have students review:

   1.4 The Subject (p. 6)

3. **Contractions** Have students write eight negative sentences with the verb *be* with different pronouns using both forms of negative contractions. Then, have students write one question for each *wh-* question word. If necessary, have students review:

   1.5 Contractions with *Be* (p. 8)
   1.9 Negative Statements with *Be* (p. 15)
   1.11 *Wh-* Questions with *Be* (p. 21–22)

4. **Articles *a/an*** Play a chain game. Have students sit in a circle. The first person says his/her name and some other information (e.g., *I'm John. I'm a mechanic.*). The second person repeats the first person's information and adds his/her own (e.g., *He's John. He's a mechanic. I'm Marta; I'm a …*). If necessary, have students review:

   1.7 *Be* with Definitions (p. 11)

5. **Statements and Questions with *Be*** Have pairs create a dialogue using forms of *be.* Say: *Use affirmative and negative statements, yes/no questions, information questions, and short answers. Use contractions wherever possible.* Have students practice their dialogs. If necessary, have students review:

   1.9 Negative Statements with *Be* (p. 15)
   1.10 *Be* in *Yes/No* Questions and Short Answers (p. 20)
   1.11 *Wh-* Questions with *Be* (pp. 21–22)
   1.13 Questions with *What* and *How* (p. 25)

6. ***This/That/These/Those*** Have students practice *this, that, these,* and *those* in pairs. Say: *Your partner is a new student in this classroom. Show him or her around the classroom.* If necessary, have students review:

   1.14 *This, That, These, Those* (p. 29)

Editing Advice

10–15 mins

Have students close their books. Write the first two sentences without editing marks or corrections on the board. For example: *1. My father he lives in Australia. 2. Is small Cuba.* Ask students to correct each sentence and explain the grammar rule that applies. After students have corrected each sentence, tell them to turn to pages 31–32. Say:

Now compare your work with the Editing Advice in the book. Have students read through all the Editing Advice. Then have them do the Editing quiz individually on pages 32–33.

Editing Quiz

ANSWERS: 1. C; **2.** C; **3.** are you; **4.** I'm; **5.** Where is Burundi? **6.** It's; **7.** a very small country; **8.** C; **9.** Is it; **10.** is a country; **11.** C; **12.** C; **13.** French is; **14.** What's; **15.** C; **16.** Are you; **17.** I am; **18.** Ø; **19.** isn't; **20.** C; **21.** C; **22.** I'm not; **23.** years old (OR Ø); **24.** the U.S.; **25.** How old is your sister? **26.** C; **27.** Is your sister in high school? **28.** C; **29.** These; **30.** Ø; **31.** is; **32.** is seven years old. (OR is seven.); **33.** Ø; **34.** an; **35.** it's

10-15 mins

1. Tell students that they are going to put the editing advice into practice. Have students read the direction line. Ask: *Do all the shaded words and phrases have mistakes?* (no) Go over the examples with the class. Then do #1 together.

2. Have students complete the quiz individually. Then have them compare answers with a partner before checking answers as a class.

3. For the items students had difficulties with, have them go back and find the relevant grammar chart and review it. Monitor and give help as necessary.

Lesson 1 Test/Review

40-60 mins

Use the Assessment CD-ROM with ExamView®, Online Workbook, and Web site for additional practice, review, and assessment materials.

PART 1

ANSWERS: 1. the; **2.** am; **3.** a; **4.** Are you; **5.** a; **6.** a; **7.** Ø; **8.** it's; **9.** Is your roommate; **10.** 's; **11.** isn't (OR 's not); **12.** isn't he; **13.** 's; **14.** are; **15.** 's; **16.** old is he; **17.** 's; **18.** old; **19.** 's; **20.** 's

1. Part 1 may be used in addition to the Assessment CD-ROM with ExamView® as an in-class test to assess student performance. Have students read the direction line. Ask:

Does every question or sentence need a word? (no) Review the examples.

2. Collect for assessment.

3. If necessary, have students review Lesson 1.

PART 2

ANSWERS: 1. we're; **2.** you aren't (OR you're not); **3.** I'm not; **4.** they're; **5.** X; **6.** X; **7.** Mary isn't (OR Mary's not); **8.** he isn't (OR he's not); **9.** what's; **10.** X

1. Part 2 may also be used as an in-class test to assess student performance, in addition to the Assessment CD-ROM with ExamView®. Have students read the direction line. Remind students to use contractions when possible. Review the example.

2. Have students complete the Part 2 individually. Collect for assessment.

3. If necessary, have students review:

   1.5   Contractions with *Be* (p. 8)

PART 3

ANSWERS: 1. 'm; **2.** I; **3.** are you; **4.** 'm; **5.** 's; **6.** She's; **7.** 's your English teacher; **8.** He's; **9.** Is he; **10.** isn't (OR 's not); **11.** a; **12.** 's; **13.** old; **14.** old is your teacher (OR old is Ms. James); **15.** is; **16.** tall is she; **17.** is; **18.** Is your class big; **19.** are; **20.** are; **21.** are; **22.** 's; **23.** from; **24.** 's not (OR isn't); **25.** are the students from; **26.** are; **27.** 're; **28.** Is your teacher (OR Is Mr. Kane); **29.** an; **30.** Is that your teacher (OR Is that Mr. Kane); **31.** 's; **32.** 'm

1. Part 3 may also be used as an in class test to assess student performance, in addition to the Assessment CD-ROM with ExamView®. Tell students that this is a conversation between two students. Review the example.

2. Have students complete Part 3 individually. Collect for assessment.

3. If necessary, have students review Lesson 1.

Expansion

These expansion activities provide opportunities for students to interact with one another and further develop their speaking and writing skills.

Encourage students to use grammar from this lesson whenever possible.

CLASSROOM ACTIVITIES

 1. Ask: *What verb do we use to describe ourselves?* (*be*) Have students complete their descriptions individually. Then collect them and read them out loud for students to guess who is being described.

10-15 mins per activity

Practice Idea: Writing

Have students write additional information about their families (e.g., *My husband is a pilot.*).

---

2. Instruct students to choose a famous person that the class would know. Have students complete the descriptions with a partner. Monitor pair work. Give help as needed. Have pairs read their descriptions to the class for other students to guess who the famous person is.

3. Try to pair students of different nationalities, if possible. If necessary, provide the option of writing out the questions before asking a partner. Ask volunteers to share what they learned about their partners.

4. Ask: *How much do you know about your native country?* Have students work in pairs. If possible, put students from the same country together. Have pairs complete the chart with information about their country. Have volunteers report interesting information to the class (e.g., *Disneyland is a popular tourist attraction in the U.S.*).

Practice Idea: Writing and Speaking

Have students make brochures about their countries. Encourage students to use drawings, pictures, photos, and other materials to illustrate their brochures. Display the brochures around the class for everyone to see. Ask volunteers to talk about their countries.

Talk About It

 Have students read the direction line and then complete the sentences with their opinions individually. Put students in small groups to compare and discuss their opinions. Monitor group work. Give help as needed. Have volunteers share their opinions with the class.

15-20 mins

Write About It

Ask students to turn to Exercise 20 on pages 17–18. Say: *Write a paragraph about yourself using this information. Write both negative and affirmative sentences.* Review the model with the students. Encourage students to add more information. Collect for assessment and/or have students present their paragraphs to a group.

20-30 mins

Practice Idea: Writing

Have students exchange first drafts with a partner. Ask students to help their partners edit their drafts. Refer students to the Editing Advice on pages 31–32.

Outside Activity

Have students interview a native speaker of English (a neighbor, a coworker, another student, or a teacher at this college). Write the following questions on the board for students to copy:

a. What city are you from?

b. Are your parents or grandparents from another country? Where are they from?

c. Is most of your family in this city?

d. Are you happy with this city? Why or why not?

e. What are your favorite places in this city?

Tell students to ask these questions and then report back to the class.

Internet Activity

Tell students to use the Internet to find the Web site of a college they are interested in. Or they can find the Web site of the college or school they are at now. Ask them to identify what information is on the home page. What links are on the home page?

Lesson 2

Lesson Overview

GRAMMAR

Ask: *What tense did we study in Lesson 1?* (the present tense of the verb *be*) *What tense are we going to study in this lesson?* (the simple present tense) *Can anyone make a sentence in the simple present tense?* (The president lives in the White House.) Have students give examples. Write them on the board.

CONTEXT

1. Ask: *What will we learn about in this lesson?* (the United States) Activate students' prior knowledge. Ask: *What do you know about the United States? Has anyone been to Washington, D.C.?*

2. Have students share their knowledge and personal experiences.

Presentation Idea

The topic for this lesson can be enhanced with the following ideas:

1. Postcards from Washington, D.C.
2. Brochures/books about the White House
3. Street map of Washington, D.C.

Context Note

George Washington, the first president of the U.S., never resided in the White House, although he did oversee its construction. John Adams, the second president of the U.S., was the first resident of the White House. The White House is the only private residence of a head of state to be open to the public free of charge. This practice has been in place since Thomas Jefferson's presidency.

Washington, D.C. READING

1. Have students look at the photo. Have them describe the building. Ask: *Do you know what the Capitol is?* (the building where the U.S. Congress meets) *Has anyone visited the Capitol?*

2. Have students look at the title of the reading. Ask: *What is the reading about? How do you know?* Have students use the title and the photo to make predictions about the reading.

3. Preteach any vocabulary words your students may not know, such as *capital, district, factories, subway,* and *law*.

Reading Glossary

capital: the official city where a state, provincial, or national government is located
district: an area officially marked for a purpose
factory: a building or group of buildings where goods are produced
law: a rule made by a government body that must be followed by the people in a nation, state, etc.
subway: a public transportation system with trains that run underground

BEFORE YOU READ

5-10 mins

1. Have students discuss the questions in pairs.
2. Ask for a few volunteers to share their answers with the class.

Reading

CD 1
TR 07

10-15 mins

1. Have students read the text silently. Tell them to pay special attention to the present tense verbs. Then play the audio and have students read along silently.

2. Check students' comprehension. Ask questions such as: *Is Washington, D.C., a state?* (no) *Are there tall buildings in Washington?* (no) *Who works in the Capitol?* (state senators and representatives)

Practice Idea: Listening

To practice listening skills, have students first listen to the audio alone. Ask a few comprehension questions such as: *What is the capital of the United States?* (Washington D.C.) *Who works on Capitol Hill?* (senators and representatives from each state) Repeat the audio if necessary. Then have students open their books and read along as they listen to the audio.

Did You Know?

New York City was the capital of the U.S. until 1790. Philadelphia temporarily served as the nation's capital from 1790 to 1800, when the capital was permanently moved to Washington, D.C.

2.1 Simple Present Tense— Forms ≡★

5-10 mins

1. Have students cover up grammar chart **2.1** on page 41. Write the verb *live* at the top of the board. Then write the subject pronouns on the board in the same order they are in the book. Ask: *How do you form the simple present tense?* (use *live* or *lives*) Write students' responses on the board.

2. Have students look at grammar chart **2.1**. Explain that the simple present tense has two forms: the base form and the *-s* form, and that the subject determines which form we use. Say: *We use the base form when the subject is* I, you, we, they, *or a plural noun. We use the* -s *form when the subject is* he, she, it, *or a singular subject.* Point out that *family* is a singular subject. Read the example sentences.

3. Explain that *have* is an irregular verb. Go over the example sentences.

Presentation Idea

Have students go back to the reading on page 40. Ask students to circle the regular *-s* form verbs and to underline the irregular *-s* form of *have.*

EXERCISE 1 ≡★

ANSWERS: 1. lives; **2.** work; **3.** has; **4.** visit; **5.** connects; **6.** lists; **7.** means

5-10 mins

1. Tell students that this exercise is about Washington, D.C. Have students read the direction line. Go over the example in the book. Then do #1 with the class. Ask: *Which form of the verb goes here?* (lives) Say: *If you need help, you can look back at the reading on page 40.*

---

2. Have students complete the rest of Exercise 1 individually. Remind them to review grammar chart **2.1** on page 41 if necessary. Check the answers as a class.

2.2 Simple Present Tense— Uses ≡★

10-15 mins

1. Have students cover up grammar chart **2.2** on page 42. Activate students' prior knowledge. Ask students if they know when to use the simple present tense. Write students' responses on the board.

2. Have students look at grammar chart **2.2**. Explain that one use of the simple present tense is to show truths or facts. Read the example sentences. Ask a volunteer to make a similar sentence about the class (e.g., *Ms. Grant teaches English. English class meets in this room.*).

3. Explain that another use of the simple present is with customs. Read the example. Point out the picture of the man waving. Then have a volunteer make a similar statement about an American custom or a custom from his or her country (e.g., *Americans shake hands when they greet each other.*).

4. Explain that the simple present tense is used to describe regular or repeated actions. Read the example and then ask a volunteer to make a similar sentence about the class (e.g., *We have English class twice a week.*).

5. Explain that the simple present tense is also used to show a place of origin. Read the example and then ask a volunteer to make a similar sentence about himself or herself (e.g., *I come from Colombia.*).

EXERCISE 2 ≡★
Answers will vary.

10-15 mins

1. Have students read the direction line. Instruct students to give facts about themselves and their countries. Go over the example in the book. Model the exercise using your own information. Write one or two of your answers on the board.

2. Have students complete Exercise 2 individually. Then have students compare answers with a partner. Remind students to review grammar chart **2.2** on page 42 if necessary. Monitor pair work. Give help as needed.

Practice Idea: Listening

Play a guessing game. Read (or have a volunteer read) a student's answers. Then have the class guess who the student is (and the student's country and native city).

2.3 Spelling of the -s Form ≡★

10-15 mins

1. Copy the base forms of the verbs from grammar chart **2.3** on the board. Elicit from students the -s forms. Write their suggestions on the board, correcting as necessary.

2. Have students cover up grammar chart **2.3** on page 43. Say: *There are four rules for adding an -s to verbs. Do you know what they are?* If students have difficulty, give them hints. Say: *Look at the endings of these four verbs* (miss, wash, catch, mix). *What do you add along with the s?* (e) *So what's the rule for these verbs?* (When the base form ends in *ss*, *sh*, *ch*, or *x* add *es* . . . , etc.) Continue with the other verbs.

3. Have students look at grammar chart **2.3**. Say: *Compare our rules with the rules in the book.* Review the rules in the grammar chart.

EXERCISE 3

ANSWERS: 1. tries; **2.** plays; **3.** has; **4.** goes; **5.** worries; **6.** finishes; **7.** does; **8.** pushes; **9.** enjoys; **10.** thinks; **11.** says; **12.** changes; **13.** brushes; **14.** obeys; **15.** reaches; **16.** fixes; **17.** works; **18.** raises; **19.** charges; **20.** sees

5-10 mins

1. Have students read the direction line. Ask: *What do we write in the blanks?* (the -s form of the verb) Go over the examples in the book. Ask students to tell you what the rules are for the spelling of

each verb in the examples. (*eat*—add -s to most verbs; *study*—consonant + *y*, change the *y* to *i* and add -*es*; *watch*—ends in *ch*, add -*es*)

2. Have students complete Exercise 3 individually. Remind them to review grammar chart **2.3** on page 43 if necessary. Check answers as a class.

2.4 Pronunciation of the -s Form

10-15 mins

1. Have students cover up grammar chart **2.4** on page 44. Say: *There are three ways to pronounce the* s. List them across the board: **1.** /s/, **2.** /z/, **3.** /əz/.

Pronounce each sound. Give an example from each list. Remind students that this is about pronunciation, not spelling or writing. Then say: *Listen to each word as I say it. Tell me which sound I'm making.* Say words from the grammar chart lists on page 44 in random order. Pronounce each word carefully. Have students guess where the word belongs and write it under the sound they tell you.

2. Have students look at grammar chart **2.4**. Say: *Compare our lists with the lists in the book.* Go over any errors. Have students practice pronouncing the -s form chorally as a class as needed.

3. Direct students to the Pronunciation Note. Pronounce *do/does* and *say/says* for the students. Tell them that these verbs end in a vowel sound and have a change in the vowel sound when the -s is added.

Presentation Idea

Have students cover up grammar chart **2.4**. Read the verbs in the first list in the grammar chart (*hopes*, *eats*, *picks*, *laughs*). Ask students to repeat what they think the /s/ sound is for that group of words. Then read the verbs from the second list and ask the students to repeat what they think the /s/ sound is for that group of words and so on. After the last group of verbs, ask students to look at the chart. Go over the rules for pronunciation.

Practice Idea: Speaking

For additional practice with pronunciation, make flash cards with the base form of the verbs in grammar chart **2.4** (or other verbs). Show students a flashcard, and have them pronounce the *-s* form. As an alternative to flashcards, you may simply say the base form of the verb and have students say the *-s* form.

EXERCISE 4

 5-10 mins Have students read the direction line. Turn to Exercise 3 on page 43. Ask: *What are we going to say?* (the base form and the *-s* form) Have a volunteer say #1. Have students finish the exercise in pairs. Circulate to help with pronunciation.

Practice Idea: Writing and Speaking

Have a Spelling and Pronunciation Bee. Make a list of about 40 verbs. Divide the class into Team A and Team B. Give one member from Team A a verb and ask him or her to spell the *-s* form on the board. Do the same with Team B. Then give another member from Team A another verb and ask him or her to pronounce the *-s* form, and so on. Make sure that team members take turns. To make the exercise more challenging, give extra points if the team can say (or act out) what the word means.

EXERCISE 5

ANSWERS: 1. flies; **2.** washes; **3.** watches; **4.** obeys; **5.** pays; **6.** fixes; **7.** studies; **8.** does; **9.** uses; **10.** teaches

 5-10 mins
1. Have students read the direction line. Go over the example in the book. Then do #1 with the class. Ask a volunteer to give an answer.
2. Have students complete the rest of Exercise 5 individually. Remind them to review grammar chart **2.4** on page 44 if necessary. Then have students practice saying the sentences in pairs. Circulate to listen to students practice the pronunciation. Finally, check the answers as a class.

EXERCISE 6

Answers will vary.

 10-15 mins
1. Have students read the direction line. Then have them say what the president does. Write one or two of their ideas on the board as full sentences (e.g., *The president attends meetings.*).
2. Have students complete Exercise 6 in pairs. Remind students to review grammar chart **2.4** on page 44 if necessary. Monitor pair work. Give help as needed.

2.5 Comparing Affirmative Statements—*Be* and Other Verbs ═★

5-10 mins
1. Have students cover up grammar chart **2.5** on page 45. Write the following on the board:
   a. *I / student*
   b. *I / study / English*
   c. *you / right*
   d. *you / know / the answer*
   e. *he / busy*
   f. *he / work / hard*
2. Tell students to write sentences using the words on the board. Then have volunteers write them on the board.
3. Have students look at grammar chart **2.5**. Compare the work on the board with the sentences in the chart. Explain to students that they can't use the verb *be* with the simple present tense of other verbs. Briefly review grammar points on the verb *be* from Lesson 1 if needed.

EXERCISE 7 ═★

ANSWERS: 1. studies; **2.** gets; **3.** has; **4.** live; **5.** 'm; **6.** study; **7.** watch; **8.** eat; **9.** use

10-15 mins
1. Have students read the direction line. Ask: *Do all sentences have the verb* be*?* (no) Go over the examples in the book. Explain that this exercise is about a student comparing himself to his friend.
2. Have students complete Exercise 7 individually. Remind them to review grammar chart **2.5** on page 45 if necessary. Check the answers as a class. Have volunteers read the sentences aloud. Check for correct pronunciation of the *-s* form.

Practice Idea: Writing

Have students make six true statements about themselves using verbs in the simple present tense. Tell them they can use Exercise 7 as a model. Then have students read their statements to a partner. Say: *If your partner's information is different from your own, write it down. For example, write:* I live in an apartment. He lives in a hotel. If possible, try to put students of different nationalities together. Have volunteers share some of their new sentences with the class.

2.6 Negative Statements with the Simple Present Tense

10-15 mins

1. Have students cover up grammar chart **2.6** on page 46. Activate students' prior knowledge. Ask students if they know how to make negative statements with the simple present tense. Have a student give an affirmative statement and write it on the board. Have the class help you rewrite it as a negative.

2. Have students look at grammar chart **2.6**. Review the examples. On the board, write: *lives* and *does not live*. Explain how to form the negative form with *he, she, it*, or a singular noun. (*does* + *not* + base form) Then show the contraction. (*doesn't* + base form) Say: *The contraction is more common than the long form.*

3. Write on the board: *pay* and *don't pay*. Explain how to form the negative form with *I, you, we, they*, or a plural noun. (*do* + *not* + base form) Then show the contraction. (*don't* + base form) Say: *The contraction is more common than the long form.*

4. Point out the Usage Note. Explain that in British English the grammar is different for the negative of *have*. Point out the examples in the book. Explain that both mean the same thing.

Presentation Idea

Ask students to find examples of negative statements in the reading on page 40. (*Washington doesn't have factories; some people who work in Washington don't live there.*) Write the examples on the board.

EXERCISE 8

ANSWERS: 1. doesn't have; **2.** don't pay; **3.** doesn't run; **4.** don't need; **5.** doesn't have; **6.** doesn't live; **7.** don't like; **8.** doesn't live; **9.** doesn't serve; **10.** don't have; **11.** doesn't make

10-15 mins

1. Tell students that this exercise contains information about Washington, D.C. Have students read the direction line. Ask: *What are we going to write in the blanks?* (the negative form of the verb) Go over the example in the book. Have a volunteer do #1. Write the answer on the board.

2. Have students complete the rest of Exercise 8 individually. Remind them to review grammar chart **2.6** on page 46 if necessary. Check the answers as a class.

Practice Idea: Writing and Speaking

Tell students to make items 3, 4, 5, 8, 9, and 10 true for their native country. Say: *Write negative and affirmative statements*. Then have students compare information in pairs. If possible, put together students from different countries. Monitor pair work. Give help as needed.

EXERCISE 9
Answers will vary.

10-15 mins

1. Tell students that this exercise is about their city or town. Have students read the direction line. Go over the examples in the book. Have a volunteer model the example, saying what is true for their city.

2. Have students complete Exercise 9 individually. Remind them to review grammar chart **2.6** on page 46 if necessary. Check the answers as a class.

EXERCISE 10
Answers will vary.

10-15 mins

1. Tell students that this exercise is about you, their teacher. Have students read the direction line. Go over the examples in the book. Have a volunteer model the example saying the one that is true about you, the teacher.

2. Have students complete Exercise 10 individually. Remind them to review grammar charts **2.3** on page 43 and **2.6** on page 46 if necessary. Check the answers as a class.

EXERCISE 11
Answers will vary.

10-15 mins

1. Tell students that this exercise is about them. Have students read the direction line. Ask: *Do you check every item?* (No. Check only the items that are true for you.) Go over the examples in the book. Model #1 with another student.

2. Have students complete the rest of Exercise 11 individually. Remind them to review grammar charts **2.3** on page 43 and **2.6** on page 46 if necessary. Then have partners exchange books and say sentences about their partner. Model with a student. Take the student's book and say sentences (e.g. *She speaks Chinese. She doesn't live alone.*).

Practice Idea: Writing

Have students do the same exercise with another student in the class. Say: *For each statement, change I to he or she. First, guess your partner's answer; then, check with your partner. If your partner's answer is negative, write the sentence out (e.g.,* He doesn't speak Chinese. He doesn't live alone.*). Remember to use the -s form of the verb.*

For an extra challenge, have students write an alternative answer. For example: *He doesn't speak Chinese. He speaks Korean.* Provide vocabulary as necessary (e.g., weather words, seasons, other languages, etc.).

2.7 Comparing Negative Statements—*Be* and Other Verbs

10-15 mins

1. Have students cover up grammar chart **2.7** on page 48. Write the following on the board:
  a. *I / not / from Washington*
  b. *I / not / work for the government*
  c. *The museums / not / open on Christmas Day*

  d. *They / not / have tours on Christmas Day*
  e. *Washington D.C. / not / a very big city*
  f. *It / not / have tall buildings*

2. Tell students to write negative statements using the words on the board. Then have volunteers write them on the board.

3. Have students look at grammar chart **2.7**. Compare the work on the board with the sentences in the chart. Explain to students that they can't use the verb *be* to make a negative of the simple present of other verbs.

EXERCISE 12
Answers will vary.

10-15 mins

1. Tell students that this exercise is about them and the things they do. Have students read the direction line. Ask: *What do you check?* (things that are true) Go over the examples in the book. Have a volunteer model the example.

2. Have students complete the rest of Exercise 12 individually. Remind them to review grammar charts **2.3** on page 43, **2.6** on page 46, and **2.7** on page 48 if necessary. Then have partners exchange information. Have students say sentences about their partners. Monitor pair work. Give help as needed.

Practice Idea: Writing

Have students do the same exercise for another student in the class. Say: *For each statement, change I to he or she. Guess the answer for your classmate. If the answer is negative, write the sentence out (e.g.,* He's not married. He doesn't have children.*).*

Remember that in this exercise, there are sentences with be *and sentences with other verbs.* For an extra challenge, have students write an alternative answer. For example: *He isn't married. He's single.*

EXERCISE 13
Answers will vary.

10-15 mins

1. Have students read the direction line. Ask: *Do you write sentences on every topic?* (No. Choose one.) Remind students to include some negative statements. Go over the example in the book.

2. Have students complete the rest of Exercise 13 individually or in pairs. Remind them to review grammar charts **2.2** on page 42, **2.3** on page 43, **2.5** on page 45, **2.6** on page 46, and **2.7** on page 48 if necessary. Have students compare sentences in groups. Monitor group work. Give help as needed. Have volunteers read their sentences to the class.

Practice Idea: Speaking

Have group discussions. Group people together who wrote on the same topic. Say: *Read your sentences to each other and discuss them.* Groups then report their findings to the class (e.g., *In our group, everyone thinks that a good friend listens to your problems.*).

 EXERCISE 14

CD 1
TR 08 ANSWERS: **1.** lives; **2.** doesn't live; **3.** isn't; **4.** doesn't need; **5.** is; **6.** uses; **7.** doesn't work; **8.** is; **9.** takes; **10.** don't need; **11.** need; **12.** isn't; **13.** has; **14.** work; **15.** work; **16.** don't have; **17.** visit; **18.** takes

10-15 mins

1. Have students read the direction line. Go over the example in the book. Do #1 and #2 with the class. Say: *When you see* not/live, *you need to write the negative. How do we write the negative?* (doesn't live)

2. Have students complete Exercise 14 individually. Remind them to review grammar charts **2.2** on page 42, **2.3** on page 43, **2.5** on page 45, **2.6** on page 46, and **2.7** on page 48 if necessary. Then play the audio and check answers as a class.

Practice Idea: Listening

To provide practice with listening skills, have students close their books and listen to the audio. Repeat the audio as needed. Ask comprehension questions, such as: *Who is Sara Harris?* (a 30-year-old woman) *Where does she live?* (in Arlington, Virginia) *Is rent cheaper in Washington or Arlington?* (in Arlington) Then have students open their books and complete Exercise 14.

Practice Idea: Writing

Have students write a paragraph about their lives. Tell students to use Exercise 14 as a model.

One Country, Many Differences READING

1. Have students look at the title of the Reading and the photo. Ask: *What country do you think the reading is about? How do you know?* Have students make predictions about what the differences referred to in the title might be.

2. Preteach any vocabulary words your students may not know, such as *religion, vote, tax, amount,* and *time zone.*

Reading Glossary

amount: a quantity of something

religion: a particular system of the belief in a god(s), such as Christianity, Islam, Judaism, Hinduism, etc.

tax: a mandatory payment on income, sales, etc., to the government

time zone: one of the 24 areas that the world is divided into, each of which has its own time

vote: to show by marking a paper which person you want to elect

BEFORE YOU READ

5-10 mins

1. Have students discuss the questions in pairs.

2. Ask for a few volunteers to share their answers with the class.

 Reading

CD 1
TR 09

10-15 mins

1. Have students read the text silently. Tell them to pay special attention to *yes/no* questions and short answers. Tell them this is a conversation about different aspects of life in the U.S. Then play the audio and have students read along silently.

2. Check students' comprehension. Ask questions such as: *What are the two most common languages in the U.S.?* (English and Spanish) *Who pays income tax?* (all citizens) *Which states don't have sales tax?* (Alaska and Montana) *How many time zones are there in the U.S.?* (six)

2.8 *Yes/No* Questions and Short Answers with the Simple Present Tense

10-15 mins

1. Have students cover up grammar chart **2.8** on page 51. Ask students if they remember how to write *yes/no* questions with *be*. Ask volunteers to write them on the board. Remind students that in a question, the subject goes before the verb.

2. Ask: *How do you write questions with the simple present tense?* If students have difficulty, write *You speak English* on the board. Say: *Try to make a question out of this sentence.* (Do you speak English?) Ask: *Is the verb before the subject?* (No, it's after the subject.) *What comes before the subject?* (Do)

3. Have students look at grammar chart **2.8**. Review the example sentences. Point out that *does* and *do* go before the subject and that the verb does not take an *-s* in the third person. Ask: *When do we use* does? (with *he, she, it, everyone, family*, or a singular subject) *When do we use* do? (with *I, we, you, they*, or a plural subject)

4. Have students go back to the reading on page 50. Ask them to underline *yes/no* questions with *do* and circle *yes/no* questions with *does*.

5. Ask students to look for short answers in the reading on page 50. *(No, it doesn't. Yes, they do.)* Then have students look at grammar chart **2.8**. Review the examples. Explain how to form the short answer. (*Yes,* + subject pronoun + *do/does* and *No,* + subject pronoun + *don't/doesn't*)

6. Direct students to the Usage Note. Explain that the British form questions and short answers differently with *have*. Say: *Americans use* do/does *as in* Does she have a car? Yes, she does/No, she doesn't. *The British say:* Has she a car? *Or* Has she got a car? No, she hasn't./Yes, she has.

7. Review the structures for statements, *yes/no* questions, and short answers with the simple present tense. Point out where *do* and *does* come in questions and answers. Point out that the *-s* form of the verb is used for *he, she, it,* etc., in statements, but in questions the base form is used.

EXERCISE 15

ANSWERS: 1. No, she doesn't. **2.** No, she doesn't. **3.** Yes, it does. **4.** No, she doesn't. **5.** No, they don't. **6.** Yes, they do. **7.** Yes, she does.

5-10 mins

1. Tell students that the information in the exercise is based on Exercise 14 on page 49. Have students read the direction line. Ask: *What do we write on the blanks?* (short answers) Go over the example in the book.

2. Have students complete Exercise 15 individually. Remind them to review grammar chart **2.8** on page 51 if necessary. Check the answers as a class.

EXERCISE 16

ANSWERS: 1. Do you like your job? **2.** Do you teach in the summer? **3.** Do you have another job?

4. Do you speak another language? **5.** Do you travel a lot? **6.** Do you know my language? **7.** Do you like to read students' homework? **8.** Do you live far from the school? **9.** Do you have a fax machine? **10.** Do you have trouble with English spelling? **11.** Do you have a scanner? **12.** Do you like soccer?

10-15 mins

1. Tell students that in this exercise they will ask you, the teacher, questions. Have students read the direction line. Go over the example in the book. Then model the example. Choose a volunteer to ask you a question.

2. Have students write the questions individually. Remind them to review grammar chart **2.8** on page 51 if necessary. Then have students interview you. Review some of the questions and answers as a class.

Practice Ideas: Writing and Speaking

1. Have students write the questions and their guesses for your answers. Then have students ask you the questions. Survey the class to see how many guessed *yes/no.* Then tell the class your real answer to the question.

2. Have students ask a partner questions 4, 5, 6, 8, 9, 10, 11, and 12 from Exercise 16.

EXERCISE 17
Answers will vary.

10-15 mins

1. Tell students that this is an activity about their native countries and customs. Have students read the direction line. Ask: *What do we check?* (customs in our native countries) Go over the examples with the class.

2. Have students check their customs individually. Then have students ask and answer questions in pairs. Remind them to use the dialogs in the examples to help them. (If necessary, students may write out the statements and questions before asking another student.) Monitor and give help as needed.

3. Review grammar chart **2.8** on page 51 if necessary.

EXERCISE 18

ANSWERS: **1.** Do they run; **2.** Do they pay; **3.** Do you need; **4.** Does it have; **5.** Does he work; **6.** Does he make

10-15 mins

1. Tell students that this exercise is about Washington, D.C. A tourist is asking questions about the city. Have students read the direction line. Go over the example with the class. Point out the photo of the Washington Monument.

2. Have students complete the exercise individually. Remind them to review grammar chart **2.8** on page 51 if necessary. Check the answers as a class.

EXERCISE 19

ANSWERS: **1.** do; **2.** have; **3.** Does she speak; **4.** speaks; **5.** talks; **6.** don't understand; **7.** gives; **8.** Does your teacher give; **9.** gives; **10.** wears; **11.** Does your teacher wear; **12.** talks; **13.** Does your teacher teach; **14.** does

1. Tell students that this exercise is a conversation two students are having about their teachers. Have students read the direction line. Go over the example with the class.

2. Have students complete Exercise 19 individually. Remind them to review grammar charts **2.3** on page 43, **2.4** on page 44, **2.6** on page 46, and **2.8** on pages 51 if necessary. Then have students check answers in small groups.

3. Have students practice the conversation in pairs. Monitor and give help as needed.

Practice Idea: Speaking

In pairs, have students write a similar dialog about their teachers. Have students work in pairs. Monitor pair work. Give help as needed. Ask volunteers to perform a role-play of their dialog in front of class.

2.9 Comparing *Yes/No* Questions—*Be* and Other Verbs

10-15 mins

1. Have students cover up grammar chart **2.9** on page 54. Write the following on the board:

   a. *you / lost?*

   b. *you / need help?*

   c. *I / right?*

   d. *I / have / the answer?*

   e. *he / from Haiti?*

   f. *he / speak French?*

2. Tell students to write *yes/no* questions using the words on the board. Then have volunteers write the questions on the board.

3. Have students look at grammar chart **2.9**. Compare the work on the board with the sentences in the chart. Ask: *Do you need the verb* be *to make questions with a simple present tense verb?* (no)

EXERCISE 20

ANSWERS: 1. Does Sara (OR she) work on the weekend? No, she doesn't. **2.** Are you interested in American government? Yes, I am. (OR No I'm not.) **3.** Does the vice president live in the White House? No, he doesn't. **4.** Is the Metro free? No, it isn't. **5.** Does Washington (OR it) have tall buildings? No, it doesn't. **6.** Does the U.S. (OR it) have a national religion? No, it doesn't. **7.** Is Los Angeles in the Eastern Time Zone? No, it isn't. **8.** Does the Metro (OR it) run after midnight on weeknights? No, it doesn't. **9.** Is the Metro (OR it) quiet? Yes, it is.

10-15 mins

1. Have students read the direction line. Ask: *What do we write on the blanks?* (a question and a short answer) Go over the examples in the book. Then do #1 together and write it on the board.

2. Have students complete the exercise individually. Remind them to review grammar chart **2.9** on page 54 if necessary. Check the answers as a class.

2.10 *Or* Questions

5-10 mins

1. Have students cover up grammar chart **2.10** on page 55. Say: *Listen. At what point in the sentence does my voice go up when I say these sentences?*

   Do you like tea or coffee?
   Is your apartment big or small?
   Do you like the city or the country?

   Write these examples on the board and use arrows to show the intonation pattern.

2. Then ask students to look at grammar chart **2.10**. Explain that *or* questions give you a choice and that the intonation rises on the first choice and falls on the second.

   Review the examples in the grammar chart. As you go down the chart, demonstrate the intonation of the questions.

3. Have students practice saying the *or* questions in the chart chorally as a class. Guide students to use correct intonation. If necessary, have students continue to practice in small groups or pairs. Circulate and provide help as needed.

EXERCISE 21
Answers will vary.

10-15 mins

1. Tell students that this exercise is about them. Have students read the direction line. Ask: *What do we circle?* (a true statement about ourselves) Point out that students must choose one of the choices listed (e.g., coffee or tea).

2. Have students complete the exercise individually. Remind them to review grammar chart **2.10** on page 55 if necessary. Then have students ask and answer questions in pairs.

Model the example with a volunteer. Say: *Don't forget to use correct intonation when you ask the questions.* If necessary, students may first write out the questions before pairing up.

The National Museum of the American Indian READING

1. Have students look at the photos on pages 56–57 and describe what they see. Activate students' prior knowledge. Ask: *What do you know about American Indians?* Write any ideas they have on the board.

2. Have students look at the title and write three questions that they think they will find the answers to in the reading (the questions don't need to be correctly formed).

3. Preteach any vocabulary words that your students may not know, such as *exhibit*, *recommend*, and *charge*.

Reading Glossary

charge: to ask someone for a certain amount of money for something

exhibit: something that you put in a public place so that people can go to see it

recommend: to advise someone to do something because it is a good idea

BEFORE YOU READ

1. Have students discuss the questions in pairs.
2. Ask for a few volunteers to share their answers with the class.

5-10 mins

Reading

CD 1
TR 10

1. Have students read the text silently. Tell them to pay special attention to *wh-* questions.

10-15 mins

2. Check students' comprehension. Ask questions such as: *What can you learn about at the museum?* (American Indian history, life, and culture) *Is it a small museum?* (no, it isn't) *Why is the museum free?* (because of taxes and members' contributions)

3. Ask students if they found the answers to their own questions.

2.11 *Wh-* Questions with the Simple Present Tense

15-20 mins

1. Have students cover up grammar chart **2.11** on page 58. Activate students' prior knowledge. Ask students to tell you all the *wh-* question words they know. Write them on the board. Write *What / the museum / have?* and *When / you / plan to go?* on the board and have students try to write the questions.

2. Have students look at grammar chart **2.11**. Ask students to compare the *wh-* question words they remembered with the ones in the chart. Ask: *Did we forget any?*

3. Have students compare their questions on the board with the ones in the chart. Explain that making a question with a *wh-* word is not much different than making a *yes/no* question. The *wh-* word goes in front of *do* or *does*. Write on the board:

Does the museum have exhibits?
What does the museum have?

(Make sure *does* lines up in each sentence.) Remind students that the verb is in the base form in a question. Review the examples with *does* and *do*.

4. Write the following on the board:

    Where…from? Who…with?

    What floor…on?

    Say: *There are two ways to write questions with these prepositions—informally and formally. With the informal, the preposition comes at the end of the sentence:*

    Where do you come **from**?

    Who does she live **with**?

    What floor do you live **on**?

    With the formal, the preposition comes *before* the question word.

    With whom does she live?

    On what floor do you live?

    Direct students to the Language Note. Explain that we use *whom* (and not *who*) after a preposition.

Presentation Idea

Activate students' prior knowledge. Say: *What wh-questions do you know?* (e.g., *What's your name? Where are you from?*) Write students' examples on the board. Have students cover up the questions column in grammar chart **1.11**. Ask volunteers to create questions from the answers in the chart (e.g., *Who is your teacher?*). Write examples on the board.

EXERCISE 22

ANSWERS WILL VARY. Some possible answers are: **1.** He lives in Washington, D.C. (OR He lives in the White House.) **2.** (*The answer depends on the current president.*) **3.** It gets a lot of visitors because it is the capital of the U.S. and because it has a lot of museums. **4.** It has the Metro and buses. **5.** It has history, science, and art museums. **6.** The museums get money from taxpayers and members.

 1. Tell students that this exercise is about Washington D.C. Have students read the direction line. Then do #1 as an example with the class.

5-10 mins

2. Have students do Exercise 22 individually. Remind them to review grammar chart **2.11** on page 58 if necessary. Check the answers as a class.

2.12 Comparing Statements and Questions with the Simple Present Tense

 1. Have students cover grammar chart **2.12** on page 59. Ask a volunteer to make a statement in the simple present tense. Write it on the board or have a volunteer write it on the board. Then ask another volunteer to make a *yes/no* question from the statement. Write it on the board, underneath the statement. Ask another volunteer to answer the question with a short answer. Finally have one more volunteer make a *wh-* question for the statement and write it on the board.

10-15 mins

2. Have students look at grammar chart **2.12**. Say: *Compare your work on the board with the chart.* Review the examples of affirmative statements and questions in the chart.

3. Review the negative statements and questions in the second chart. Tell students that they should use contractions (*don't/doesn't*) in negative questions. Explain that if they don't use contractions, they must change the word order: *Why do they not like taxes? Why does she not get a tax refund?*

EXERCISE 23

ANSWERS: 1. Do you like museums?, What kind of museums do you like? **2.** Do you like to learn about American history?, Why do you like to learn about American history? **3.** Do you visit museums in this city?, Which museums do you visit? **4.** Do you know a lot about American Indians?, Which American Indians do you know a lot about? **5.** Do you plan to take a vacation?, Where do you plan to go? **6.** Do you travel with someone?, Who do you travel with? (OR With whom do you travel?)

1. Tell students that this exercise is about them. Have students read the direction line. Ask: *What kind of question do you ask first?* (a *yes/no* question) Go over the examples with the class.

10-15 mins

2. Have students ask and answer questions with a partner. Remind them to review grammar chart **2.12** on page 59 if necessary. Monitor pair work. Give help as needed. If needed, students may write out the questions before asking another student.

EXERCISE 24

ANSWERS: 1. What kinds of plants does it have? **2.** Why don't we have to pay to go into the museum? **3.** What kinds of programs do they have (in the theater)? **4.** What time does the museum (OR it) close? **5.** Why doesn't the U.S. (OR it) have an official language?

10-15 mins

1. Tell students that in this exercise they will ask questions about the museum in the reading on pages 56–57. Have students read the direction line. Ask: *What do you do with the words in parentheses?* (write a *wh-* question) Model the example with a student.

2. Have students complete the exercise individually or in pairs. Remind them to review grammar chart **2.12** on page 59 if necessary. Check the answers as a class.

EXERCISE 25

CD 1
TR 11

ANSWERS: 1. don't you like; **2.** do you want to; **3.** don't you like history; **4.** does; **5.** have; **6.** does it (OR the museum) close; **7.** does it start

10-15 mins

1. Tell students that they will be completing a conversation in which two people are making plans for the weekend. Have students read the direction line. Model the example with a student.

2. Have students complete the conversation in pairs and then practice it. Remind them to review grammar chart **2.12** on page 59 if necessary. Monitor pair work. Give help as needed. Play the audio and check answers as a class.

Practice Idea: Speaking

In pairs, have students role play the dialog using different information to make plans for the weekend. Before they begin, elicit ideas about things to do/ places to go and write them on the board (e.g., the mall, the movies, a gallery, the park, the sports club).

2.13 Questions About Meaning, Spelling, Cost, and Time

5-10 mins

1. Have students cover up grammar chart **2.13** on page 61. Elicit question words. Ask students: *When you want to know the meaning of a word, what do you say?* (What does X mean?) *When you want to know how to spell something, what do you say?* (How do you spell X?) *When you want to know how to say something in another language, what do you say?* (How do you say X in your language?) *When you want to know how much something costs, what do you say?* (How much does X cost?) *When you want to know how much time something takes?* (How long does X take?)

2. Have students look at grammar chart **2.13**. Review the example sentences.

3. Explain to students that *mean, spell, say, cost,* and *take* are all verbs that go in the verb position in a question. For example, it's incorrect to say *What means "D.C."?*

EXERCISE 26

ANSWERS: 1. does it take (to see everything); **2.** do you spell; **3.** does, mean; **4.** do you say

10-15 mins

1. Have students read the direction line. Remind students to read the first statement for help in writing the question. Go over the example in the book.

2. Have students complete the exercise individually. Remind them to review grammar chart **2.13** on page 61 if necessary. Go over the answers as a class.

EXERCISE 27

ANSWERS: 1. do you; **2.** from; **3.** not; **4.** do; **5.** from; **6.** do; **7.** speak; **8.** Is; **9.** isn't; **10.** does a phone card (OR it); **11.** costs; **12.** do you say; **13.** does; **14.** mean

15-20 mins

1. Have students read the direction line. Go over the example with the class.

2. Have students complete the exercise individually or in pairs. Remind them to use grammar charts **2.9** on page 54, **2.11** on

page 58, **2.12** on page 59, and **2.13** on page 61 if necessary. Check the answers as a class.

3. Have students practice the conversation. Monitor pair work. Give help as needed.

Practice Idea: Speaking

Have pairs rewrite the conversation making it true for them. Tell students they can change information and make it shorter. Have the pairs practice their new conversation. Monitor pair work. Have volunteers share their conversation with the class.

2.14 Comparing *Wh-* Questions— *Be* and Other Verbs

10-15 mins

1. Have students cover up grammar chart **2.14** on page 63. Write the following on the board:

   a. *who / she?*
   b. *where / she / live?*
   c. *how / you?*
   d. *how / you / feel?*
   e. *where / I?*
   f. *what / I / need?*

2. Tell students to write *wh-* questions using the words above. Say: *Write the missing verbs.* Then have volunteers write them on the board.

3. Have students look at grammar chart **2.14**. Compare the work on the board with the sentences in the chart. Say: *Don't forget to use* do *or* does *in a question. Also, remember that you can't use the verb* be *to make questions with a simple present tense verb.*

 EXERCISE 28

CD 1
TR 12

ANSWERS: 1. Does he (OR Brian) work; **2.** does he do; **3.** does, mean; **4.** Does he live; **5.** does he live; **6.** does it take; **7.** does she live; **8.** do you spell it (OR "Fallston"); **9.** does she; **10.** Does she work; **11.** does "ciao" mean; **12.** do you say

10-15 mins

1. Have students read the direction line. Tell students that this is a conversation between two students. Remind students to look at the

answer for help writing the question. Go over the example in the book.

2. Have students complete Exercise 28 individually. Remind them to review grammar chart **2.14** on page 63 if necessary. Then play the audio and check answers as a class.

3. Have students practice the conversation in pairs. Monitor pair work. Give help as needed.

Practice Idea: Listening

To provide practice with listening skills, have students close their books and listen to the audio. Repeat the audio as needed. Ask comprehension questions such as: *Where does Jessica live?* (New York) *Does Brian work for the government?* (Yes, he does.) *How long does it take to drive to D.C.?* (about five hours) Then have students open their books and complete Exercise 28.

Summary of Lesson 1

20-30 mins

1. **Forms of the simple present tense** Have students make sentences for each subject in the chart. If necessary, review:

   2.1 Simple Present Tense—Forms (p. 41)

2. **Simple present-tense patterns with the -s form** Have students close their books. Say: *Write one sentence for each sentence type listed. Use a subject that takes the -s form. Then compare your sentences with those in the book.* If necessary, review:

   2.3 Spelling of the *-s* Form (p. 43)
   2.6 Negative Statements with the Simple Present Tense (p. 46)
   2.8 *Yes/No* Questions and Short Answers with the Simple Present Tense (p. 51)
   2.10 *Or* Questions (p. 55)
   2.11 *Wh-* Questions with the Simple Present Tense (p. 58)

3. **Simple present-tense patterns with the base form** Have students close their books. Say: *Write one sentence for each sentence type listed. Use a subject that takes the base form.*

Then compare your sentences with those in the book. If necessary, review:

2.6 Negative Statements with the Simple Present Tense (p. 46)

2.8 *Yes/No* Questions and Short Answers with the Simple Present Tense (p. 51)

2.10 *Or* Questions (p. 55)

2.11 *Wh-* Questions with the Simple Present Tense (p. 58)

4. **Present-tense patterns with the verb *be*** Have students close their books. Say: *Write one sentence for each sentence type listed. Use the verb* be. *Then compare your sentences with those in the book.* If necessary, review:

2.5 Comparing Affirmative Statements—*Be* and Other Verbs (p. 45)

2.7 Comparing Negative Statements—*Be* and Other Verbs (p. 48)

2.9 Comparing *Yes/No* Questions—*Be* and Other Verbs (p. 54)

2.14 Comparing *Wh-* Questions—*Be* and Other Verbs (p. 63)

5. **Uses of the simple present tense** Have students write an affirmative sentence in the simple present tense for each use. If necessary, review:

2.2 Simple Present Tense—Uses (p. 42)

Editing Advice

10-15 mins

Have students close their books. Write the example sentences without editing marks or corrections on the board. For example:

1. *He need more money.*

   This school have a big library.

2. *My father doesn't has a car.*

   Does your mother speaks English well?

Ask students to correct each sentence. This activity can be done individually, in pairs, or as a class. After students have corrected each sentence, tell them to turn to pages 65–67. Say: *Now compare your work with the Editing Advice in the book.* Have students read through all the advice.

Editing Quiz

ANSWERS: Part A: 1. likes; **2.** go; **3.** has; **4.** doesn't have; **5.** C; **6.** likes; **7.** watches; **8.** doesn't like; **9.** cries; **10.** don't want; **11.** C; **12.** She likes; **13.** eat

Part B: 1. Do you live; **2.** How long does it take you to get to school? **3.** How do you get to school? **4.** What does "transfer" mean? **5.** How much does the transfer cost? **6.** Why don't you drive to school? **7.** How much does parking cost at school? **8.** Where does your friend live? **9.** Does he live; **10.** doesn't; **11.** C; **12.** How do you spell Dmitry? **13.** How do you say "see you later"

10-15 mins

1. Tell students they are going to put the editing advice into practice. Have students read the direction line. Ask: *Do all the shaded words and phrases have mistakes?* (no) Go over the examples in Part A and Part B with the class. Then do Part A, #1 together.

2. Have students complete the quiz individually, Parts A and B. Then have them compare answers with a partner before checking answers as a class.

3. For the items students had difficulties with, have them go back and find the relevant grammar chart and review it. Monitor and give help as necessary.

Lesson 2 Test/Review

40-60 mins

Use the Assessment CD-ROM with Exam*View*®, Online Workbook, and Web site for additional practice, review, and assessment materials.

PART 1

ANSWERS: 1. goes; **2.** carries; **3.** mixes; **4.** drinks; **5.** plays; **6.** studies; **7.** catches; **8.** says

1. Part 1 may be used in addition to the Assessment CD-ROM with Exam*View*® as an in-class test to assess student performance. Have students read the direction line. Go over the examples with the class.

2. Collect for assessment.

3. If necessary, have students review:

   2.3 Spelling of the *-s* Form (p. 43)

PART 2

ANSWERS: **1.** uses, doesn't use; **2.** speak, don't speak; **3.** has, doesn't have; **4.** are, aren't; **5.** pronounce, don't pronounce; **6.** teaches, doesn't teach; **7.** means, doesn't mean; **8.** come, don't come; **9.** is, isn't

1. Part 2 may also be used as an in-class test to assess student performance, in addition to the Assessment CD-ROM with ExamView®. Have students read the direction line. Ask: *Is the first or second sentence in the negative?* (second) Go over the examples with the class.

2. Have students complete Part 2 individually. Collect for assessment.

3. If necessary, have students review:
   2.5 Comparing Affirmative Statements— *Be* and Other Verbs (p. 45)
   2.7 Comparing Negative Statements— *Be* and Other Verbs (p. 48)

PART 3

ANSWERS: **1.** Does Mexico have 50 states? No, it doesn't. **2.** Does the bank sell stamps? No, it doesn't. **3.** Is Los Angeles in California? Yes, it is. **4.** Do Americans (OR they) pay income tax? Yes, they do. **5.** Do April and June have 31 days? No, they don't. **6.** Does the president work on Capitol Hill? No, he doesn't. **7.** Do Canadians speak English? Yes, they do. **8.** Does the teacher come to class on time? Yes, he (OR she) does.

1. Part 3 may also be used as an in-class test to assess student performance, in addition to the Assessment CD-ROM with ExamView®. Have students read the direction line. Ask: *Do we use* wh- *words in these questions?* (no) Go over the example as a class.

2. Have students complete Part 3 individually. Collect for assessment.

3. If necessary, have students review:
   2.8 *Yes/No* Questions and Short Answers with the Simple Present Tense (p. 51)
   2.9 Comparing *Yes/No* Questions—*Be* and Other Verbs (p. 54)

PART 4

ANSWERS: **1.** What (language) do Canadians speak? **2.** How many museums does Washington, D.C. (OR it) have? **3.** How often does the president meet with foreign leaders? **4.** When is Christmas? **5.** How do you spell "tomorrow"? **6.** What does "occasion" mean? **7.** Why doesn't the president make the laws? **8.** What country do you come from?

1. Part 4 may also be used as an in-class test to assess student performance, in addition to the Assessment CD-ROM with ExamView®. Point out that it isn't necessary to answer the question. Go over the examples with the class.

2. Have students complete Part 4 individually. Collect for assessment.

3. If necessary, have students review:
   2.11 *Wh-* Questions with the Simple Present Tense (p. 58)
   2.12 Comparing Statements and Questions with the Simple Present Tense (p. 59)

PART 5

ANSWERS: **1.** Are you; **2.** Do you live; **3.** don't you live; **4.** do they live; **5.** Do; **6.** like; **7.** do you like; **8.** do they (OR your parents) visit you; **9.** do they love; **10.** do you have; **11.** does "commerce" mean; **12.** do you spell it (OR "commerce"); **13.** Do you like; **14.** Where do you live; **15.** Do you; **16.** do you go; **17.** does it (OR a taxi ride) cost; **18.** Is the Metro; **19.** Does it (OR the Metro) run; **20.** do you say

1. Part 5 may also be used as an in-class test to assess student performance, in addition to the Assessment CD-ROM with ExamView®. Have students read the direction line. Point out that this conversation is an interview. Go over the example with the class.

2. Have students complete Part 5 individually. Collect for assessment.

3. If necessary, have students review:
   2.8 *Yes/No* Questions and Short Answers with the Simple Present Tense (p. 51)
   2.9 Comparing *Yes/No* Questions—*Be* and Other Verbs (p. 54)
   2.11 *Wh-* Questions with the Simple Present Tense (p. 58)

Expansion

These expansion activities provide opportunities for students to interact with one another and further develop their speaking and writing skills. Encourage students to use grammar from this lesson whenever possible.

CLASSROOM ACTIVITIES

10-15 mins per activity

Have students read the direction line. Model the first item with a student. Have students complete the checklist on their own. Then instruct students to compare lists and write sentences about themselves and their partners (*I have a cell phone. Pedro doesn't have a cell phone.*). Monitor pair work. Give help as needed.

Practice Ideas: Speaking

1. Do a class survey. In groups, have students compare information. Have students report their results to the class. Record the information on the board for selected categories (e.g., *All of the students in the class have a cell phone.*).

2. Have students read the direction line. Go over the sample questions and briefly model the activity. Before the game, brainstorm *wh-* question words and write them on the board. Point out that both *yes/no* questions and *wh-* questions may be asked.

3. Have students read the direction line. Go over the example and briefly model the activity. Point out that the answer to the example is a lion.

4. Tell students that this activity is about making comparisons between schools. Have students read the direction line. Go over the example with the class. Have students work in groups. Monitor group work. Give help as needed.

TALK ABOUT IT

15-20 mins

Write these headings on the board: *taxes, public transportation, languages, elections.* Ask questions such as: *What kind of taxes do we pay? Whom do we pay taxes to? What kinds of public transportation are there? What languages do the students in this class speak? Who do we vote for in elections?* etc. Write the vocabulary that these questions elicit under each heading on the board. Then have students discuss the questions in pairs or small groups. Monitor and give help as needed.

WRITE ABOUT IT

20-30 mins

Have students read the direction line. Go over the example with them. Briefly model the activity with the class. Choose a tourist attraction in the U.S. and elicit sentences about it from the students (e.g., *I love New York City. It's very exciting. It has tall buildings. It has wonderful stores and restaurants.*). Then write a few sentences about your tourist attraction on the board, following the model in the example. Then have students write their own paragraphs. Collect for assessment and/or have students present their paragraphs to the class.

Practice Idea: Writing

Have students make brochures about the tourist attractions. Encourage students to use drawings, pictures, photos, and other materials to illustrate their brochures. Display the brochures around the class for everyone to see. Ask volunteers to talk about the tourist attractions. Have each student exchange first drafts with a partner. Ask students to help their partners edit their drafts. Refer students to the Editing Advice on pages 65–66.

OUTSIDE ACTIVITY

Have students interview an American about his or her favorite tourist place in the U.S. Tell them to ask these questions: Why does you like this place? What does this place have? Then have students report back to the class.

INTERNET ACTIVITY

1. Have students use the Internet to find information about one of the following places: Disneyland, the White House, the Holocaust Museum, Ellis Island, Epcot Center, the Alamo, or any other American tourist attraction that interests them. Have them answer these questions: What is it? What does it cost to enter? Where is it? What does it have?

2. Have students use the Internet to find information about a museum or place of special interest in this city. Have them answer these questions: What is it? What does it cost to enter? Where is it? What does it have?

Lesson 3

Lesson Overview

GRAMMAR

1. Briefly review other tenses students have learned.

   Ask: *What tense did we study in Lesson 1?* (present tense of the verb *be*) *What tense did we study in Lesson 2?* (simple present tense)

2. Ask: *What tense are we going to study in this lesson?* (simple present tense) *What else will we study?* (frequency words and prepositions of time) *Do you know any frequency words or prepositions of time that we use with the simple present tense?* (e.g., *sometimes* and *in the morning*). Have students give examples. Write the examples on the board.

CONTEXT

1. Ask: *What are we going to learn about in this lesson?* (American holidays, celebrating holidays) Activate students' prior knowledge. Ask: *What do you know about holidays in the United States?*

2. Have students share their knowledge and personal experiences. Write their ideas on the board.

Presentation Idea

The topic for this lesson can be enhanced with the following ideas:

1. Magazine pictures of Fourth of July picnics and celebrations

2. Photos from home of family Fourth of July picnics

Three Special Days in the United States READING

1. Have students look at the photos. Ask: *Who are the people?* (a couple; a little boy; a mother and son)

What are they doing? (giving gifts, giving flowers/chocolates/candies; laughing; hugging)

2. Have students look at the title of the reading. Ask: *What is the reading about? How do you know?* Have students use the photos and title to make predictions about the reading.

3. Preteach any vocabulary words your students may not know, such as *sweetheart, manufacturer, valentine, florist, parade, shamrock*, and *greeting card*. For *sweetheart* and *shamrock*, point out the pictures on page 76. For *parade*, direct students to the picture on page 77.

Reading Glossary

florist: a person who owns or runs a flower shop

greeting card: a card, usually folded and printed with a message inside, such as "Get Well" or "Happy Birthday"

manufacturer: a business that makes things

parade: an orderly movement of people in fanciful or formal dress or in uniforms, usually to show pride or to honor a special day or event

shamrock: a tiny green plant with three leaves; the symbol of Ireland

sweetheart: someone who is loved with tender affection

valentine: a love letter or greeting card given to a person to show affection or love on Valentine's Day

BEFORE YOU READ

5-10 mins

1. Have students discuss the questions in pairs. Try to pair students of different cultures together.

2. Ask for a few volunteers to share their answers with the class.

 Reading ━★
CD 1 TR 13

10-15 mins

1. Have students read the text silently. Tell them to pay special attention to frequency words such as *always* and *often*. Then play the audio and have students read along silently.

2. Check students' comprehension. Ask questions such as: *What kinds of gifts do people give on Valentine's Day?* (flowers, candy, and cards called valentines) *Who celebrates St. Patrick's Day?* (Irish people and many other Americans) *When is Mother's Day?* (the second Sunday in May)

Did You Know?

Explain that several holidays have their origins in Ancient Rome, including Easter and Christmas. Say: *Describe any holidays celebrated in your native country. Are any connected to ancient rituals?*

Practice Idea: Listening

To practice listening skills, have students first listen to the audio alone. Ask a few comprehension questions such as: *When is Valentine's Day?* (February 14) *What color do people wear on St. Patrick's Day?* (green) *How do people celebrate Mother's Day?* (buying presents for their mothers and grandmothers, sending special cards, having dinner at a restaurant) Repeat the audio if necessary. Then have students open their books and read along as they listen to the audio.

Context Note

Here are some other interesting American holidays:

April Fool's Day is celebrated on April 1. People play practical jokes on each other.

Memorial Day is a day of remembrance for those who died in military service. It is celebrated on the last Monday of May.

Labor Day is celebrated on the first Monday in September. It is a day that honors American workers.

Halloween is celebrated on October 31. Children dress up in costumes and go through their neighborhoods collecting candy and other treats.

Thanksgiving is celebrated on the fourth Thursday in November. Americans get together with family and friends to give thanks and eat a large meal.

3.1 Frequency Words with the Simple Present Tense

🕐 10-15 mins
1. Have students cover up grammar chart **3.1** on page 77. Write all the frequency words on the board in scrambled order. Have students find sentences from the reading that contain frequency words. Write a few of the sentences on the board. For example, write: *It is always on February 14.*

2. On the board, draw a scale from 0 percent to 100 percent. Ask students to place the frequency words on the scale. Ask: *Where is* never *on the scale?*

3. Have students look at grammar chart **3.1**. Ask students to compare the scale on the board with the scale in the book. Ask: *Is our scale the same as the scale in the book?* Point out that *rarely* and *seldom* have the same frequency.

4. Review the example sentences in the grammar chart. Remind students that frequency words are used with the simple present tense.

Presentation Idea

Have students come to the board and write the frequency words on the scale. Or have students draw a scale from 0 percent to 100 percent in their notebooks. Have them look at the reading and try to write the frequency words on the scale.

EXERCISE 1

ANSWERS: 1. always; **2.** often; **3.** usually; **4.** usually; **5.** always; **6.** never; **7.** always; **8.** always; **9.** never; **10.** never

---

🕐 10-15 mins
1. Tell students that this exercise is about the holidays they just read about. Have students read the direction line. Ask: *What words do we use here?* (frequency words) Go over the example in the book. Then do #1 with the class.

2. Have students complete Exercise 1 individually. Remind them to review grammar chart **3.1** on page 77 if necessary. Then have them check their answers in pairs and

compare their answers with the reading. Monitor the pair work. If necessary, check the answers as a class.

EXERCISE 2
Answers will vary.

1. Tell students that this exercise is about this class or this school. Have students read the direction line. Ask: *What words do we use here?* (frequency words) Go over the example in the book. Do #1 together.

2. Have students complete Exercise 2 individually. Then have them check their answers in pairs. Remind them to review grammar chart **3.1** on page 77 if necessary. Monitor the pair work. If necessary, check the answers as a class.

Practice Idea: Speaking

In pairs, have students tell each other how they spend Mother's Day in their native country. Say: *Your partner wants to know what your family does for Mother's Day. Your partner says, "Please tell me about Mother's Day in your home." Tell your partner about Mother's Day in your home or in your native country. Say three sentences about Mother's Day. Use frequency words to talk about what you do or do not do.* Instruct students to switch roles and repeat.

3.2 Position of Frequency Words and Expressions

1. Have students cover up grammar chart **3.2** on page 78. Then have students find sentences from the reading on page 76 that contain frequency words and the verb *be*. Have them find sentences with other verbs and frequency words. Write several of the sentences with *be* and several sentences with other verbs on the board. For example, write: *It is always on February 14.*

   Businesses are never closed for Valentine's Day or St. Patrick's Day.

A valentine usually has a red heart and a message of love.

(Make sure the verbs of each sentence line up on the board.)

2. Ask students to guess the rule for the position of frequency words with *be* and other verbs. If students have difficulty guessing the rule, ask: *Do frequency words come before or after* be? (after) *Do frequency words come before or after other verbs?* (before)

3. Have students look at grammar chart **3.2**. Review the example sentences in the grammar chart. Point out to students that *sometimes, usually,* and *often* can also come at the beginning of the sentence.

Presentation Idea

Ask students to cover up the Explanation side of the grammar chart. Elicit the rules from the students. Ask: *Does the frequency verb come before or after the verb* be? (after) *Does the frequency verb come before or after other verbs?* (before) *Do* usually *and* sometimes *always come at the beginning of the sentence?* (no, but they can)

EXERCISE 3
Answers will vary.

1. Tell students that this exercise is about their personal customs and routines. Have students read the direction line. Ask: *What words do we use here?* (frequency words)

2. Go over the example in the book. Then do #1 with the class. Ask a volunteer to give an answer.

3. If students need speaking practice, have them say true statements in pairs. If students need writing practice, have them complete the exercise in writing. Remind them to review grammar chart **3.2** on page 78 if necessary. Then have them compare their answers in pairs. Finally, check the answers as a class.

Practice Idea: Speaking

Have students survey the answers to Exercise 3 in groups. Model the questions: *How many cook meals in their homes? How many stay home on Sundays?* and so on. Circulate to observe the group work. Give help as needed. Then put the results of the survey on the board.

EXERCISE 4

Answers will vary.

10-15 mins

1. Tell students that this exercise is about customs and routines from their countries or cultural groups. Have students read the direction line. Go over the example. Then do #1 with the class. Ask a volunteer to give an answer.

2. Have students complete the rest of Exercise 4 individually. Remind them to review grammar chart **3.2** on page 78 if necessary. Then have them compare their answers in pairs. Try to pair students from different cultural groups. Finally, check the answers as a class.

Practice Idea: Speaking

Try and find similarities between cultures. Ask volunteers to talk about what they wrote in Exercise 4. Write examples on the board and ask students if there are similarities with other cultures.

EXERCISE 5

Answers will vary.

10-15 mins

1. Tell students that this exercise is about their personal customs and routines. Have students read the direction line. Go over the example in the book. Ask: *What tense is the first example in?* (simple present tense) *And the second example?* (present tense of *be*) Encourage students to use both the verb *be* and other verbs in their statements.

2. Have students complete the rest of Exercise 5 individually. Remind them to review grammar chart **3.2** on page 78 if necessary. Then have them compare their answers in pairs. Finally, check the answers as a class.

Practice Idea: Speaking

Put students in groups. Ask students to make true or false statements about themselves. Have the other students guess whether the statements are true or false. Model an example. Say: *I always wake up early on Sundays. True or false?* Students guess whether you're telling the truth.

EXERCISE 6

Answers will vary.

10-15 mins

1. Tell students that this exercise is about their observations and opinions. Have students read the direction line. Go over the example in the book.

2. Have students complete the rest of Exercise 6 in pairs. Remind them to review grammar chart **3.2** on page 78 if necessary. Monitor pair work. Give help as needed.

Practice Idea: Speaking

Take a survey of the class. How did students complete the statements? Have them discuss their ideas as a class or in small groups.

The Fourth of July READING

1. Have students look at the title. Ask: *What do you think you are going to find out about this celebration?*

2. Preteach any vocabulary words your students may not know, such as *barbecue*, *grill*, *backyard*, and *fireworks*. For *fireworks*, direct students to the picture on page 75.

Reading Glossary

barbecue: a party where food is grilled or barbecued

fireworks: bright, colorful light explosives used for celebrations

grill: a frame of metal bars on which food is cooked, usually outside

backyard: an outdoor area behind a house

BEFORE YOU READ

1. Activate students' prior knowledge of American customs. Quickly brainstorm a list of American holidays with the class and write them on the board. Ask: *What other American holidays do you know?* (e.g., April Fool's Day, Memorial Day, Labor Day, Halloween, and Thanksgiving)

2. Have students discuss the questions in pairs.

3. Ask for a few volunteers to share their answers with the class.

Reading ≡★

CD 1
TR 14

1. Have students read the text silently. Tell them to pay special attention to prepositions of time, such as *in* and *at*. Then play the audio and have students read along.

2. Check students' comprehension. Ask questions such as: *What is another name for Independence Day?* (the Fourth of July) *What do the writer and her family eat on the Fourth of July?* (hamburgers and hot dogs) *When do they usually eat?* (at about three o'clock) *Where do they go in the evening?* (to the park)

Practice Idea: Listening

To practice listening skills, have students first listen to the audio alone. Ask a few comprehension questions such as: *What is the student's favorite holiday in the U.S.?* (Independence Day OR the Fourth of July) *What do they do at night on the Fourth of July?* (watch fireworks) Repeat the audio if necessary. Then have students open their books and read along as they listen to the audio.

Context Note

Many towns and cities have Fourth of July parades with floats, marching bands, military veterans, and other participants.

3.3 Prepositions of Time ≡★

1. Have students cover up grammar chart **3.3** on page 82. Then have students find sentences from the reading on page 81 that contain prepositions of time. Write several of the sentences on the board. For example, write: *We celebrate it on July 4; We usually start to eat at about three o'clock,* etc.

2. Have students look at grammar chart **3.3**. Review the example sentences in the grammar chart.

Practice Idea: Reading

Have students underline every prepositional phrase of time in the reading (e.g., *on July 4*). Then have them match the preposition with the explanation in the grammar chart.

EXERCISE 7 ≡★
Answers will vary.

---

1. Tell students that this exercise is about their personal routines and customs. Have students read the direction line. Ask: *What kind of questions are these?* (information questions or *wh-* questions) Model the exercise. Do #1 with the class. Ask a volunteer to give an answer. Remind students to use the appropriate preposition in their answer.

2. Have students complete the rest of Exercise 7 individually. Remind them to review grammar chart **3.3** on page 82 if necessary. Then have them interview each other in pairs. Say: *Now ask your partner the questions and write down his or her answers.* Finally, check the answers as a class.

Practice Idea: Speaking

Create two rings of students. Have half of the students stand in an outer ring around the classroom. Have the other half stand in an inner ring, facing the outer ring. Instruct students to interview each other using the questions from Exercise 7. Call out *turn* every minute or so. Students in the inner ring should move one space clockwise. Students now interview their new partners. Make sure students look up at each other when they're asking and answering questions.

3.4 Questions with *Ever*

1. Have students cover up grammar chart **3.4** on page 83. Review *yes/no* questions with students. Write statements on the board based on the reading. For example, write: *The Fourth of July is my favorite holiday. We cook hamburgers and hot dogs on the grill.* Then have students write questions in their notebooks for the statements. Check answers with the class. (*Is the Fourth of July your favorite holiday? Do you cook hamburgers and hot dogs on the grill?*)

2. Have students look at grammar chart **3.4**. Say: *We use* ever *in a question when we want an answer that has a frequency word.* Review the example sentences in the grammar chart.

3. Review the Language Notes. Ask students to look at the frequency word in short answers. Ask: *Where is the frequency word?* (It's between the subject and the verb.)

Remind students not to use a negative verb with *never*. Write on the board:

Correct: No, it never is.

Wrong: No, it never isn't.

EXERCISE 8

Answers will vary.

1. Tell students that this exercise is about personal preferences and customs. Have students read the direction line. Ask: *What word do we add to the questions?* (ever) Ask: *What words are in the answers?* (frequency words)

2. Direct students to the examples in the book. Model the first example with a student. Then have two other students model the next example.

3. Have students complete the exercise in pairs. Remind them to review grammar chart **3.4** on page 83 if necessary. Check the answers as a class.

EXERCISE 9

Answers will vary.

1. Tell students that this exercise is about American customs. Have students read the direction line. Ask: *What word do we add to the questions?* (ever) Ask: *What words are in the answers?* (frequency words) Go over the examples in the book. Model the first example with a student. Then have two other students model the next example.

2. Have students complete the exercise in pairs. Remind them to review grammar chart **3.4** on page 83 if necessary. Check the answers as a class.

Practice Idea: Speaking

If possible, put students of different nationalities together. Tell them to interview each other with questions 1–4, 7, and 9 from Exercise 9. Say: *Substitute the word* American *for your partner's nationality. For example: Do Colombians ever eat with chopsticks?* Monitor pair work. Give help when needed. Have students switch roles.

EXERCISE 10

Answers will vary.

1. Tell students that this exercise is about their personal customs and habits. Have students read the direction line. Ask: *What word do we put in the blank?* (a frequency word) Ask: *Then what do we do?* (Write a question with *ever*.) Model the example with a student. Then have two other students model #1.

2. Have students fill in the blanks and write the questions individually. Remind them to review grammar chart **3.4** on page 83 if necessary. Then have students ask and answer questions in pairs. Check the answers as a class.

3.5 Questions with *How Often* and Answers with Frequency Expressions ≡★

10-15 mins

1. Have students cover up grammar chart **3.5** on page 85. Write frequency expressions from the chart on the board. For example, write: *every day*, *every month*, and *twice a week*. Ask: *What do you do every day? What do you do every other day? What do you do twice a week?* Have volunteers answer. Write their responses on the board.

2. Write *How often* on the board. Make a question with one of the students' sentences. Write: *How often do you take a shower?* Write an answer. (*every day*) Ask volunteers to make questions with *how often* and the information on the board.

3. Have students look at grammar chart **3.5**. Say: *We ask a question with* how often *when we want to know the frequency of an activity.* Review the example sentences and the expressions that show frequency in the grammar chart. Tell students that frequency expressions can come at the beginning or at the end of a sentence.

EXERCISE 11 ≡★
Answers will vary.

10-15 mins

1. Tell students that this exercise is about their personal customs and habits. Have students

read the direction line. Ask: *What words do we use to make the question?* (How often do you) Model the example with a student. Then have two other students model #1.

2. Have students ask and answer questions in pairs. Remind them to review grammar chart **3.5** on page 85 if necessary. If necessary, students may write the questions before working with a partner. Check the answers as a class.

EXERCISE 12 ≡★

ANSWERS: 1. How often does she pick up her son at baseball practice? She picks up her son at baseball practice twice a week. **2.** How often does she shop for groceries? She shops for groceries once a week. **3.** How often does she take the dog for a haircut? She takes the dog for a haircut once a month. **4.** How often does she go to the beauty salon? She goes to the beauty salon once a month. **5.** How often does she visit her mother? She visits her mother once a week. **6.** How often does she go to the gym? She goes to the gym three times a week. **7.** How often does she prepare the kids' lunches? She prepares the kids' lunches five days a week (OR every day). **8.** How often does she change the oil in her car? She changes the oil in her car four times a year.

10-15 mins

1. Tell students that this exercise is about Linda's activities. Have students read the direction line. Ask: *What question words will you use in the question?* (how often) Model the example with a student. Then have two other students model #1.

2. Have students complete the exercise individually. Remind them to review grammar chart **3.5** on page 85 if necessary. Then have them check answers in pairs. Check answers as a class if needed.

2. Have students complete Exercise 14 individually. Remind them to review grammar charts **3.1** on page 77 and **3.5** on page 85 if necessary. Then play the audio and check answers as a class.

3. Have students practice the dialog in pairs.

Practice Idea: Speaking

Have students write their own list of things they do on a regular basis. Tell students not to include when or how often they do the activity. Have students exchange lists and interview each other. Ask students to report interesting activities to the class (e.g., *John goes to karate class every other day.*). Monitor pair work. Give help when needed.

Practice Idea: Listening

To provide practice with listening skills, have students close their books and listen to the audio before they do Exercise 14. Ask comprehension questions, such as: *What does person A want to do tonight?* (go to a movie) *What does person B's mother do on Friday nights?* (make dinner for person B) *Is person B's mother young or old?* (old) Then have students open their books and complete Exercise 14.

EXERCISE 13

Answers will vary.

10-15 mins

1. Tell students that this exercise is about their family members' habits and routines. Have students read the direction line. Ask: *What words will we use in the sentences?* (frequency words) Go over the example in the book.

2. Have students complete the exercise individually. Remind them to review grammar charts **3.1** on page 77 and **3.5** on page 85 if necessary. Collect for assessment or have students read their sentences to a partner.

EXERCISE 14

CD 1
TR 15

ANSWERS: 1. usually complains; **2.** How often do you call; **3.** I call her every day; **4.** 's often; **5.** always watches; **6.** Does she ever; **7.** rarely does; **8.** usually cooks; **9.** never changes; **10.** do you usually do; **11.** usually buy; **12.** usually says; **13.** always die; **14.** Is she always; **15.** Is she ever; **16.** always says

10-15 mins

1. Tell students that this exercise is a conversation between two friends. Have students read the direction line. Remind students that the verbs should be in the simple present tense. Go over the example in the book. Point out the picture of someone knitting.

EXERCISE 15

ANSWERS: 1. My friends and I always get; **2.** usually cook; **3.** cook; **4.** They rarely; **5.** we have; **6.** have; **7.** bakes; **8.** on; **9.** to; **10.** At; **11.** is always; **12.** it; **13.** happens; **14.** are; **15.** are always; **16.** I; **17.** works; **18.** stay; **19.** forget; **20.** have; **21.** in

10-15 mins

1. Tell students that this exercise is about how one person celebrates the Fourth of July. Have students read the direction line. Ask: *Does every sentence have a mistake?* (no) Go over the examples.

2. Have students complete the exercise individually. Collect for assessment or check answers as a class.

3. If necessary, review Lessons 1, 2, and 3.

Context Note

Americans often show patriotism on special days by hanging the American flag outside their homes. You will often see flags out on Memorial Day (the last Monday in May), the Fourth of July (July 4), and on Flag Day (June 14). Some people even hang their flags out all year round.

Summary of Lesson 3

20-30 mins

1. **Frequency Words** Have students practice frequency words in pairs using the reading on page 76. Say: *Go back to the reading on page 76. One student says, "True or false? St. Patrick's Day is sometimes on March 17." The other student says, "False. St. Patrick's Day is always on March 17." Each partner makes four true or false statements.* If necessary, have students review:

   3.1 Frequency Words with the Simple Present Tense (p. 77)

   3.2 Position of Frequency Words and Expressions (p. 78)

2–3. **The Position of Frequency Words and Frequency Expressions** Have students close their books. Instruct students to write down at least five frequency words and five frequency expressions on a piece of paper. Have students practice in pairs.

   Say: *One student says, "Every other day." The other student gives an example about himself or herself, such as, "I have English class every other day" or "Every other day I have English class."* Instruct students to switch roles and repeat. If necessary, have students review:

   3.2 Position of Frequency Words and Expressions (p. 78)

   3.5 Questions with *How Often* and Answers with Frequency Expressions (p. 85)

4. **Frequency Questions and Answers** Have students write ten questions using *ever* and *how often*. Remind students to use *ever* with the simple present tense and also with the present tense of *be*. Then have students ask and answer the questions in pairs. If necessary, have students review:

   3.4 Questions with *Ever* (p. 83)

   3.5 Questions with *How Often* and Answers with Frequency Expressions (p. 85)

5. **Prepositions of Time** Write three to five questions on the board to elicit prepositions of time. For example, write:

   What time do you eat breakfast/dinner?

   When do you go shopping?

When do you do your homework?

When do you go to work/school?

What time do you get home?

Have students answer the questions in their notebooks. Then instruct students to go around the room and ask other students the same questions. Ask: *How many students have the same information as you?* If necessary, have students review:

   3.3 Prepositions of Time (p. 82)

Editing Advice

5-10 mins

Have students close their books. Write the example sentences without editing marks or corrections on the board. For example:

1. *I never am bored in class.*

   Always I drink coffee in the morning.

Ask students to correct each sentence. This activity can be done individually, in pairs, or as a class. After students have corrected each sentence, tell them to turn to page 90. Say: *Now compare your work with the Editing Advice in the book.*

Editing Quiz

ANSWERS: 1. never; **2.** C; **3.** I never mail; **4.** I always visit; **5.** How often; **6.** Do you tell them once in a while? **7.** C; **8.** C; **9.** you ever think; **10.** I always do

10-15 mins

1. Tell students that they are going to put the editing advice into practice. Have students read the direction line. Ask: *Do all the shaded words and phrases have mistakes?* (no) Go over the examples with the class. Then do #1 together.

2. Have students complete the quiz individually. Then have them compare answers with a partner before checking answers as a class.

3. For the items students had difficulties with, have them go back and find the relevant grammar chart and review it. Monitor and give help as necessary.

Lesson 3 Test/Review

 40-60 mins Use the Assessment CD-ROM with Exam*View*®, Online Workbook, and Web site for additional practice, review, and assessment materials.

PART 1

ANSWERS: 1. is (OR 's); **2.** Do you like; **3.** Does; **4.** doesn't; **5.** wears; **6.** How old is he; **7.** Is (OR 's); **8.** Does he speak; **9.** speaks; **10.** When (OR How often); **11.** meets; **12.** Is (OR 's); **13.** wears; **14.** always; **15.** doesn't speak; **16.** speaks; **17.** gives; **18.** How often; **19.** don't; **20.** Does; **21.** ever; **22.** teach; **23.** does; **24.** does your class use; **25.** does "context" mean; **26.** do you spell "context" (OR it)

1. Part 1 may be used as an in-class test to assess student performance, in addition to the Assessment CD-ROM with Exam*View*®. Tell students that this is a conversation between two students. Words and phrases are missing. Review the example. Then do #1 as a class. Ask: *What goes in the first blank?* (*is*)

2. Have students complete Part 1 individually. Collect for assessment.

3. If necessary, have students review Lessons 1, 2, and 3.

PART 2

ANSWERS: 1. in; **2.** in; **3.** on; **4.** at; **5.** at; **6.** in; **7.** from, to (OR till OR until); **8.** in; **9.** in

1. Part 2 may also be used as an in-class test to assess student performance, in addition to the Assessment CD-ROM with Exam*View*®. Tell students that prepositions of time are missing. Review the example. Then do #1 as a class. Ask: *What goes in the first blank?* (*in*)

2. Have students complete Part 2 individually. Collect for assessment.

3. If necessary, have students review:
   3.3 Prepositions of Time (p. 82)

PART 3

ANSWERS: 1. She's; **2.** C; **3.** gives; **4.** C; **5.** English is; **6.** C; **7.** C; **8.** C; **9.** she explains; **10.** C; **11.** has; **12.** are; **13.** say; **14.** C; **15.** C; **16.** C; **17.** makes; **18.** often brings; **19.** C; **20.** C; **21.** I always; **22.** sometimes go; **23.** She's very; **24.** tries; **25.** C; **26.** C; **27.** she usually wears; **28.** She's about; **29.** she looks; **30.** a teacher never wears; **31.** I'm very; **32.** understands; **33.** C; **34.** She comes; **35.** C; **36.** knows

1. Part 3 may also be used as an in-class test to assess student performance, in addition to the Assessment CD-ROM with Exam*View*®. Tell students that this is a composition a student wrote about his teacher. Have students read the direction line.

   Ask: *Do all the shaded words and phrases have mistakes?* (no) Do #1 together.

2. Have students complete Part 3 individually. Collect for assessment.

3. If necessary, have students review Lessons 1, 2, and 3.

Expansion

These expansion activities provide opportunities for students to interact with one another and further develop their speaking and writing skills. Encourage students to use grammar from this lesson whenever possible.

CLASSROOM ACTIVITIES

 10-15 mins per activity

1. Tell students that this activity is about usual activities. Ask: *What tense do we use to talk about usual activities?* (the simple present tense) Remind students to use frequency words and expressions, prepositions of time, and questions with *ever*. If necessary, provide the option of writing out the questions before asking a partner. Have two volunteers read the example interview.

2. As a class, brainstorm a list of famous people from the U.S. and from other parts of the world. Write the names on the board. Say: *Let's find out how much we know about well-known people. Who should we talk about? How about Prince William?* Elicit other names. In groups, or as a class, have students make statements about the activities of the list of people you brainstormed.

Practice Idea: Speaking

Bring in magazine pictures of famous people from all over the world. Distribute three to five pictures to each group. Ask students to make statements about these well-known people.

3. Try to pair students of different nationalities, if possible. If necessary, provide the option of writing out the questions before asking a partner.

Practice Idea: Speaking

Bring in photos from home of special occasions. Tell students about your family's traditions. Or have students ask you questions about your pictures.

4. Instruct students to write a list of activities, but not to say when or how often they do them. Tell students to read their partners' lists and ask questions. Say: *Remember to ask your partners how often and when they do the activity.*

TALK ABOUT IT

15-20 mins

Write on the board: *customs.* Ask questions such as, *What do you usually do when you greet people? Do you shake hands/kiss/hug? What do you usually say before you begin a meal? What kind of clothes do you usually wear to work?* Write the students' responses on the board. Then have students complete the chart about American customs and their customs. Have students discuss their answers in small groups. Monitor and give help as needed.

WRITE ABOUT IT

40-60 mins

1. Brainstorm classroom activities. Ask: *What kinds of activities does your teacher do in class?* (e.g., *teach, talk, write on the board, give homework, correct papers, prepare assignments*) Write them on the board. Say: *Now use these ideas to write about one of your teachers.* Encourage students to use frequency words and expressions in their writing.

2. Have students read the paragraph about the Day of the Dead. Then have them write a paragraph about a holiday or special occasion using it as a model. Say: *Write about the way you celebrate birthdays or a special holiday in your family. Give details about what you usually do, always do, never do, and sometimes do.* Collect for assessment and/or have students present their paragraphs to a group.

Practice Idea: Writing

Have students exchange first drafts with a partner. Ask students to help their partners edit their drafts. Refer students to the Editing Advice on page 90.

OUTSIDE ACTIVITIES

1. Have students ask an American-born person to do Exercise 4 on page 79. See how your answers compare to this person's answers. Report this person's answers to the class.

2. Have students go to a drugstore, supermarket, or card store. Is there a special holiday (for example, Father's Day, Thanksgiving, Christmas, Chanukah)? Read the messages in a few cards. Have students make a card for someone they know and write their own message. Have them share their cards with the class.

INTERNET ACTIVITIES

1. Tell students to find a greeting card Web site and send an electronic greeting card to someone they know.

2. Have students use the Internet to find the answers to these questions:

   a. When is Father's Day in the U.S.?
   b. What is the origin of Mother's Day?
   c. When is Thanksgiving?
   d. What is the history of the Fourth of July?

Lesson 4

Lesson Overview

GRAMMAR

Ask: *What did we study in Lesson 3?* (frequency words and prepositions of time) *What are we going to study in this lesson?* (the singular and plural; *there* + *be* + noun; articles and quantity words) Activate students' prior knowledge. Have volunteers give examples. Write them on the board. Ask: *What's the plural of teacher?* (teachers) *What about child?* (children) *Name two articles that we've already studied.* (*a, an*) *Do you know any quantity words?* (*some, many*)

CONTEXT

1. Ask: *What will we learn about in this lesson?* (where Americans live) Activate students' prior knowledge. Ask: *Which of you live in an apartment? A house?*

2. Have students share their knowledge and personal experiences.

Presentation Idea

The topic for this lesson can be enhanced with the following ideas:

1. Interior and exterior pictures of your house or apartment

2. Pictures of houses and apartments from magazines

Americans and Where They Live READING

1. Have students look at the photo. Ask: *Who are these people?* (a family) *Where are they?* (in front of a house)

2. Have students look at the title of the reading. Ask: *What is the reading about? How do you know?* Have students make predictions.

3. Preteach any vocabulary words your students may not know, such as *household, homeowner,* and *renter.*

Reading Glossary

homeowner: a property owner, especially of a house or apartment

household: the person or people living together in one home

renter: a person or business that rents things, such as apartments, from the owner(s)

BEFORE YOU READ

 5-10 mins

1. Have students discuss the questions in pairs.

2. Ask for a few volunteers to share their answers with the class.

 CD 1 TR 16   ### Reading

1. Have students read the text silently. Tell them to pay special attention to plural nouns.

 10-15 mins

2. Check students' comprehension. Ask questions such as: *How many people live in the U.S.?* (over 300 million) *How many have cats?* (31 percent) *Are homes in San Diego inexpensive?* (no)

Practice Idea: Listening

To practice listening skills, have students first listen to the audio alone. Ask a few comprehension questions such as: *How many people does the average American family have?* (3.19) *What percent of Americans live alone?* (27 percent) Repeat the audio if necessary. Then have students open their books and read along as they listen to the audio.

4.1 Singular and Plural—An Overview

5-10 mins

1. Have students close their books. Write a brief list of nouns in the singular on the board. (kid, beach, American, man) Ask: *Are these nouns singular or plural?* (singular)

2. Ask volunteers to write the plural of each word on the board. (*kids, beaches, Americans, men*) Explain that the plural usually ends in -*s* or -*es*, although some plural forms are irregular—for example, *men*.

3. Go through the examples in the grammar chart with the class.

EXERCISE 1

ANSWERS: **1.** F; **2.** T; **3.** F; **4.** F; **5.** F; **6.** T; **7.** T; **8.** T; **9.** F; **10.** T; **11.** T

1. Tell students that this true-or-false exercise is based on the reading on page 98. Have students read the direction line. Go over the example in the book. Say: *If you need help, you can look back at the reading on page 98.*

2. Have students complete Exercise 1 individually. Remind them to review grammar chart **4.1** on page 99 if necessary. Check the answers as a class.

Practice Idea: Speaking

Have students research similar statistics for their native countries. If possible, put students of the same nationality in the same group. Have group members compare information. Finally, have groups present their information to the class.

4.2 Spelling of Regular Noun Plurals =★

1. Copy the lists of nouns (example words and plural forms) from grammar chart **4.2** on the board. Keep nouns in the same groups and in the same order as in the chart in the book. For example:

Singular	Plural
bee	*bees*
banana	*bananas*
pie	*pies*
bed	*beds*
pin	*pins*
month	*months*

2. Have students cover up grammar chart **4.2** on page 100. Say: *Study these spelling changes. Can you guess what the rules for adding an -s are?* If students have difficulty, give them hints. Say: *Look at the endings of the four nouns in row 3* (*ss, sh, ch,* and *x*). *What do you add?* (*es*) *So what's the rule?* (When the noun ends in *ss, sh, ch,* or *x*, add *es*.)

3. Have students look at grammar chart **4.2**. Say: *Compare our rules with the rules in the book.* Review the rules in the grammar chart.

4. Point out the exceptions. Some nouns ending in a consonant + *o* that do not add an -*e* are: *photos, pianos, solos, altos, sopranos, autos,* and *avocados.* Nouns that end in *f* or *fe* that don't change to -*ves* are: *beliefs, chiefs, roofs,* and *chefs.*

Presentation Idea

Have students cover up grammar chart **4.2** on page 100. Write the singular nouns from the chart on the board. Ask students to go up to the board and write the plural forms next to them. Then ask students to look at grammar chart **4.2** and check the board. Go over the rules for spelling.

EXERCISE 2 =★

ANSWERS: **1.** dishes; **2.** countries; **3.** halves; **4.** books; **5.** boys; **6.** girls; **7.** benches; **8.** boxes; **9.** sharks; **10.** stereos; **11.** knives; **12.** stories; **13.** sofas; **14.** keys; **15.** movies; **16.** squirrels; **17.** mosquitoes; **18.** lions; **19.** flies; **20.** cows; **21.** tables; **22.** roaches; **23.** foxes; **24.** houses; **25.** turkeys; **26.** chickens; **27.** wolves; **28.** dogs; **29.** baths; **30.** ponies; **31.** ducks; **32.** moths

1. Have students read the direction line. Ask: *What do we write in the blanks?* (the plural form of the noun) Go over the examples in the book. Ask students to tell you what the rules are for the spelling of each noun in the examples. (Words that end in *f*, add -*ves*; vowel + *y*, add –*s*; etc.)

2. Have students complete Exercise 2 individually. Remind them to review grammar chart **4.2** on page 100 if necessary. Check answers as a class.

4.3 Pronunciation of Plural Nouns

1. Have students cover up grammar chart **4.3** on page 101. Say: *There are three ways to pronounce the endings of plural nouns.* Across the board, write:

   1. /s/
   2. /z/
   3. /əz/

   Then pronounce each sound. Remind students that this is about pronunciation, not spelling or writing. Then say: *Listen to each word as I say it. Tell me which sound I'm making.* Say words from the grammar chart **4.3** in random order. Pronounce each word carefully. Have students guess where the word belongs and write it under the sound they tell you.

2. Have students look at grammar chart **4.3**. Say: *Compare our lists with the lists in the book.* Go over any errors. Have volunteers pronounce words.

EXERCISE 3

Have students read the direction line. Turn to Exercise 2 on page 100. Have students complete the exercise in pairs. Circulate to help with pronunciation. Go over pronunciation in class, if necessary.

4.4 Irregular Noun Plurals

1. Have students cover up grammar chart **4.4** on page 102. Activate students' prior knowledge. Write the list of the singular nouns from the chart on the board. Ask volunteers to come up to the board and write the plural spellings.

2. Have students look at grammar chart **4.2**. Say: *Compare our nouns on the board with the plurals in the book. How many did we get right?* Review the information in the grammar chart. Explain to students that there are no rules for spelling changes with these nouns. English learners have to memorize the plural forms.

3. Point out that some nouns do not have a singular form (e.g., *pajamas*, *clothes*, and *pants/slacks*). Point out that exact numbers use the singular form, and the plural form of a number such as *thousand*, i.e., *thousands*, is not exact.

4. Go over the Pronunciation Note and Language Note. Demonstrate the pronunciation differences between *woman* and *women*. Say them several times and have students guess if you're saying the singular or plural. Explain that sometimes you can use *persons* as the plural for *person*—but that it's not common.

EXERCISE 4

ANSWERS: 1. feet; **2.** women; **3.** policemen; **4.** children; **5.** fish; **6.** mice; **7.** sheep; **8.** teeth

1. Have students read the direction line. Ask: *What do we write in the blanks?* (the plural form of the noun) Go over the example in the book.

2. Have students complete Exercise 4 individually. Remind them to review grammar chart **4.4** on page 102 if necessary. Check answers as a class.

Practice Idea: Speaking

Have a spelling and pronunciation bee. Make a list of approximately 40 nouns. Divide the class into Team A and Team B. Give one member from Team A a noun, and tell them to write the plural form on the board. Do the same with Team B. Then give a member from Team A a plural noun to pronounce. Do the same with Team B. To make the exercise more challenging, give extra points if the team can say (or act out) what the word means.

EXERCISE 5

ANSWERS: 1. families; **2.** people; **3.** times; **4.** women, husbands; **5.** Homes, cities; **6.** countries; **7.** children; **8.** feet; **9.** kids, grandparents; **10.** people; **11.** mice; **12.** Pets; **13.** Dogs, cats; **14.** Fish

1. Have students read the direction line. Go over the example. Then do #1 with the class. Ask a volunteer to give an answer.

2. Have students complete the rest of Exercise 5 individually. Then have students practice saying the sentences in pairs. Finally, check the answers as a class.

3. If necessary, review grammar charts **4.2** on page 100, **4.3** on page 101, and **4.4** on page 102.

Practice Idea: Writing

Have students write an e-mail to a friend in another country. Say: *Talk about life here in the U.S. How many people are there? Where do people live?* Tell students to use information from the reading and from Exercise 5.

Finding an Apartment READING

1. Have students look at the ad on page 105. Ask: *What is it an ad for?* (an apartment for rent) *Do you live in an apartment? How many bedrooms does this apartment have?* (five)

2. Have students look at the title of the reading. Ask: *What is the reading about? How do you know?* Have students use the ad and the title to make predictions about the reading.

3. Preteach any vocabulary words your students may not know, such as *ad, listing, appointment,* and *janitor.*

Reading Glossary

ad: short for advertisement
appointment: a time, place, and date to see someone
janitor: a person in charge of cleaning and fixing things in a building
listing: an advertisement

BEFORE YOU READ

1. Have students discuss the questions in pairs.

2. Ask for a few volunteers to share their answers with the class.

5-10 mins

Reading ≡★

CD 1
TR 17

10-15 mins

1. Have students read the text silently. Tell them to pay special attention to *there + be* followed by singular and plural nouns. Then play the audio and have students read along silently.

2. Check students' comprehension. Say: *Name two ways to look for an apartment.* (ads in a newspaper, "For Rent" signs in front of buildings) *What are some questions you should ask about the apartment* (Is there a lease? Are there smoke detectors?)

Practice Idea: Listening

To practice listening skills, have students first listen to the audio alone. Ask a few comprehension questions such as: *What are some questions to ask when calling about an apartment?* (How much is the rent? Is heat included?) *What should you do before you sign a lease?* (You should check the apartment over carefully and ask the landlord to fix anything that's broken before you move in). Repeat the audio if necessary. Then have students open their books and read along as they listen to the audio.

Did You Know?

Point out the information to students. Explain that Craigslist has ads for many different things (housing, jobs, things for sale, etc.). Ask: *If you rent an apartment or house, how did you find it?*

4.5 Using *There + Is/Are* ≡★

10-15 mins

1. Have students turn to the reading on pages 104–105. Ask students to find examples of *there is* and *there are* in the reading (e.g., *There is usually a number on the sign. There are also ads for houses for rent and houses for sale.*). Write students' responses on the board. Now have students identify the nouns that follow *there is* and *there are* (a number, ad). Ask: *Which ones are plural and which ones are singular?*

2. Have students look at grammar chart **4.5** on page 106. Review the examples. Point out the contraction *there's.* Explain that there are two forms of contraction for the negative: *there isn't* and *there's no.* Tell students that there is no contraction for *there are.* However, there is a contraction for the negative of *there are: there aren't.* Tell students that they can also use *there are no.*

3. Have students cover up grammar chart **4.5.** Write on the board:

   _____ *a dining room and living room.*
   _____ *three bathrooms and a laundry room.*
   _____ *a closet in the hall and two closets in the master bedroom.*
   Ask students to complete the sentences using *there is* or *there are.*

4. Ask students to look at grammar chart **4.5** on page 106. Review the Language Notes at the bottom. Say: *When two nouns follow* there, *use the singular if the first noun is singular and use the plural if the first noun is plural.*

5. Explain that *there is* and *there are* are not used before nouns preceded by the definite article *the*. Review the example in the Language Note.

Presentation Idea

Ask students to describe the classroom. Say: *Describe the classroom. Tell me what's in here.* Model an example (*There are desks in the classroom.*).

EXERCISE 6

Answers will vary.

10-15 mins

1. Tell students that this exercise is about them and where they live. Have students read the direction line. Ask: *Who should do this exercise?* (people who live in a house or an apartment) Go over the examples in the book. Have a volunteer model #1. Point out the pictures of the porch, fireplace, blinds, and smoke detector.

2. Have students complete the rest of Exercise 6 individually. Remind them to review grammar chart **4.5** on page 106 if necessary. Check the answers as a class.

EXERCISE 7

Answers will vary.

10-15 mins

1. Tell students that this exercise is about them and where they live. Have students read the direction line. Ask: *Who should do this exercise?* (people who live in a dorm) Go over the examples in the book. Have a volunteer model #1. Point out the picture of window shades.

2. Have students complete the rest of Exercise 7 individually. Remind them to review grammar chart **4.5** on page 106 if necessary. Check the answers as a class.

Practice Idea: Speaking

Have students compare information about their house, apartment, or dorm with a partner. Say: *You tell your partner:* There's carpet in the living room. *Your partner says:* There's no carpet in my living room. Monitor pair work. Give help as needed.

4.6 Questions and Short Answers Using *There*

10-15 mins

1. Have students turn to the reading on pages 104–105. Ask students to find examples of *is there* and *are there* in the reading (e.g., *Is there an elevator? Are there smoke detectors?*). Write students' examples on the board.

2. Have students look at grammar chart **4.6** on page 108. Review the examples for both singular and plural statements. Go over the word order for *yes/no* questions with *there + be*. Review short answers. Point out that *Yes, there is* doesn't have a contraction. There are two contractions for short negative answers in the singular: *No, there isn't* and *No, there's not*. In the plural, *Yes, there are* is not contracted. The contraction for the negative is *No, there aren't*.

3. Explain that *any* is often used in questions and negatives with plural nouns. *Any*, which means *some*, is not used in affirmative statements.

4. Have students ask and answer questions about the classroom or school using *there is/there are*. Model an example: *Is there a library at this school? Yes, there is.*

5. Review word order with information questions. (*How many + plural noun + are there…?*)

EXERCISE 8

ANSWERS: 1. Are there any children in your building? **2.** Is there a dishwasher in the kitchen? **3.** Is there a yard in front of your building? **4.** Are there (any) trees in front of your building? **5.** Is there a basement in the building? **6.** Is there a laundry room in the building? **7.** Is there a janitor in the building? **8.** Are there (any) noisy neighbors in the building? **9.** Are there (any) nosy neighbors in the building? **10.** Is there an elevator in the building? **11.** Are there (any) parking spaces for the tenants? **12.** Are there a lot of closets in the apartment? **13.** How many apartments are there in your building? **14.** How many parking spaces are there in front of your building?

10-15 mins

1. Tell students that this exercise is about their apartments. Have students read the direction line. Ask: *Do students who live in dorms do this exercise?* (No. Students who live in dorms should do Exercise 9.) Go over the examples. Have two volunteers model the examples.

2. Have students complete Exercise 8 in pairs. Remind them to review grammar chart **4.6** on page 108 if necessary. Monitor pair work. Give help as needed.

Practice Idea: Speaking

Create two rings of students. Have half of the students stand in an outer ring around the classroom. Have the other half stand in an inner ring, facing the outer ring. Instruct students to ask and answer the questions from Exercise 8. Call out *turn* every minute or so. Students in the inner ring should move one space clockwise. Students now ask and answer with their new partner. Have students ask questions in random order. Make sure students look at each other when they're speaking.

EXERCISE 9

Answers: 1. Are there (any) married students in your dorm? **2.** Are there (any) private rooms in your dorm? **3.** Is there a bicycle room in your dorm? **4.** Is there a computer room in your dorm? **5.** Is there an elevator in your dorm? **6.** Is there a bulletin board in your dorm? **7.** Are there any graduate students in your dorm? **8.** Is there a quiet place to study in your dorm? **9.** Is there an air conditioner in your room? **10.** Is there a parking lot for your dorm? **11.** How many rooms are there in your dorm? **12.** How many floors are there in your dorm?

10-15 mins

1. Tell students that this exercise is about their dorms. Have students read the direction line. Ask: *Do students who live in apartments do this exercise?* (No. Students who live in apartments should do Exercise 8.) Go over the example. Have two volunteers model the example.

2. Have students complete Exercise 9 in pairs. Remind them to review grammar chart **4.6** on page 108 if necessary. Monitor pair work. Give help as needed.

Practice Idea: Speaking

Create two rings of students. Have half of the students stand in an outer ring around the classroom. Have the other half stand in an inner ring, facing the outer ring. Instruct students to ask and answer the questions from Exercise 9. Call out *turn* every minute or so. Students in the inner ring should move one space clockwise. Students now ask and answer with their new partner. Have students ask questions in random order. Make sure students look at each other when they're speaking.

EXERCISE 10

Answers: 1. Is there a phone in your office? **2.** Is there a file cabinet in your office? **3.** Are there (any) photos of your family in your office? **4.** Is there a radio in your office? **5.** Is there a copy machine in your office? **6.** Are there (any) windows in your office? **7.** Is there a calendar in your office? **8.** Are there (any) bookshelves in your office? **9.** Are there (any) plants in your office? **10.** Are there (any) pictures in your office? **11.** Is there a fax machine in your office? **12.** Is there a computer in your office?

10-15 mins

1. Tell students that in this exercise they will ask you, the teacher, questions. Have students read the direction line. Go over the examples in the book. Then model the examples. Ask a volunteer to ask you the questions.

2. Have students interview you in groups. Review some of the questions and answers as a class. Review grammar chart **4.6** on page 108 if necessary.

Practice Idea: Speaking

Have students pair up and ask each other questions about their living rooms or bedrooms. Students can use ideas from Exercise 10.

 EXERCISE 11 ≡★

CD 1
TR 18
ANSWERS: 1. Is there; **2.** are there; **3.** There are; **4.** Are there (any); **5.** There are; **6.** many; **7.** are there; **8.** There are; **9.** there aren't; **10.** there are; **11.** Is there; **12.** There are

1. Have students read the direction line. Go over the example in the book. Explain that this is a phone conversation between a student who is looking for an apartment and the landlord. Remind students to use contractions wherever possible.

10-15 mins

2. Have students complete Exercise 11 individually. Remind them to review grammar chart **4.6** on page 108 if necessary. Then play the audio and check answers as a class.

Practice Idea: Listening

To provide practice with listening skills, have students close their books and listen to the audio. Explain that this is a phone conversation between a student who is looking for an apartment and the landlord. Ask comprehension questions, such as: *Where is the apartment?* (on Grover Street) *How many rooms does the apartment on the first floor have?* (four) *Does the student want a large apartment?* (no) Then have students open their books and complete Exercise 11.

Practice Idea: Speaking

Have students practice the conversation in pairs. Monitor pair work and give help as needed. Ask volunteers to role-play all or part of the conversation in front of the class.

4.7 *There* vs. *They* and Other Pronouns ≡★

1. Have students look at grammar chart **4.7** on page 111. Explain that *there + is/are* is used to introduce new nouns. When we use the noun again, we use a pronoun: *he, she, it,* or *they*.

10-15 mins

2. Review the examples in the chart. Have volunteers make sentences using *there is/are* and pronouns with *be*. For example: *There is a big chalkboard in the room. It is at the front of the room.*

3. Go over the Pronunciation Note and the Spelling Note. Point out that people often get confused with *there* and *they're*—especially since their pronunciations are exactly the same. Demonstrate their pronunciations. Have students practice the pronunciation chorally.

EXERCISE 12 ≡★

ANSWERS: 1. There are, They're; **2.** There's, It's; **3.** They're; **4.** They're; **5.** It's; **6.** It's; **7.** It's; **8.** there are; **9.** It's; **10.** it's; **11.** There are; **12.** It's

1. Have students read the direction line. Go over the examples in the book. Have a volunteer do #1.

10-15 mins

2. Have students complete the rest of Exercise 12 individually. Remind them to review grammar chart **4.7** on page 111 if necessary. Check the answers as a class.

EXERCISE 13 ≡★

ANSWERS: 1. Is there a library at this school? **2.** Are there (any) vending machines at this school? **3.** Are there (any) public telephones at this school? **4.** Is there a computer room at this school? **5.** Is there a cafeteria at this school? **6.** Is there a gym at this school? **7.** Is there a swimming pool at this school? **8.** Are there (any) tennis courts at this school? **9.** Are there (any) dormitories at this school? **10.** Is there a parking lot at this school? **11.** Is there a bookstore at this school? **12.** Are there (any) copy machines at this school? **13.** Is there a student lounge at this school? **14.** Is there an auditorium at this school?

1. Tell students that this exercise is about their school. Have students read the direction line. Ask: *What kind of question do you ask if the answer is "yes" to the first question?* (a question with *where*) Go over the examples with the class. Have two students model the example.

2. Have students complete the exercise in pairs. Remind them to review grammar chart **4.6** on page 108 if necessary. Monitor pair work. Give help as needed.

Practice Idea: Speaking

Have students ask and answer questions about a school in their hometown. Tell students to use the words from Exercise 13.

Calling About an Apartment READING

1. Have students look at the floor plan. Ask: *What is this?* (the floor plan to a house or an apartment) *Is there a bathroom?* (yes) *Is there a bedroom?* (no) *Is there a living room?* (yes)

2. Have students look at the title of the reading. Ask: *What is the reading about? How do you know?* Have students use the title and the illustration to make predictions about the reading.

3. Preteach any vocabulary words your students may not know, such as *landlord, roommate, snake,* and *permit.* For *snake,* point out the illustration on page 114.

Reading Glossary

landlord: a man or business that owns real estate, especially that which is rented to others
permit: allow someone to do something
roommate: a person who lives with one in a room, apartment, or house
snake: a long, slender reptile with no legs that moves with a curvy, winding motion

BEFORE YOU READ

1. Have students discuss the questions in pairs.
2. Ask for a few volunteers to share their answers with the class.

 ## Reading

CD 1
TR 19

1. Have students read the text silently. Explain that this is a phone conversation between a student and the manager of a building. Tell students to pay special attention to the definite article (*the*), the indefinite articles (*a, an*), and indefinite quantity words (*some, any*). Then play the audio and have students read along silently.

2. Check students' comprehension. Ask questions such as: *Why does the student want a new apartment?* (because his roommate is moving out) *Is there an apartment available in the manager's building?* (Yes, there's one on the third floor.) *What kind of pet does the student have?* (a snake)

Presentation Idea

The topic for this reading can be enhanced with the following ideas:

1. Online listings of apartments
2. Real estate brochures of apartment listings with full descriptions of the apartments for rent
3. Floor plans of apartments

Practice Idea: Listening

To practice listening skills, have students first listen to the audio alone. Ask a few comprehension questions such as: *Where does the student live now?* (in a big apartment on Wright Street) *Is there a small apartment available?* (yes, on the third floor). Repeat the audio if necessary. Then have students open their books and read along as they listen to the audio.

4.8 Articles with Definite and Indefinite Nouns

1. Have students go to the reading on pages 113–114. Ask them to:
   a. underline articles *a/an* + noun
   b. double underline definite article *the* + noun
   c. circle nouns without articles

2. Ask volunteers to discuss why a noun in the reading has *a/an* and not *the* and vice versa.

3. Ask why some of the nouns don't have an article.

4. Have students look at grammar chart **4.8** on pages 114–115. Read through the examples and explanations.

5. Explain that *a/an* are used for general nouns and that *the* is used for specific nouns. Singular nouns are introduced with *a/an*. Later, when they are referred to again, we use *the*. Plural nouns are introduced with *some, any,* or no article. Later, when they are referred to again, we use *the*.

6. Explain that *the* is also used if this noun is the only one or if the speaker and listener share the same experience. Review the examples in the chart. Point out that when students refer to you, they may say "the teacher" because they share the same experience (same classroom, same teacher).

Presentation Idea

Have students close their books. Write a part of the conversation from the reading on pages 113–114 on the board. However, change the articles. For example, write:

M: I'm a **manager** of a **building**.

S: I need to **find new apartment**.

Ask students to correct the mistakes.

EXERCISE 14

ANSWERS: Conversation 1: 1. the; **2.** the; **3.** some (OR any) **4.** the; **5.** a; **6.** The; **Conversation 2: 7.** a; **8.** the; **9.** an; **10.** a; **11.** The

10-15 mins

1. Have students read the direction line. Point out that the conversations are between two students. Ask: *What words go in the blanks?* (*the, a, an, some,* or *any*) Go over the example in the book.

2. Have students complete the exercise individually. Remind them to review grammar chart **4.8** on pages 114–115 if necessary. Check answers as a class. Then have students practice the conversations in pairs. Monitor pair work.

 EXERCISE 15 ⭐

CD 1
TR 20

ANSWERS: 1. the; **2.** The; **3.** a; **4.** an; **5.** the; **6.** the; **7.** the; **8.** a; **9.** the; **10.** a; **11.** a; **12.** a; **13.** The; **14.** the; **15.** a; **16.** the; **17.** the; **18.** the; **19.** a; **20.** the; **21.** the; **22.** the; **23.** any; **24.** some; **25.** a; **26.** the; **27.** a; **28.** an

10-15 mins

1. Have students read the direction line. Go over the example in the book. Have a volunteer do #1.

2. Have students complete Exercise 15 individually. Remind them to review grammar chart **4.8** on pages 114–115 if necessary. Play the audio and check answers as a class.

3. Then have students practice the conversation in pairs. Monitor pair work.

Practice Idea: Listening

To provide practice with listening skills, have students close their books and listen to the audio. Repeat the audio as needed. Ask comprehension questions, such as: *What is person A's problem?* (The landlord doesn't provide enough heat.) *What does person A have to wear in the apartment?* (a sweater or a coat) *Who should person A write a letter to?* (the Department of Housing) Then have students open their books and complete Exercise 15.

Practice Idea: Speaking

Have students write a new conversation based on the one in Exercise 15. Ask students to change some details (e.g., the air-conditioning is broken, not the heat). Monitor pair work. Give help as needed. Then have volunteers role-play the new conversation in front of the class.

4.9 Making Generalizations ⭐

10-15 mins

1. Explain to students that a generalization says that something is true of all members of a group. Give an example. Say: *Students are noisy. That means that all students, everywhere are noisy. Is this true?* (no)

2. Have students look at grammar chart **4.9** on page 117. Review the information. Say: *To make a generalization about a singular noun, use* a *or* an. *To make a generalization about a plural noun, don't use any article. To make a generalization about an object, use a plural noun with no article.*

3. Write the following words on the board:

   1. houses
   2. cat
   3. sharks
   4. subway
   5. bus
   6. taxes

Ask students to write two sentences for each item. Say: *Write a generalization and write a sentence about something specific.* Have volunteers write their sentences on the board.

Presentation Idea

Have students close their books. Write the second part of the conversation from the reading on pages 113–114 on the board. However, change the articles. For example, write:

*Do you have **the dog**?*

*We don't permit **the dogs**.*

Have students correct the errors.

EXERCISE 16

ANSWERS: **1.** Houses in San Diego are expensive. **2.** Homeowners pay property tax. **3.** Dogs are part of the family. **4.** Renters don't have freedom to make changes. **5.** Owners have freedom to make changes.

1. Have students read the direction line. Ask: *What do you change from singular to plural?* (the subject) *What else are we going to change?* (articles and verbs) Go over the example in the book.

⏱ 10-15 mins

2. Have students complete Exercise 16 individually. Remind them to review grammar chart **4.9** on page 117 if necessary. Check answers as a class.

EXERCISE 17
Answers will vary.

⏱ 10-15 mins

1. Tell students that they will be making generalizations about their native countries or hometowns. Have students read the direction line. Ask: *Will you use plural or singular nouns?* (plural) *Will you use an article?* (no) Go over the example. Have a volunteer model the example.

2. Have students complete Exercise 17 individually. Remind them to review grammar chart **4.9** on page 117 if necessary. Collect for assessment.

Practice Idea: Speaking

Have students compare answers in groups. If possible, put students with different nationalities together.

EXERCISE 18
Answers will vary.

⏱ 5-10 mins

1. Have students read the direction line. Remind students that this exercise is about making generalizations. Go over the example in the book.

2. Have students complete Exercise 18 individually. Remind them to review grammar chart **4.9** on page 117 if necessary. Check answers with the class. Have volunteers read their sentences aloud.

Practice Idea: Speaking

Take a class survey. Compare answers as a class. Write the results of the survey on the board.

EXERCISE 19
Answers will vary.

⏱ 5-10 mins

1. Tell students that this exercise is about their likes and dislikes. Have students read the direction line. Ask: *Do you use singular or plural*

nouns? (plural) *Do you use articles?* (no) Go over the example in the book. Have a volunteer model the example. Point out the pictures of curtains and hardwood floor.

2. Have students complete Exercise 19 individually. Remind them to review grammar chart **4.9** on page 117 if necessary. Then have students compare answers in pairs. Monitor pair work. Give help as needed.

EXERCISE 20

ANSWERS: 1. Do you like cats? **2.** Do you like dogs? **3.** Do you like hamburgers? **4.** Do you like American cars? **5.** Do you like American movies? **6.** Do you like fashion magazines? **7.** Do you like comic books? **8.** Do you like computers? **9.** Do you like computer games? **10.** Do you like strict teachers? **11.** Do you like American supermarkets? **12.** Do you like American textbooks?

10-15 mins
1. Tell students that this exercise is about their likes and dislikes. Have students read the direction line. Go over the examples in the book. Have two volunteers model #1.

2. Have students complete the rest of Exercise 20 in pairs. Remind them to review grammar chart **4.9** on page 117 if necessary. Monitor pair work. Give help as needed.

Practice Idea: Speaking

Take a class survey. Compare answers as a class. Write the results of the survey on the board.

EXERCISE 21

ANSWERS: 1. the; **2.** the; **3.** a; **4.** the; **5.** Some (OR X); **6.** a; **7.** the; **8.** X; **9.** X; **10.** X

10-15 mins
1. Have students read the direction line. Explain that this is a conversation between two students. Ask: *Will you always use an article?* (no) Go over the example in the book.

2. Have students complete Exercise 21 individually. Remind them to review grammar chart **4.8** on pages 114–115 if necessary. Play the audio and check answers as a class.

Practice Idea: Listening

To provide practice with listening skills, have students close their books and listen to the audio. Explain that this is a conversation between two students. Repeat the audio as needed. Ask comprehension questions, such as: *How many copy machines are there in the library?* (several) *Does it cost money to use the copy machines?* (yes) *What does person A want to copy?* (a classmate's textbook) Then have students open their books and complete Exercise 21.

Practice Idea: Speaking

Have students practice the conversation in pairs. Monitor students. Give help as needed. Have volunteers role-play the conversation in front of the class.

Summary of Lesson 4

20-30 mins
1. **Singular and Plural** Review the rules for forming the plural of nouns. Go over the examples in the book. If necessary, have students review:

   4.1 Singular and Plural—An Overview (p. 99)
   4.2 Spelling of Regular Noun Plurals (p. 100)
   4.4 Irregular Noun Plurals (p. 102)

2. ***There + be*** Have students close their books. On the board, write:

   affirmative
   negative
   yes/no *question with short answer*
   how many

   Instruct students to write two affirmative sentences (singular and plural); two negative sentences (singular and plural); two *yes/no* questions with short answers (singular and plural); and one question using *how many*. Say: *You can write the questions about this classroom or about where you live.* Then go over the examples in the book. If necessary, have students review:

    4.5 Using *There + Is/Are* (p. 106)

    4.6 Questions and Short Answers Using *There* (p. 108)

3. **Articles** Have students read the examples and write sentences of their own. Then put students in pairs to compare work. Circulate to observe and give help as needed. If necessary, have students review:

    4.8 Articles with Definite and Indefinite Nouns (p. 114)

    4.9 Making Generalizations (p. 117)

Editing Advice

Have students close their books. Write the sentences without editing marks or corrections on the board. For example:

10-15 mins

1. *People in my country is very poor.*
2. *The dogs are friendly animals.*

Ask students to correct each sentence and provide a rule or explanation for each correction. This activity can be done individually, in pairs, or as a class. After students have corrected each sentence, tell them to turn to page 121. Say: *Now compare your work with the Editing Advice in the book.*

Editing Quiz

ANSWERS: 1. There's a large closet in each bedroom. **2.** There's; **3.** C; **4.** C; **5.** C; **6.** Are there any; **7.** C; **8.** there are; **9.** Are there; **10.** In my building there are 30 apartments (OR There are 30 apartments in my building.) **11.** Is there a janitor; **12.** C; **13.** C; **14.** C

10-15 mins

1. Tell students they are going to put the editing advice into practice. Have students read the direction line. Ask: *Do all the shaded words and phrases have mistakes?* (No) Go over the examples with the class. Then do #1 together.

2. Have students complete the quiz individually. Then have them compare answers with a partner before checking answers as a class.

3. For the items students had difficulties with, have them go back and find the relevant grammar chart and review it. Monitor and give help as necessary.

Lesson 4 Test/Review

40-60 mins

Use the Assessment CD-ROM with Exam*View*®, Online Workbook, and Web site for additional practice, review, and assessment materials.

PART 1

ANSWERS: boxes; cards; feet; potatoes; women; months; matches; shelves; radios; mice; children; desks; keys; stories; bushes

1. Part 1 may also be used as an in-class test to assess student performance, in addition to the Assessment CD-ROM with Exam*View*®. Have students read the direction line. Review the example.

2. Have students complete Part 1 individually. Collect for assessment.

3. If necessary, have students review:

    4.2 Spelling of Regular Noun Plurals (p. 100)

PART 2

ANSWERS: 1. There are; **2.** They're; **3.** Is there; **4.** there is; **5.** is (OR 's) **6.** It's; **7.** Are there; **8.** They're; **9.** Is there; **10.** It's; **11.** are there; **12.** There are; **13.** Is there; **14.** there is; **15.** it's

1. Part 2 may also be used as an in-class test to assess student performance, in addition to the Assessment CD-ROM with Exam*View*®. Have students read the direction line. Review the example.

2. Have students complete Part 2 individually. Collect for assessment.

3. If necessary, have students review:

    4.5 Using *There + Is/Are* (p. 106)

    4.6 Questions and Short Answers Using *There* (p. 108)

    4.7 *There* vs. *They* and Other Pronouns (p. 111)

PART 3

1. Part 3 may also be used as an in-class test to assess student performance, in addition to the Assessment CD-ROM with Exam*View*®. Have students read the direction line. Ask: *Will all nouns have an article?* (no) Review the example.

2. Have students complete Part 3 individually. Collect for assessment.

3. If necessary, have students review:

   4.8 Articles with Definite and Indefinite Nouns (pp. 114–115)

   4.9 Making Generalizations (p. 117)

Expansion

These expansion activities provide opportunities for students to interact with one another and further develop their speaking and writing skills. Encourage students to use grammar from this lesson whenever possible.

CLASSROOM ACTIVITIES

1. Have students read the direction line. Go over the list of items to make sure everyone knows the meanings of the words. Point out the pictures of a scale and an orange juice squeezer. Model the activity for the class. Have students complete the chart on their own. Then instruct students to compare lists. Monitor pair work. Give help as needed.

10-15 mins per activity

Practice Idea: Speaking

Do a class survey. In groups, have students compare information. Have students report their results to the class. Record the information on the board for selected categories (e.g., *All of the students in the class have a blow dryer.*).

2. Have students bring in the classifieds section of a newspaper. Put students in groups to compare apartments. Monitor group work. Give help as needed. Have groups report

"good apartment deals" to the class (e.g., *There's a really nice apartment by the park. It's only $600 a month.*).

Practice Idea: Speaking

Find or create ads for apartments and houses for half of the class. Make sure the ads include some details. Make copies of each ad. Put each of the ads on small identical cards. Pass out the cards randomly to students. Ask students to circulate around the room to find their match. Say: *Don't show your card to anyone. Describe the apartment or house. For example, say: There's a backyard, a swimming pool, etc.*

3. Instruct groups to explore the rest of the newspaper. Go over the examples in the book. Have volunteers report their findings to the class.

4. Have students read the direction line. Briefly model the activity with a volunteer.

5. Instruct students to bring in pictures of their homes. Ask volunteers to describe their homes to a group or to the class.

6. Have students read the direction line. Say: *Ask and answer questions about the apartment.* Brainstorm questions to ask a landlord (e.g., *Is there an elevator? Is there a garage?*). Then have students work in pairs to write the conversations. Monitor pair work. Give help as needed.

TALK ABOUT IT

Write on the board: *Renting an apartment.* Ask questions such as, *How do you find an apartment to rent in this city? How do you find one in your hometown? Is it easy to rent an apartment in your hometown?* and so on. Write the vocabulary that these questions elicit on the board. Then have students discuss the questions in pairs or small groups. Monitor and give help as needed.

15-20 mins

WRITE ABOUT IT

30–40 mins per activity

1. Have students read the direction line. Go over the example. Have students complete the assignment individually. Collect for assessment and/or have students present their paragraph to a group.

2. Tell students that for this activity, they'll write a comparison. Have students read the direction line. Instruct students to work individually.

Practice Idea: Writing

Have students exchange first drafts with a partner. Ask students to help their partners edit their drafts. Refer students to the Editing Advice on page 121.

INTERNET ACTIVITY

Tell students to use the Internet to look for apartments for rent and houses for sale in this city (or nearby suburbs). Tell them to find out what parts of the city or the suburbs have the highest rents and housing prices.

Lesson 5

Lesson Overview

GRAMMAR

Ask: *What did we study in Lesson 4?* (singular and plural nouns; articles and quantity words; *there + be + noun*) *What are we going to study in this lesson?* (possession; object pronouns; questions about the subject) Activate students' prior knowledge. Have volunteers give examples. Ask: *Can you give me examples of possessives?* (father's, children's) Write them on the board.

CONTEXT

1. Ask: *What will we learn about in this lesson?* (families and names) Activate prior knowledge. Ask a few students their names. Ask them if their last name is their father's, mother's, husband's, etc.

2. Have students share their knowledge and personal experiences.

Presentation Idea

The topic for this lesson can be enhanced with the following ideas:

1. Pictures of your family or someone else's family
2. Pictures of extended families
3. A family tree

Names  READING

1. Have students look at the illustration.

   Ask: *What is it?* (a check) *What's the name of the person who wrote the check?* (Mark Robert Smith)

2. Have students look at the title of the reading.

   Ask: *What is the reading about? How do you know?* Have students use the title to make predictions about the reading.

3. Preteach any vocabulary words your students may not know, such as *surname, initial,* and *hyphen.*

Reading Glossary

hyphen: the punctuation mark (-)
initial: the first letter of a word or name
surname: family name or last name

BEFORE YOU READ

1. Have students discuss the questions in pairs.
2. Ask for a few volunteers to share their answers with the class.

5-10 mins

Reading

CD 1 TR 21

1. Have students read the text silently. Tell them to pay special attention to possessive forms. Then play the audio and have students read along silently.

5-10 mins

2. Check students' comprehension. Ask questions such as: *How many names do Americans usually have?* (three) *Do women always change their last names when they get married?* (No, some keep their maiden names.) *Do men usually change their last names?* (no)

Did You Know?

Have students read what it says about last names. Then ask them to say common last names in their countries. Then ask about popular first names. Tell them about first names in the U.S.: *In 1900, the most popular male name was John, and the most popular female name was Mary. In 2005, the most popular male and female names were James and Mary.*

Practice Idea: Listening

To practice listening skills, have students first listen to the audio alone. Ask a few comprehension questions such as: *What is another word for last name?* (surname) *Do women always change their last names when they get married?* (No, some keep their maiden names.) Then have students open their books and read along as they listen to the audio.

5.1 Possessive Form of Nouns

10-15 mins

1. Have students close their books. Put students into pairs. Write grammar chart **5.1** on the board. Keep the middle column ("Ending") empty. Say: *Study the nouns and the examples of possessives, and try to guess the rule for the endings.* Have volunteers write the rules on the board.

2. Then ask students to look at grammar chart **5.1** on page 131 to compare their chart with the chart in the book.

3. Make sure to point out that possession by inanimate objects is expressed in the following way: *the ___ of ___.*

EXERCISE 1
Answers will vary.

5-10 mins

1. Tell students that this exercise is based on the reading on page 130. Have students read the direction line. Review the example. Have a volunteer model #1.

2. Have students complete Exercise 1 individually. Remind them to review grammar chart **5.1** on page 131 if necessary. Check the answers as a class.

EXERCISE 2

ANSWERS: 1. The teacher always corrects the students' homework. **2.** No change. **3.** The teacher's job is to explain the grammar. **4.** What are your parents' names? **5.** No change. **6.** Do you use your father's last name? **7.** What is your dog's name? **8.** The children's names are Jason and Jessica.

10-15 mins

1. Have students read the direction line. Ask: *Do we always use 's or '?* (No. Some of the sentences have inanimate objects.) Review the examples.

2. Have students complete Exercise 2 individually. Then have them compare answers in pairs. Remind them to review

grammar chart **5.1** on page 131 if necessary. Monitor pair work. Give help as needed. Check answers as a class.

Practice Idea: Listening

Have students make questions from the statements in Exercise 2. Then have pairs ask and answer the questions. Monitor pair work. Give help as needed.

5.2 Possessive Adjectives

10-15 mins

1. Have students cover up grammar chart **5.2** on page 133. Activate students' prior knowledge. Ask: *What are the subject pronouns?* (I, you, he, etc.) Write them on the board. Then ask: *Do you know what the possessive adjectives are for these pronouns?* (my, your, his, etc.) Write them on the board next to the subject pronouns.

2. Have students look at grammar chart **5.2**. Say: *Compare our lists with the grammar chart.* Go over any errors.

3. Review the examples in the chart. Point out that English learners sometimes confuse *his* and *her.* Point out the difference between *its* (the possessive adjective) and *it's* (the contraction for *it is*). Show how we can use possessive adjectives and nouns together.

EXERCISE 3

ANSWERS: 1. his; **2.** her; **3.** its; **4.** their; **5.** her, her; **6.** their; **7.** your; **8.** my; **9.** our; **10.** your; **11.** my

5-10 mins

1. Have students read the direction line. Ask: *What will we write in the blanks?* (possessive adjectives) Review the example in the book. Have a volunteer do #1.

2. Have students complete the rest of Exercise 3 individually. Remind them to review grammar chart **5.2** on page 133 if necessary. Check the answers as a class.

5.3 Questions with *Whose*

 5–10 mins
1. Have students cover up grammar chart **5.3** on page 134. Pick up a book from a student's desk. Ask: *Whose book is this?* (Tina's book) Write it on the board. Then ask: *What was the question I asked?* Have a volunteer write it on the board.

2. Have students look at grammar chart **5.3**. Say: Whose + noun *asks about possession or ownership.* Go over the pattern for questions with *whose.*

EXERCISE 4 ⭐

ANSWERS: 1. Whose office is this? This is (OR It's) the dean's office. **2.** Whose offices are those? Those are (OR They're) the teachers' offices. **3.** Whose dictionary is that? That's (OR It's) the teacher's dictionary. **4.** Whose books are those? Those are (OR They're) the students' books. **5.** Whose car is that? That's (OR It's) my parents' car. **6.** Whose house is this? This is (OR It's) my cousin's house. **7.** Whose papers are those? Those are (OR They're) Mr. Ross's (OR Mr. Ross') papers. **8.** Whose pencils are these? These are (OR They're) the teacher's pencils.

 10–15 mins
1. Have students read the direction line. Review the examples in the book. Have a volunteer do #1.

2. Have students complete the rest of Exercise 4 individually. Remind them to review grammar chart **5.3** on page 134 if necessary. Check the answers as a class.

5.4 Possessive Pronouns

 5–10 mins
1. Have students cover up grammar chart **5.4** on page 135. Activate students' prior knowledge. Say: *OK. Let's review. What are the subject pronouns?* Write them on the board. *What are the possessive adjectives?* (my, your, his, etc.) Write them on the board. Then ask: *Do you know what the possessive pronouns are?* (mine, yours, his, hers, etc.) Write them on the board next to the possessive adjectives.

2. Have students look at grammar chart **5.4**. Say: *Compare our lists with the grammar chart.* Go over any errors.

3. Review the examples in the chart. Say: *We use possessive pronouns to avoid repetition of a noun.* Direct students to the first example in the chart. Say: *Instead of repeating* name (i.e., my name, your name), *we can just say* yours.

4. Explain that after a possessive noun, the noun can be omitted. Review the example in the book.

EXERCISE 5 ⭐

ANSWERS: 1. mine; **2.** yours; **3.** his; **4.** Hers; **5.** Theirs; **6.** Ours

 5–10 mins
1. Have students read the direction line. Ask: *What do we replace the underlined words with?* (a possessive pronoun) Go over the example in the book. Have a volunteer do #1.

2. Have students complete the rest of Exercise 5 individually. Remind them to review grammar chart **5.4** on page 135 if necessary. Check the answers as a class.

EXERCISE **6** =★

CD 1
TR 22

ANSWERS: 1. yours; **2.** my; **3.** Our; **4.** my; **5.** Your; **6.** our; **7.** your; **8.** our; **9.** mine; **10.** their; **11.** their; **12.** your; **13.** my; **14.** theirs

10–15 mins

1. Have students read the direction line. Go over the example in the book. Have a volunteer do #1.

2. Have students complete Exercise 6 individually. Remind them to review grammar chart **5.4** on page 135 if necessary. Check answers as a class.

3. Have pairs practice the conversation.

5.5 The Subject and the Object =★

10–15 mins

1. Have students turn to Exercise 3 on page 133. Say: *Underline the subject in each sentence.* Then say: *Find the object in each sentence and circle it.* If students have difficulty, say: *The object is the noun after the verb.* Check that students have found all the subjects and objects. Go over any errors.

2. Have students look at grammar chart **5.5** on page 136. Review the examples in the chart.

3. Point out that pronouns can be used for both subjects and objects. Explain that a sentence with two clauses will have more than one subject and more than one object.

William Madison's Name

READING

1. Have students look at the photo. Ask: *Who are these people?* (a family; mother, father and two children)

2. Have students look at the title of the reading. Ask: *What is the reading about? How do you know?* Have students use the title and photo to make predictions about the reading.

3. Preteach any vocabulary words your students may not know, such as *nickname*.

Reading Glossary

nickname: an informal name given to a person in addition to a legal one

BEFORE YOU READ

5–10 mins

1. Have students discuss the questions in pairs.

2. Ask for a few volunteers to share their answers with the class.

 Reading =★

CD 1
TR 23

10–15 mins

1. Have students first read the text silently. Tell them to pay special attention to object pronouns. Then play the audio and have students read along silently.

2. Check students' comprehension. Ask questions such as: *How many names does William have?* (three) *Why do William's friends call him Bill?* (It's a common nickname for William.) *Why does William include "Junior" when he signs his name?* (because he has the same name as his father)

Practice Idea: Listening

To practice listening skills, have students first listen to the audio alone. Ask a few comprehension questions such as: *What is William's full name?* (William Michael Madison) *What does "junior" mean?* (it means that a son has the same name as his father). Then have students open their books and read along as they listen to the audio.

5.6 Object Pronouns

 1. Have students cover up grammar chart **5.6** on
10-15 mins pages 138–139. Write the subject pronouns on the board. Activate prior knowledge. Say: *Here are the subject pronouns. Can you write the object pronouns?* If students have difficulty, have them look back at the reading on pages 137–138 and find the object pronouns. Have a volunteer write them on the board.

2. Have students look at grammar chart **5.6**. Say: *Compare our list with the grammar chart.* Go over any errors.

3. Review the examples in the chart. Say: *We can use an object pronoun after the verb or after a preposition.* Then go back to the reading on pages 137–138. Ask students to circle the verbs and the object pronouns.

4. Explain that after a preposition, an object pronoun is used. Ask: *What prepositions do you know?* (*of, about, to, from, in,* etc.) Go over the examples in the chart. Point out that we use *them* for both plural people and plural things.

EXERCISE 7

ANSWERS: 1. me; **2.** it; **3.** them; **4.** her; **5.** you; **6.** us; **7.** him

 1. Have students read the direction line. Ask:
5-10 mins *What do we replace the underlined words with?* (an object pronoun) Review the example. Have a volunteer do #1.

2. Have students complete the rest of Exercise 7 individually. Remind them to review grammar chart **5.6** on pages 138–139 if necessary. Check the answers as a class.

EXERCISE 8

CD 1
TR 24 **ANSWERS: 1.** you; **2.** her; **3.** him; **4.** me; **5.** them; **6.** her; **7.** it; **8.** it; **9.** her; **10.** It (OR that); **11.** her; **12.** it; **13.** her; **14.** me; **15.** them

 1. Tell students that this is a conversation
10-15 mins between a Chinese student and an American student. Have students read the direction line. Ask: *What do we put on the blank?* (an object pronoun) Review the example.

2. Have students complete Exercise 8 individually. Remind them to review grammar chart **5.6** on pages 138–139 if necessary. Then check answers as a class or in small groups.

3. Have students practice the conversation in pairs. Monitor pair work. Give help as needed.

Practice Idea: Listening

To provide practice with listening skills, have students close their books and listen to the audio. Repeat the audio as needed. Ask comprehension questions, such as: *How do American teachers call their students?* (by their first names) *How do Chinese teachers call their students?* (using *miss, madam, sir,* etc.) *Do Chinese students call their teachers by their first names?* (no) Then have students open their books and complete Exercise 8.

Practice Idea: Speaking

Have pairs rewrite the conversation. Say: *You can change the information to make it true for you.* Have them practice their conversations.

EXERCISE 9

ANSWERS: 1. My, Mine; **2.** My, me; **3.** I; **4.** My; **5.** I'm; **6.** My; **7.** My, me

 1. Have students read the direction line. Ask:
5-10 mins *What do we write on the blanks?* (*I, I'm, my, mine,* or *me*) Review the examples in the book.

2. Have students complete Exercise 9 individually. Remind them to review grammar charts **5.4** on page 135, **5.5** on page 136, and **5.6** on pages 138–139 if necessary. Check the answers as a class.

EXERCISE 10

ANSWERS: **1.** He's; **2.** He; **3.** He's; **4.** His, him, his; **5.** He's, His; **6.** his; **7.** His

5-10 mins

1. Have students read the direction line. Ask: *What do we write on the blanks? (he, he's, his,* or *him)* Go over the examples in the book.

2. Have students complete Exercise 10 individually. Remind them to review grammar charts **5.4** on page 135, **5.5** on page 136, and **5.6** on pages 138–139 if necessary. Check the answers as a class.

EXERCISE 11

Answers: **1.** She's; **2.** her; **3.** She's; **4.** She; **5.** Hers; **6.** She's, She, her; **7.** Her

5-10 mins

1. Have students read the direction line. Ask: *What do we write on the blanks? (she, she's, her,* or *hers)* Review the examples in the book.

2. Have students complete Exercise 11 individually. Remind them to review grammar charts **5.4** on page 135, **5.5** on page 136, and **5.6** on pages 138–139 if necessary. Check the answers as a class.

EXERCISE 12

ANSWERS: **1.** They're; **2.** They; **3.** They; **4.** Their; **5.** Theirs; **6.** They're; **7.** them

5-10 mins

1. Have students read the direction line. Ask: *What do we write on the blanks? (they, they're, their, theirs,* or *them)* Review the examples in the book.

2. Have students complete Exercise 12 individually. Remind them to review grammar charts **5.4** on page 135, **5.5** on page 136, and **5.6** on pages 138–139 if necessary. Check the answers as a class.

EXERCISE 13

ANSWERS: **1.** It; **2.** It's; **3.** Its; **4.** It; **5.** Its; **6.** It's; **7.** it

5-10 mins

1. Have students read the direction line. Ask: *What do we write on the blanks? (it, it's,* or *its)* Review the examples in the book.

2. Have students complete Exercise 13 individually. Remind them to review grammar charts **5.4** on page 135, **5.5** on page 136, and **5.6** on pages 138–139 if necessary. Check the answers as a class.

EXERCISE 14

ANSWERS: **1.** We; **2.** We're; **3.** Our; **4.** us; **5.** Ours; **6.** We're

5-10 mins

1. Have students read the direction line. Ask: *What do we write on the blanks? (we, we're, our, ours,* or *us)* Review the examples in the book.

2. Have students complete Exercise 14 individually. Remind them to review grammar charts **5.4** on page 135, **5.5** on page 136, and **5.6** on pages 138–139 if necessary. Check the answers as a class.

EXERCISE 15

ANSWERS: **1.** You; **2.** you; **3.** Yours; **4.** You're; **5.** Your; **6.** You

5-10 mins

1. Have students read the direction line. Ask: *What do we write on the blanks? (you, you're, your,* or *yours)* Review the examples in the book.

2. Have students complete Exercise 15 individually. Remind them to review grammar charts **5.4** on page 135, **5.5** on page 136, and **5.6** on pages 138–139 if necessary. Check the answers as a class.

Practice Idea: Writing

Have students write an e-mail to a friend in another city or country. Say: *Write about yourself, or a friend or friends. Use the sentences in Exercises 9–15 as models.* Remind students to use all forms of pronouns. Have students exchange e-mails with a partner. Say: *Correct your partner's e-mail.* Circulate to give help as needed.

Who Helps Your Parents?

READING

1. Have students look at the photo. Ask: *Who are these people?* (a family)

2. Have students look at the title of the reading. Ask: *What is the reading about? How do you know?* Have students use the title and the photo to make predictions about the reading.

3. Preteach any vocabulary words your students may not know, such as *health*, *so-so*, and *take care of*.

Reading Glossary

health: the condition of a living thing's body and mind
so-so: not wonderful; fair; mediocre
take care of: to attend to or provide for the needs, operation, or treatment of

BEFORE YOU READ

1. Have students discuss the questions in pairs.
2. Ask for a few volunteers to share their answers with the class.

10-15 mins

 Reading =★

CD 1
TR 25

10-15 mins

1. Have students read the text silently. Tell them to pay special attention to questions. Then play the audio and have students read along silently.

2. Check students' comprehension. Ask questions such as: *Where does person B's dad live?* (with person B's brother and his wife) *Do Americans typically live with their parents after the age of 25?* (no) *Where does person A's dad live?* (in another state)

Practice Idea: Listening

To practice listening skills, have students first listen to the audio alone. Ask a few comprehension questions such as: *Does person A live with his parents?* (no) *Who takes care of person A's parents?* (no one) Then have students open their books and read along as they listen to the audio.

Context Note

Most senior citizens in the U.S. do not live with their children after retirement. They usually live with their spouses or alone. Most senior citizens (80 percent) live in houses that they own. Only 4.5 percent of the population lives in nursing homes. About 5 percent of the elderly lives in senior housing of various types, which typically offers services for the elderly, such as transportation, meals, and even social events.

5.7 Questions About the Subject or About the Complement =★

10-15 mins

1. Have students turn to the reading on pages 143–144. Ask them to look at the questions in the reading. Say: *Underline the questions with* do *or* does. *Circle the questions with a verb in the* -s *form.*

2. Have students look at grammar chart **5.7** on page 144. Explain that when we use *do* or *does* in a question, we are asking about the complement of the sentence, not the subject. Read the examples and the explanation. Then explain that when we use the *-s* form in a question, we are asking a question about the subject. Read the examples and the explanation.

3. Have students look back again at the reading on pages 143–144 to compare.

EXERCISE 16

ANSWERS: 1. Who dusts the furniture in your house? **2.** Who shops for groceries in your house? **3.** Who pays the bills in your house? **4.** Who washes the dishes in your house? **5.** Who makes your bed in your house? **6.** Who takes in the mail in your house? **7.** Who washes the clothes in your house? **8.** Who cooks the meals in your house? **9.** Who sweeps the floor in your house?

10-15 mins

1. Have students read the direction line. Go over the examples in the book. Have volunteers model the examples.

2. Have students complete Exercise 16 in pairs. Remind them to review grammar chart **5.7** on page 144 if necessary. Monitor pair work. Give help as needed.

Practice Idea: Speaking

Create two rings of students. Have half of the students stand in an outer ring around the classroom. Have the other half stand in an inner ring, facing the outer ring. Instruct students to ask and answer the questions from Exercise 16. Call out *turn* every minute or so. Students in the inner ring should move one space clockwise. Students now ask and answer with their new partners. Have students ask questions in random order. Make sure students look at each other when they're speaking.

EXERCISE 17

ANSWERS: 1. takes care; **2.** Do they live; **3.** Is she single; **4.** kids do they have; **5.** takes care of; **6.** do you talk to; **7.** does it (OR a phone card) cost; **8.** knows

1. Have students read the direction line. Go over the examples with the class.

   10-15 mins

2. Have students complete Exercise 17 individually. Remind them to review grammar chart **5.7** on page 144 if necessary. Check answers as a class.

Practice Idea: Speaking

Have students practice the conversation from Exercise 17 in pairs. Ask volunteers to role-play all or part of the conversation in front of the class.

5.8 *Who, Whom, Who's, Whose*

1. Have students cover up grammar chart **5.8** on page 146. Write the following on the board:

   5-10 mins

   1. who   a. who is
   2. whose   b. object
   3. who's   c. possession (ownership)
   4. who(m)   d. subject

   Then ask students to match the columns.

2. Have students look at grammar chart **5.8**. Go over the examples. Point out that *whom* is now considered formal and that it is more common to hear *who* as the object.

EXERCISE 18

ANSWERS: 1. Who(m); **2.** Who's; **3.** Who; **4.** Whose; **5.** Who

1. Have students read the direction line. Ask: *What do we write in the blanks?* (who, whom, who's, or whose) Review the example.

   10-15 mins

2. Have students complete Exercise 18 individually. Remind them to review grammar chart **5.8** on page 146 if necessary. Check the answers as a class.

EXERCISE 19

CD 1 TR 26

ANSWERS: 1. My; **2.** Mine; **3.** hers; **4.** her; **5.** husband's; **6.** Whose; **7.** Their; **8.** your; **9.** her; **10.** our; **11.** ours; **12.** his; **13.** him; **14.** He's; **15.** her; **16.** She; **17.** our; **18.** their; **19.** mine; **20.** we're

1. Have students read the direction line. Go over the example.

   10-15 mins

2. Have students complete Exercise 19 individually. Remind them to review the grammar charts in Lesson 5 if necessary. Check the answers as a class. Then have students practice the conversation in pairs.

Practice Idea: Speaking

Have pairs write a conversation using subject pronouns, object pronouns, possessive pronouns, possessive nouns, and possessive adjectives. Ask volunteers to role-play their conversations in front of the class.

Summary of Lesson 5

1. Possessive Forms of Nouns

15-20 mins

Review the example sentences. Then have students talk about things in the classroom using possessive pronouns (e.g., *Maria's notebook is blue and white.*). If necessary, have students review:

5.1 Possessive Forms of Nouns (p. 131)

2. Pronouns and Possessive Forms

Have students close their books. Write the chart headings across the top of the board. Write the subject pronouns in the first column. Have students come up to the board to fill in the chart with pronouns and possessive forms. Then have volunteers write sentences and questions with the pronouns and possessive forms. Have students open their books and compare their charts with the charts in the book. Go over the example sentences in the book. If necessary, have students review:

5.2 Possessive Adjectives (p. 133)

5.4 Possessive Pronouns (p. 135)

5.6 Object Pronouns (pp. 138–139)

Editing Advice

10-15 mins

Have students close their books. Write a few sentences without editing marks or corrections on the board. For example:

1. Your a good person.

Where's you're book?

Ask students to correct each sentence and provide a rule or an explanation for each correction. This activity can be done individually, in pairs, or as a class. After students have corrected each sentence, tell them to turn to pages 149–150. Say: *Now compare your work with the Editing Advice in the book.* Then have students read through all the editing advice.

Editing Quiz

ANSWERS: 1. It's; **2.** names; **3.** C; **4.** C; **5.** C; **6.** parents'; **7.** Their; **8.** C; **9.** C; **10.** His; **11.** He's; **12.** his; **13.** C; **14.** boy's; **15.** girl's; **16.** His; **17.** C;

18. I; **19.** C; **20.** Her; **21.** her; **22.** who has; **23.** Its; **24.** My neighbor's dog; **25.** her; **26.** She; **27.** C; **28.** its; **29.** Whose coat is that? **30.** yours; **31.** mine; **32.** C; **33.** C; **34.** mine; **35.** the name of the book? **36.** mine; **37.** It's; **38.** C; **39.** Whose; **40.** C; **41.** C;

10-15 mins

1. Tell students they are going to put the editing advice into practice. Have students read the direction line. Ask: Do all the shaded words and phrases have mistakes? (no) Go over the examples with the class. Then do #1 together.

2. Have students complete the quiz individually. Then have them compare answers with a partner before checking the answers as a class.

3. For the items students had difficulties with, have them go back and find the relevant grammar chart and review it. Monitor and give help as necessary.

Lesson 5 Test/Review

Use the Assessment CD-ROM with Exam*View*®, Online Workbook, and Web site for additional practice, review, and assessment materials.

PART 1

ANSWERS: 1. a; **2.** a; **3.** b; **4.** c; **5.** b; **6.** a; **7.** c; **8.** a; **9.** a; **10.** b; **11.** c; **12.** d; **13.** b; **14.** c; **15.** c; **16.** a; **17.** d

20-30 mins

1. Part 1 may be used as an in-class test to assess student performance, in addition to the Assessment CD-ROM with Exam*View*®. Have students read the direction line. Review the example with the class.

2. Have students complete Part 1 individually. Collect for assessment.

3. If necessary, have students review Lesson 5.

PART 2

ANSWERS: 1. my; **2.** your; **3.** I; **4.** it (OR mine); **5.** your; **6.** you; **7.** '; **8.** her; **9.** '; **10.** her; **11.** 's; **12.** her; **13.** 's; **14.** her; **15.** 's; **16.** Her; **17.** our (OR her OR my); **18.** 's; **19.** 's; **20.** Their; **21.** '; **22.** ours; **23.** 's; **24.** them; **25.** their; **26.** 's; **27.** her; **28.** Her; **29.** 's; **30.** his; **31.** him; **32.** He's; **33.** his; **34.** him

1. Part 2 may also be used as an in-class test to assess student performance, in addition to the Assessment CD-ROM with Exam*View*®.

Have students read the direction line. Explain that this conversation is between two women who are talking about names. Review the example.

2. Have students complete Part 2 individually. Collect for assessment.

3. If necessary, have students review:
   5.1 Possessive Forms of Nouns (p. 131)
   5.2 Possessive Adjectives (p. 133)
   5.4 Possessive Pronouns (p. 135)
   5.5 The Subject and the Object (p. 136)
   5.6 Object Pronouns (pp. 138–139)

Expansion

These expansion activities provide opportunities for students to interact with one another and further develop their speaking and writing skills. Encourage students to use grammar from this lesson whenever possible.

CLASSROOM ACTIVITIES

20-30 mins per activity

1. Review the example. Model the activity with a volunteer. Have pairs make comparisons Monitor pair work. Give help as needed. Then have them present their facts to a group or to the class.

2. This activity can be done as a whole class activity or in groups. If necessary, review the meanings of vocabulary such as *cartoons*, *vegetarian*, etc. Have different volunteers ask the questions.

3. Decide whether the class is going to do the original activity or the variation. Have students read the direction line. Review the examples.

TALK ABOUT IT

15-20 mins

Put students in small groups to discuss the questions and compare the differences in their different cultures and countries. Try to put students

from different countries together. Monitor group work. Give help as needed. Have volunteers share their responses with the class.

WRITE ABOUT IT

15-20 mins

Have students read the direction line. Review the model with the students. Begin writing a paragraph about your name on the board. Then have students write their paragraphs. Encourage students to add more information about their name and their families' names. Collect for assessment and/or have students present their paragraphs to a group.

Practice Idea: Writing

Have students exchange first drafts with a partner. Ask students to help their partners edit their drafts. Refer students to the Editing Advice on pages 149–150.

OUTSIDE ACTIVITY

Have students ask an American about his or her name. Brainstorm questions they can ask. Write them on the board (e.g., *Your name is interesting—tell me about it. Do you have your father's name? Is your last name your father's name or your mother's name?*). Tell students to ask these questions and then report back to the class.

INTERNET ACTIVITY

Have students use an Internet telephone directory. Tell them: *You're going to look for phone directories on the Internet. Then you're going to find out how many people in this city (or a major U.S. city such as New York City) have your last name.* Ask students if they ever look for phone numbers on the Internet. On the board, write a list of phone directory Web sites you and your students use.

Lesson 6

Lesson Overview

GRAMMAR

Ask: *What did we study in Lesson 5?* (possession; object pronouns; questions about the subject) *What are we going to study in this lesson?* (the present continuous tense) Point out the footnote that says the present continuous tense is also called the present progressive tense. Activate prior knowledge that students may have. Have volunteers give examples. Write them on the board. Walk across the room. Ask: *What am I doing now?* (walking)

CONTEXT

1. Ask: *What will we learn about in this lesson?* (things about American life, pets, sports) Activate students' prior knowledge. Ask students if they have a dog or other pet, and if they play any sports.

2. Have students share their knowledge and personal experiences.

Observations in the Park READING

1. Have students look at the title of the reading. Ask: *What is the reading about? How do you know?* Have students make predictions.

2. Preteach any vocabulary words your students may not know, such as *journal, observe,* and *behavior.*

Reading Glossary

behavior: a way of acting
journal: a written record, a diary
observe: to view, watch, especially for anything unusual

BEFORE YOU READ

1. Have students discuss the questions in pairs.

5-10 mins

2. Ask for a few volunteers to share their answers with the class.

 Reading =★

CD 1
TR 27

10-15 mins

1. Have students read the text silently. Tell them to pay special attention to the present continuous tense. Then play the audio and have students read along silently.

2. Check students' comprehension. Ask questions such as: *What is Dan doing?* (writing in his journal) *Why is he writing in a journal?* (He is doing homework for his ESL class.) *Who is making a lot of noise?* (teenagers)

Practice Idea: Listening

To practice listening skills, have students first listen to the audio alone. Ask a few comprehension questions such as: *Where is Dan?* (in the park) *Is it cold outside?* (No, it's warm and people are wearing shorts.) *What surprised Dan?* (even old people are wearing shorts). Then have students open their books and read along as they listen to the audio.

6.1 The Present Continuous Tense =★

10-15 mins

1. Have students look at the reading on page 158. Say: *All the words in bold in the reading are in the present continuous.* Write several examples from the reading on the board. (*I'm taking an ESL course. The sun is shining. They are barbecuing.*) Say: *Study these verbs and try to guess the rule for forming the present continuous tense.* Have volunteers write their guesses on the board.

2. Then ask students to compare their guesses with grammar chart **6.1** on page 159. Review how to form the present continuous: *be* + verb + *-ing*. Explain that the present continuous is used to describe an action

in progress at this moment. Demonstrate, or have volunteers demonstrate, various actions. Narrate the actions (e.g., *I'm running. He's writing.*). Review all of the examples and explanations.

3. Explain that contractions are made with the pronoun and the verb *be*. Also point out that most nouns can form a contraction with *is*.

4. Review how to form the negative: *be + not + verb + -ing*. Remind students to use contractions in the negative (*isn't* and *aren't*). Explain that there is no contraction for *am not*.

5. Point out to students that when the subject is doing two or more things, we don't repeat the verb *be* after *and*.

EXERCISE 1

ANSWERS: 1. ing; **2.** are; **3.** ing; **4.** are; **5.** m; **6.** is; **7.** ing

---

⏱ **5-10 mins**

1. Have students read the direction line. Go over the example in the book. Say: *The verb might be missing or the -ing might be missing.*

2. Have students complete Exercise 1 individually. Remind them to review grammar chart **6.1** on page 159 if necessary. Review the answers as a class.

Practice Idea: Speaking

Put students in groups. Say: *One member mimes an activity and the other students in the group guess.* Tell students to use the present continuous tense to describe the activity (e.g., *Pedro's watching TV.*).

6.2 Spelling of the *-ing* Form

⏱ **10-15 mins**

1. Copy the lists of verbs (base form and *-ing* form) from grammar chart **6.2** on the board. Make sure you separate the six sets of verbs. For example:

eat   eating

go   going

study   studying
plan   planning
stop   stopping
sit   sitting

2. Have students cover up grammar chart **6.2** on page 160. Say: *There are six rules for spelling the -ing form. Can you guess what they are?* Give them hints. Say: *The first row is the category that most verbs belong to. In the second row, pay attention to syllables and consonant and vowel patterns. The verbs in the third row are exceptions to the verbs in the second row. In the fourth and fifth rows, pay attention to syllables and consonant and vowel patterns.* Write the rules that the students come up with on the board.

3. Have students look at grammar chart **6.2**. Say: *Compare our rules with the rules in the book.* Review the rules in the grammar chart.

Presentation Idea

Have students cover up grammar chart **6.2** on page 160. Write the base form of the verbs from the chart on the board. Ask students to go up to the board and write the *-ing* form next to it. (Have students go up in groups so that their answers remain somewhat anonymous.) Then ask students to look at grammar chart **6.2** and check what's on the board. Go over the rules for spelling.

EXERCISE 2

ANSWERS: 1. planning; **2.** opening; **3.** sitting; **4.** beginning; **5.** hurrying; **6.** happening; **7.** staying; **8.** growing; **9.** marrying; **10.** grabbing; **11.** writing; **12.** fixing; **13.** wiping; **14.** carrying; **15.** drinking; **16.** driving; **17.** waiting; **18.** serving; **19.** visiting; **20.** occurring

---

⏱ **5-10 mins**

1. Have students read the direction line. Ask: *What do we write in the blanks?* (the *-ing* form of the verb) Point out that the accent marks show which syllable is stressed. Go over the examples in the book. Ask students to tell you what the rules are for the spelling of each verb in the examples (*Do not double a final* y; *ends in consonant +* e *drop* e *add* -ing.).

2. Have students complete Exercise 2 individually. Remind them to review grammar chart **6.2** on page 160 if necessary. Check answers as a class.

EXERCISE 3

ANSWERS: 1. 's writing; **2.** are playing; **3.** 's riding; **4.** are jogging; **5.** 's shining; **6.** 's sitting; **7.** are going; **8.** are carrying

10-15 mins

1. Have students read the direction line. Go over the example. Then do #1 with the class. Ask a volunteer to give an answer.

2. Have students complete Exercise 3 individually. Remind them to review grammar chart **6.2** on page 160 if necessary. Then have students practice saying the sentences in pairs. Finally, check the answers as a class.

6.3 The Present Continuous Tense—Uses

5-10 mins

1. Have students cover up grammar chart **6.3** on page 161. Write the following sentences and explanations from the grammar chart on the board:

    a. *I am writing in my journal now.*
    b. *I'm taking an ESL course this semester.*
    c. *Most people are wearing shorts.*

    1. *To show a long-term action that is in progress.*
    2. *To describe a state or condition.*
    3. *To show that an action is in progress now, at this moment.*
    Say: *Match the examples to the rule.*

2. Have students look at grammar chart **6.3**. Say: *Compare our answers with the grammar chart.* Go over any errors.

3. Review the examples in the chart.

Presentation Idea

In pairs, have students write two sentences for each of the three rules. Say: *Look at the classroom right now. What is happening?* Monitor pair work. Have volunteers write their sentences on the board. Then go through the examples in grammar chart **6.3**.

EXERCISE 4
Answers will vary.

10-15 mins

1. Tell students that this exercise is about what they're doing in the classroom now. Have students read the direction line. Go over the examples in the book. Have volunteers model the examples.

2. Have students complete Exercise 4 individually. Then have pairs compare answers. Remind them to review grammar chart **6.3** on page 161 if necessary. Monitor pair work. Give help as needed.

EXERCISE 5
Answers will vary.

10-15 mins

1. Have students read the direction line. Say: *You're going to be making affirmative or negative sentences based on what's true for you.* Go over the examples in the book. Have volunteers model the examples.

2. Have students complete Exercise 5 individually. Remind them to review grammar chart **6.3** on page 161 if necessary. Then have pairs compare answers. Monitor pair work. Give help as needed.

Practice Idea: Writing

Have students write an e-mail to a friend. Say: *Tell your friend what you're doing now, at this moment, and what your long-term actions are.*

Observations Downtown
READING

1. Have students look at the title of the reading and the photo. Ask: *What is the reading about? How do you know?* Have students make predictions.

2. Preteach any vocabulary words your students may not know, such as *dress shoes*, *comfortable*, and *couriers*.

Reading Glossary

comfortable: something that makes you feel relaxed
courier: someone whose job is to take packages and documents somewhere
dress shoes: shoes that are worn with smart clothes, such as a suit

BEFORE YOU READ

5-10 mins

1. Have students discuss the questions in pairs.
2. Ask for a few volunteers to share their answers with the class.

Reading

CD 1
TR 28

10-15 mins

1. Have students read the text silently. Tell them to pay special attention to questions with the present continuous tense. Then play the audio and have students read along silently.
2. Check students' comprehension. Ask questions such as: *What are Dan and Peter waiting for?* (the bus) *What are the couriers doing?* (riding their bicycles fast, riding between the cars) *Where is Peter going?* (to the library)

Practice Idea: Listening

To practice listening skills, have students first listen to the audio alone. Ask a few comprehension questions such as: *Why are the women wearing running shoes?* (because they want to be comfortable on the way to work) *What does Dan think is dangerous?* (talking on the phone and driving at the same time). Then have students open their books and read along as they listen to the audio.

6.4 Questions with the Present Continuous Tense

10-15 mins

1. Have students cover up grammar chart **6.4** on page 164. Write on the board: *Women are wearing running shoes.* Underneath write: *suits.* Now say: *Write a* yes/no *question about women wearing suits.* Have a volunteer write it on the board. Then say: *Now write a* why *question about women wearing running shoes.* Ask another volunteer to write it on the board.

2. Have students look at grammar chart **6.4**. Say: *Compare our answers with the grammar chart.* Review all of the examples, including negative statements and questions. Go over contractions with the negative.

3. Direct students to the Language Notes. Demonstrate *What … doing?* Ask the class about the actions of different students. Elicit responses. Ask: *What's Farid doing? What's Karmen doing? What are Sylvia and Andrea doing?* Write the questions on the board and their responses. Explain that when we ask a *What … doing?* question, we usually respond with another verb.

EXERCISE 6

ANSWERS: 1. No, he isn't. **2.** Yes, they are. **3.** She's wearing running shoes. **4.** She wants to be comfortable. **5.** They're waiting for a bus. **6.** Peter is going to the library.

10-15 mins

1. Tell students that this exercise is about the reading on page 163. Have students read the direction line. Say: *Some of the questions are* yes/no *questions, and some are* wh- *questions.* Do #1 with the class.

2. Have students complete the exercise in pairs. Remind them to review grammar chart **6.4** on page 164 if necessary. Tell students to alternate asking and answering questions. Monitor pair work. Give help as needed.

EXERCISE 7

ANSWERS: 1. Is the teacher writing on the board? **2.** Is the teaching sitting at the desk? **3.** Is the teacher helping the students? **4.** Are we practicing the past tense? **5.** Are we reviewing Lesson 5? **6.** Where is the teacher standing? **7.** What exercise are we doing? **8.** What are you thinking about?

10-15 mins

1. Tell students that this exercise is about what people in the class are doing now. Have students read the direction line. Ask: *What kind of questions are we asking?* (yes/no questions) Go over the example with the class. Have two students model the example.

2. Have students complete the exercise in pairs. Tell students to alternate asking and

answering questions. Remind them to review grammar chart **6.4** on page 164 if necessary. Monitor pair work. Give help as needed.

Practice Idea: Speaking

Create two rings of students. Have half of the students stand in an outer ring around the classroom. Have the other half stand in an inner ring, facing the outer ring. Instruct students to ask and answer the questions from Exercise 7. Call out *turn* every minute or so. Students in the inner ring should move one space clockwise. Students now ask and answer with their new partner. Have students ask questions in random order. Make sure students look at each other when they're speaking.

EXERCISE [8]

ANSWERS: 1. Are you planning to buy a car? **2.** Are you studying biology this semester? **3.** Are you taking other courses this semester? **4.** Are you looking for a new apartment? **5.** Are you looking for a job? **6.** Is your English improving? **7.** Is your vocabulary growing? **8.** Is the teacher helping you? **9.** Are the students making progress? **10.** Are you learning about other students' countries?

10-15 mins

1. Tell students that this exercise is about them and their long-term actions. Have students read the direction line. Ask: *What kind of questions are we asking?* (*yes/no* questions) Go over the example with the class. Have two students model the example.

2. Have students complete the exercise in pairs. Tell students to alternate asking and answering questions. Remind them to review grammar chart **6.4** on page 164 if necessary. Monitor pair work. Give help as needed.

EXERCISE [9]

ANSWERS: 1. I'm (not) wearing; **2.** I'm (not) holding; **3.** I'm (not) chewing; **4.** I'm (not) thinking; **5.** I'm (not) living; **6.** I'm (not) planning; **7.** I'm (not) looking; **8.** I'm (not) planning; **9.** I'm (not) taking;

10. I'm (not) getting; **11.** I'm (not) gaining; **12.** I'm (not) learning; **13.** I'm (not) learning

10-15 mins

1. Have students read the direction line. Say: *You're going to write what's true for you. And then you're going to ask your partner the same questions.* Go over the examples with the class. Have two students model the examples.

2. First have students fill in the blanks individually. Then tell students to ask and answer questions in pairs. Remind them to review grammar chart **6.4** on page 164 if necessary. Monitor pair work. Give help as needed.

EXERCISE [10]

ANSWERS: 1. are they looking at people; **2.** are they waiting (for the bus); **3.** are people (OR they) walking fast; **4.** is he talking; **5.** isn't she wearing dress shoes; **6.** isn't he writing (in his journal) now; **7.** is (OR 's) riding a bicycle

10-15 mins

1. Have students read the direction line. Ask: *What kind of question do we ask?* (a *wh*-question) Go over the example with the class. Do #1 with the class.

2. Have students complete the exercise individually. Remind them to review grammar chart **6.4** on page 164 if necessary. Check answers as a class.

EXERCISE [11]
CD 1
TR 29

ANSWERS: 1. 'm calling; **2.** 'm using; **3.** are you driving (OR going OR coming); **4.** are you driving (OR going); **5.** are flying; **6.** 'm talking; **7.** am driving; **8.** is arriving (OR landing); **9.** aren't they; **10.** Are you wearing your seat belt; **11.** are you doing; **12.** 'm using; **13.** 'm looking; **14.** are the kids; **15.** 's watching; **16.** 's doing; **17.** isn't; **18.** Are you making (OR preparing OR cooking); **19.** 'm waiting

15-20 mins

1. Have students read the direction line. Point out that this conversation is between a woman (Betty) and her husband. Direct students to the picture on page 167. Ask: *Where is Betty calling from?* (her car; the airport; her cell phone)

2. Go over the example in the book. Remind students to use contractions wherever possible.

3. Have students complete Exercise 11 individually. Remind them to review grammar chart **6.4** on page 164 if necessary. Then play the audio and check answers as a class.

4. Then have students practice the conversation in pairs. Monitor pair work. Give help as needed.

Practice Idea: Listening

To provide practice with listening skills, have students close their books and listen to the audio. Repeat the audio as needed. Ask comprehension questions, such as: *Why is Betty driving to the airport?* (to pick up a client) *Why is it so noisy at the airport?* (because airplanes are flying overhead and they're very low) *Why is Betty late?* (because she's stuck in traffic) Then have students open their books and complete Exercise 11 on page 167.

Practice Idea: Speaking

Have volunteers role-play all or part of the conversation in Exercise 11 in front of the class.

Observations in the School Cafeteria READING

1. Have students look at the illustration. Ask: *Where are these people?* (in a cafeteria) *What are they doing?* (eating, talking, reading, etc.)

2. Have students look at the title of the reading. Ask: *What is the reading about? How do you know?* Have students use the title and the picture to make predictions about the reading.

3. Preteach any vocabulary words your students may not know, such as *kiss*, *feed*, and *bother*.

Reading Glossary

bother: to disturb or give unwanted attention
feed: to provide with food
kiss: to press one's lips against someone or something

5-10 mins

1. Have students discuss the questions in pairs.
2. Ask for a few volunteers to share their answers with the class.

 Reading

CD 1
TR 30

10-15 mins

1. Have students read the text silently. Tell them to pay special attention to simple present and present continuous verbs. Then play the audio and have students read along silently.

2. Check students' comprehension. Ask questions such as: *What is Dan doing?* (observing people) *Who is feeding the baby?* (the man) *Is Dan surprised at the behavior of the people in the cafeteria?* (Yes. He thinks they're being rude.)

Practice Idea: Listening

To practice listening skills, have students first listen to the audio alone. Ask a few comprehension questions such as: *Where is Dan?* (in the school cafeteria) *What actions does Dan think are impolite?* (public displays of affection, women putting on makeup in public, students listening to loud music, a man resting his feet on a chair) Then have students open their books and read along as they listen to the audio.

6.5 Present Continuous and Simple Present ≡★

10-15 mins

1. Have students go to the reading on page 169. Say: *Underline the verbs in the simple present and circle the verbs in the present continuous.* Have volunteers give examples of what they circled and underlined. Elicit students' prior knowledge. Ask: *What do we use the simple present tense for?* (to talk about a habitual activity, a custom, or a general truth or fact) *What do we use the present continuous for?* (to show actions in progress at this moment, to show long-term action in progress, to describe a state or condition)

2. Have students look at grammar chart **6.5** on pages 169–170. Go over the examples and the explanations.

3. Explain that the question *What does she do?* is used to ask about a profession or job. *What is she doing?* asks about a present activity. Review the example sentences. Go around the room asking students both questions: *What are you doing?* and *What do you do?*

 EXERCISE 12 =★

CD 1
TR 31

ANSWERS: 1. am eating; **2.** eat; **3.** observe; **4.** is wearing; **5.** wear; **6.** is wearing; **7.** is wearing; **8.** use; **9.** is using; **10.** write; **11.** belong; **12.** sits; **13.** stands; **14.** stand up; **15.** enters; **16.** study; **17.** is taking; **18.** are you taking; **19.** take; **20.** is waiting

 1. Have students read the direction line. Point out that this conversation takes place in a cafeteria and is between two students discussing American customs and those of their native countries. Go over the example in the book. Remind students to use contractions wherever possible.

10-15 mins

2. Have students complete Exercise 12 individually. Remind them to review grammar chart **6.5** on pages 169–170 if necessary. Check answers as a class.

Practice Idea: Listening

To provide practice with listening skills, have students close their books and listen to the audio. Repeat the audio as needed. Ask comprehension questions such as: *Why does person B think the man looks strange?* (because he's wearing an earring) *Do women in person B's country wear earrings?* (yes) *Why does person A think the woman looks strange?* (because she's wearing three earrings in one ear) Then have students open their books and complete Exercise 12.

Practice Idea: Speaking

Have students role-play all or part of the conversation in front of the class. If possible, have students go to the cafeteria to observe people. Then have them work in pairs to create a similar dialog.

6.6 Nonaction Verbs =★

 1. Have students cover up grammar chart **6.6** on page 172. Ask: *What are nonaction verbs? Can you give me any examples?* If students have difficulty, tell them that nonaction words describe a state or condition, not an action. Give them an example. Then ask them to go to the reading on page 169. Say: *Double-underline the nonaction verbs.* (*want, see, think, care, hear,* and *look*) Have volunteers give examples of what they underlined. Write them on the board.

10-15 mins

2. Have students look at grammar chart **6.6**. Say: *Are the verbs you found in the reading on this list?* Go over the examples and the explanations.

3. Direct students to the Language Note. Say: *Compare the verbs* hear, see, listen, *and* look. Hear *and* see *are nonaction verbs because they are involuntary—you do them without necessarily wanting to.* Listen *and* look *are action verbs because they are voluntary actions.* Go over the examples.

EXERCISE 13 =★

ANSWERS: 1. 'm studying; **2.** 're using; **3.** need; **4.** 're comparing; **5.** don't remember; **6.** see; **7.** 'm not looking, 'm looking; **8.** don't need; **9.** aren't writing; **10.** don't hear; **11.** are learning; **12.** know

---

 1. Have students read the direction line. Say: *You have to decide between using the simple present and the present continuous.* Go over the examples.

10-15 mins

2. Have students complete Exercise 13 individually. Remind them to review grammar chart **6.6** on page 172 if necessary. Check the answers as a class.

Practice Idea: Speaking

Have students explain why they used the simple present or the present continuous in each statement in Exercise 13 (e.g., 1. *understand*—simple present because *understand* is a nonaction word).

6.7 *Think, Have,* and the Sense Perception Verbs

10-15 mins

1. Have students cover up grammar chart **6.7** on page 173. Write all of the example sentences from the grammar chart on the board. Write them without the verb in place. Don't label the sentences with "action" or "nonaction." Don't write the explanations. For example:

   (think)

   He about his mother's cooking.

   He it is wrong to kiss in public.

2. Say: *Some verbs can be action or nonaction verbs depending on the use. Study these sentences. Which sentence needs an action verb, and which sentence needs a nonaction verb?* (action—*He is thinking about his mother's cooking;* nonaction—*He thinks it is wrong to kiss in public.*)

3. Have students look at grammar chart **6.7**. Say: *Compare our sentences on the board with the chart.* Review the examples and the explanations. Go over any errors.

Presentation Idea

Have students cover up the examples side of grammar chart **6.7**. Write the sentences without the verbs in place (as described above). Go over the explanations in the book. Then have students complete the sentences on the board using the right form of each verb.

EXERCISE 14

ANSWERS: 1. 's smelling; **2.** smell; **3.** 's thinking; **4.** thinks; **5.** am having; **6.** have; **7.** don't have; **8.** has, 'm having

10-15 mins

1. Have students read the direction line. *You have to decide between using the simple present and the present continuous.* Go over the examples.

2. Have students complete Exercise 14 individually. Remind them to review grammar chart **6.7** on page 173 if necessary. Check the answers as a class.

Practice Idea: Speaking

Have students explain why they used the simple present or the present continuous in each statement in Exercise 14 (e.g., 1. *smelling*—present continuous because *smell* is an action word here. I'm smelling the flowers right now.).

EXERCISE 15

ANSWERS: 1. 's writing; **2.** 's sitting; **3.** sees; **4.** goes; **5.** writes; **6.** thinks, wants; **7.** 's looking, 're holding; **8.** looks; **9.** 's thinking; **10.** are wearing; **11.** wear; **12.** seem

10-15 mins

1. Have students read the direction line. Point out that students should use the simple present with action verbs that are regular activities (e.g., *He thinks about his mother's cooking every night.*) and with nonaction verbs (e.g., *He thinks it is wrong to kiss in public.*) Go over the examples.

2. Have students complete Exercise 15 individually. Remind them to review grammar charts **6.5** on pages 169–170, **6.6** on page 172, and **6.7** on page 173 if necessary. Check the answers as a class.

EXERCISE 16

ANSWERS: 1. The mother isn't feeding the baby. **2.** Dan (OR He) isn't sitting in class. **3.** He doesn't understand American customs. **4.** Men and women in his country don't kiss in public. **5.** Americans (OR They) don't use their hands to eat spaghetti. **6.** The man (OR He) isn't wearing a bracelet. **7.** Americans (OR They) don't seem strange to me. **8.** Dan doesn't like to take care of babies. **9.** Women in Dan's country don't wear shorts in the summer.

10-15 mins

1. Have students read the direction line. Ask: *What do we write?* (the negative form of the verb) Go over the examples in the book. Remind students to use contractions wherever possible.

2. Have students complete Exercise 16 individually. Then have students compare answers in pairs. Remind them to review grammar chart **6.1** on page 159 if necessary. Monitor pair work. Give help as needed.

EXERCISE 17

ANSWERS: 1. Is Dan (OR he) writing his homework? No, he isn't. **2.** Is he watching American people? Yes, he is. **3.** Does he understand American customs? No, he doesn't. **4.** Do American women wear shorts in the summer? Yes, they do. **5.** Is the man eating a hot dog? No, he isn't.

10-15 mins

1. Have students read the direction line. Ask: *What do we write?* (a *yes/no* question and a short answer) Go over the examples in the book.

2. Have students complete the exercise individually. Remind them to review grammar chart **6.4** on page 164 if necessary. Check the answers as a class.

EXERCISE 18

ANSWERS: 1. To whom is Dan (OR he) writing a letter? OR Who is Dan (OR he) writing a letter to? **2.** Why does Dan (OR he) want to know about American customs? **3.** Where are two women putting on makeup? **4.** Why do American men and women touch and hold hands in public? **5.** How often does Dan (OR he) write to his family? **6.** Why isn't the man (OR he) using a fork? **7.** Why don't women wear shorts in some countries? **8.** Why do Americans (OR they) often wear jeans? **9.** What does "behavior" mean?

10-15 mins

1. Have students read the direction line. Ask: *What do we write?* (a *wh-* question) Point out that students do not need to write an answer. Go over the examples in the book.

2. Have students complete the exercise individually. Then have students compare answers in pairs. Remind them to review grammar chart **6.4** on page 164 if necessary. Monitor pair work. Give help as needed.

EXERCISE 19

CD 1
TR 32

ANSWERS: 1. 're; **2.** do you like; **3.** like; **4.** 'm having; **5.** Why aren't you studying; **6.** 'm meeting; **7.** 'm thinking; **8.** are doing; **9.** don't care; **10.** don't need; **11.** need; **12.** Are you getting; **13.** know; **14.** 'm getting; **15.** Are you practicing; **16.** don't have; **17.** 'm taking; **18.** usually take; **19.** does "freshman" mean; **20.** Are you getting;

21. 'm gaining; **22.** do not like; **23.** don't you like; **24.** doesn't taste; **25.** miss; **26.** 'm making; **27.** 'm getting; **28.** always think; **29.** 's working; **30.** 'm wearing; **31.** Do you have; **32.** 's starting; **33.** are getting; **34.** are changing; **35.** 'm looking; **36.** see; **37.** prefer; **38.** 'm making; **39.** 's making; **40.** Does she want; **41.** don't think; **42.** 's watching; **43.** Is she getting; **44.** spends; **45.** 's coming; **46.** wants

15-20 mins

1. Have students read the direction line. Explain that this is a phone conversation between Dave and his mother. Point out the picture of Dave on page 177. Go over the example in the book. Remind students to use contractions wherever possible.

2. Have students complete Exercise 19 individually. Remind them to review grammar chart **6.5** on pages 169–170, **6.6** on page 172, and **6.7** on page 173 if necessary. Play the audio and check answers as a class.

3. Then have students practice the conversation in pairs. Monitor pair work. Give help as needed.

Practice Idea: Listening

To provide practice with listening skills, have students close their books and listen to the audio. Ask comprehension questions, such as: *Where is Dave's college?* (in the U.S.) *What does Dave think of college?* (fun, great) *What is Dave thinking of doing?* (getting an earring) Then have students open their books and complete Exercise 19.

Practice Idea: Speaking

Have pairs write their own conversations. Tell students they can use Exercise 19 as a model. Monitor pair work. Give help as needed. Have volunteers role-play their conversations in front of the class.

Summary of Lesson 6

20-30 mins

Uses of Tenses Have students close their books. Create two matching exercises. Write the sentences from the simple present tense chart on the board. Choose one sentence from each row and write them in random order.

Then write the uses in random order. For example: *Oranges grow in Florida. Japanese people bow.* Do the same with the present continuous chart. Have students match the uses with the example sentences.

Then have students open their books and compare their work with the charts in the book. Go over the example sentences in the book. Have students write a sentence of their own for each use. If necessary, have students review:

- **6.1** The Present Continuous Tense (p. 159)
- **6.3** The Present Continuous Tense— Uses (p. 161)
- **6.5** Present Continuous and Simple Present (pp. 169–170)
- **6.6** Nonaction Verbs (p. 172)
- **6.7** *Think, Have,* and the Sense Perception Verbs (p. 173)

Lesson 2 The Simple Present Tense

Editing Advice

10-15 mins

Have students close their books. Write the first few sentences without editing marks or corrections on the board. For example:

1. *He working now.*
2. *Where you're going?*

Ask students to correct each sentence and provide a rule or explanation for each correction. This activity can be done individually, in pairs, or as a class. After students have corrected each sentence, tell them to turn to page 181.

Say: *Now compare your work with the Editing Advice in the book.* Refer students to the Editing Advice on pages 65–67 for the simple present tense.

Editing Quiz

ANSWERS: **1.** 'm writing; **2.** why are you doing; **3.** do you have; **4.** We need; **5.** I think; **6.** C; **7.** C; **8.** How do you spell "earring"; **9.** are you writing; **10.** is wearing; **11.** C; **12.** C

10-15 mins

1. Tell students they are going to put the editing advice into practice. Have students read the direction line. Ask: *Do all the shaded words and phrases have mistakes?* (no) Go over the examples with the class. Then do #1 together.

2. Have students complete the quiz individually. Then have them compare answers with a partner before checking answers as a class.

3. For the items students had difficulties with, have them go back and find the relevant grammar chart and review it. Monitor and give help as necessary.

Lesson 6 Test/Review

40-60 mins

Use the Assessment CD-ROM with Exam*View®*, Online Workbook, and Web site for additional practice, review, and assessment materials.

PART 1

ANSWERS: **1.** 'm looking ; **2.** 'm returning; **3.** Do you want; **4.** 'm waiting; **5.** are working; **6.** need; **7.** Do you like; **8.** like; **9.** wears; **10.** has; **11.** seems; **12.** think; **13.** does Bob teach; **14.** usually work; **15.** helps; **16.** Does he give; **17.** doesn't believe; **18.** doesn't he believe; **19.** thinks; **20.** says; **21.** 're working; **22.** sounds; **23.** are you asking; **24.** 'm thinking; **25.** fill; **26.** see; **27.** 's walking

1. Part 1 may also be used as an in-class test to assess student performance, in addition to the Assessment CD-ROM with Exam*View®*. Have students read the direction line. Explain that this is a conversation between two students, Alicia and Teresa, that takes place in the school library. Go over the example with the class.

2. Have students complete Part 1 individually. Collect for assessment.

3. If necessary, have students review Lesson 6.

PART 2

ANSWERS: **1.** doesn't want; **2.** isn't looking;
3. aren't talking; **4.** don't have; **5.** don't work;
6. doesn't give; **7.** isn't waiting; **8.** doesn't seem;
9. isn't returning

1. Part 2 may also be used as an in-class test to assess student performance, in addition to the Assessment CD-ROM with Exam*View*®. Have students read the direction line. Point out that students need to use the negative form of the underlined word. Go over the example with the class.

2. Have students complete Part 2 individually. Collect for assessment.

3. If necessary, have students review:
   6.1 The Present Continuous Tense (p. 159)
   6.5 Present Continuous and Simple Present (pp. 169–170)

PART 3

ANSWERS: **1.** Does Bob (OR he) like tests? No, he doesn't. **2.** Does Teresa (OR she) have time now? No, she doesn't. **3.** Are they talking about their teachers? Yes, they are. **4.** Does Bob (OR he) ever wear a suit to class? No, he doesn't. **5.** Does Teresa (OR she) want to go for coffee? No, she doesn't. **6.** Do American teachers seem strange to Teresa? No, they don't. **7.** Is Alicia working on a geography project? No, she isn't.

1. Part 3 may also be used as an in-class test to assess student performance, in addition to the Assessment CD-ROM with Exam*View*®. Have students read the direction line. Explain that students should write a *yes/no* question and a short answer. Go over the example with the class.

2. Have students complete Part 3 individually. Collect for assessment.

3. If necessary, have students review:
   6.4 Questions with the Present Continuous Tense (p. 164)
   6.5 Present Continuous and Simple Present (pp. 169–170)

PART 4

ANSWERS: **1.** Why does he sound interesting?
2. Why doesn't he like tests? **3.** What kind of project are they working on? **4.** How often does Teresa (OR she) study in the library? **5.** What kind of book is she looking for? **6.** Why is she waiting for her friend? **7.** Why aren't her classmates (OR they) writing in a journal?

1. Part 4 may also be used as an in-class test to assess student performance, in addition to the Assessment CD-ROM with Exam*View*®. Have students read the direction line. Ask: *Do we write answers?* (no) Go over the example with the class.

2. Have students complete Part 4 individually. Collect for assessment.

3. If necessary, have students review:
   6.4 Questions with the Present Continuous Tense (p. 164)
   6.5 Present Continuous and Simple Present (pp. 169–170)

Expansion

These expansion activities provide opportunities for students to interact with one another and further develop their speaking and writing skills. Encourage students to use grammar from this lesson whenever possible.

CLASSROOM ACTIVITIES

10-15 mins per activity

1. This guessing activity can be done in groups or as a whole class. Have students read the direction line. Go over the example. Model the activity with a volunteer. Have students write their sentences and then read them to a partner or their group to guess where they are.

2. Have students read the direction line. Model letter "a" for the class. Say: *First complete the sentences on your own. Then compare your sentences with a partner.*

Practice Idea: Speaking

Have students create mini cell-phone dialogs based on the ideas from Activity 2. Ask volunteers to role-play their dialogs in front of the class.

TALK ABOUT IT

10-15 mins

Write on the board: *Cultural differences: behavior.* Ask questions such as: *What kind of things do Americans do that are strange in your culture?* Elicit one or two ideas and write them on the board. Then have students discuss behaviors that are strange to them in groups. Have groups report the results of their discussions to the class (e.g., *We think it's strange that Americans don't have much physical contact when they greet each other.*). If possible, put students from different countries together in the same group.

WRITE ABOUT IT

10-15 mins

Have students read the direction line and the example text. Have students help you write a similar text on the board about the class. Then have students carry out the activity. Encourage them to write as much as they can.

Practice Idea: Writing

Have students exchange first drafts with a partner. Ask students to help their partners edit their drafts. Refer students to the Editing Advice on page 181.

OUTSIDE ACTIVITY

Ask students to observe behaviors in public places. Say: *Write down all the actions you see.* Have students report their observations in groups or have volunteers report their observations to the class.

INTERNET ACTIVITY

Tell students to use the Internet to find the Web site of a college in this city and answer the following questions:

1. Where is it?
2. What's the tuition?
3. Does this college have evening classes?
4. Does this college have more than one location?
5. Does it have a graduate program?
6. Does it have dormitories?
7. Does it have ESL classes?
8. When is the next registration?
9. What are the vacation days?

Have students brainstorm a list of local colleges. Go over the questions to make sure that students understand everything.

Practice Idea: Writing

Have students create a poster for the college they research. Display the posters around the room.

Lesson 7

Lesson Overview

GRAMMAR

1. Briefly review other tenses students have learned. Ask: *What tense did we study in Lessons 1, 2, and 3?* (simple present tense) *What tense did we study in Lesson 6?* (present continuous tense)

2. Ask: *What tenses are we going to study in this lesson?* (future tenses) *What words do we use to talk about the future?* (*will* and *be going to*) Have volunteers give examples. Write the examples on the board.

CONTEXT

1. Ask: *What will we learn about in this lesson?* (weddings) Elicit students' prior knowledge. Ask: *Have you ever been to a wedding in the U.S.? Are weddings here different from weddings in your country?*

2. Have students share their knowledge and personal experiences.

> ### Presentation Idea
>
> The topic for this lesson can be enhanced with the following ideas:
>
> 1. Photos of your wedding or of another wedding
> 2. Newspaper articles about weddings or wedding announcements
> 3. A registry list from a department store
> 4. Newspaper articles on unusual weddings or honeymoon trips

Planning for a Wedding
READING

1. Have students look at the photo. Ask: *Who are the people?* (a couple) *Where are they?* (at a store) *What are they doing?* (choosing gifts for their gift registry)

2. Have students look at the title of the reading. Ask: *What is the reading about?* Have students use the title and photo to make predictions.

3. Preteach any vocabulary words students may not know, such as *engaged, invitations, reception, rehearsal, honeymoon, duplicate,* and *debt.* For *invitation,* direct students to the picture on page 194. For *reception,* point out the footnote at the bottom of the page.

Reading Glossary

debt: a sum of money owed to another
duplicate: an exact copy
engaged: having a formal agreement to get married
honeymoon: a trip people take after they get married
invitation: a card or spoken request asking someone to come to an event
reception: a type of party planned so people can meet a special guest and each other
rehearsal: a practice session

BEFORE YOU READ

5-10 mins

1. Have students discuss the questions in pairs. Try to pair students of different cultures together.

2. Ask for a few volunteers to share their answers with the class.

 ### Reading ─⭐
CD 1 TR 33

10-15 mins

1. Have students read the text silently. Tell them to pay special attention to the future tense verbs *will* and *be going to.* Then play the audio and have students read along.

2. Check students' comprehension. Ask questions such as: *What do Karyn and Steve need to do before the wedding?* (choose photographers, invitations, a wedding dress, etc.)

3. Direct students to the wedding cost chart on page 191. Ask: *Are American weddings expensive? Are weddings in your native country expensive?*

Practice Idea: Listening

To practice listening skills, have students first listen to the audio alone. Ask a few comprehension questions such as: *When are Karyn and Steve going to get married?* (a year and a half after they graduate) *How many people are they going to invite to the wedding?* (250) Then have students open their books and read along as they listen to the audio.

Did You Know?

Have students read the information. Ask: *Do couples often spend more than they planned on weddings in your country?*

Context Note

Bridal registries usually include items for the kitchen, the bedroom, and the bathroom. They don't usually include large pieces of furniture or personal items such as clothing.

7.1 Future with *Will*

1. Have students cover up grammar chart **7.1** on page 191. Then have students find sentences from the reading on page 190 that contain *will*. Write a few of the sentences on the board. For example, write: *They will need to rent a limousine.* Below that write: *They will register for gifts.* Make sure the subject, *will*, and the verb line up. Ask: *What do all the sentences have?* (subject + *will* + verb) Write these labels above the sentences.

2. Demonstrate how to form the contraction of *will* (by adding *'ll*). On the board, write: *They will register for gifts.* Ask: *How can we make a contraction with the subject and* will? (subject + *'ll*) Write: *They'll register for gifts.* Elicit contractions for other subject pronouns. Write them on the board.

3. Demonstrate how to form the negative. On the board, write: *They will register for gifts.* Ask: *How can we make this sentence negative?* (add *not* after *will*) Write: *They will not register for*

gifts. Then ask: *How can we make a contraction?* (will + not = won't) Write: *will + not = won't. They won't register for gifts.*

4. Demonstrate the use of an adverb in sentences with *will*. Say: *We want to use* probably *in the sentence* They will register for gifts. *Where does it go?* (after *will*) On the board, write: *They will probably register for gifts.*

5. Have students look at grammar chart **7.1**. Review the forms of *will*. Point out that unlike in the simple present and present continuous tenses, there is only one form of *will* for different subject pronouns.

6. Discuss the function of the future tenses. Ask: *In the reading, are Karyn and Steve married?* (no) *When do they want to marry?* (a year and a half after they graduate from college) Say: *The reading says, "The wedding will take place a year and a half after they graduate from college." When do we use* will? (to talk about future events)

Presentation Idea

Draw a time line on the board. Draw a mark in the center and label it *present (now)/Karyn and Steve—engaged*. Label the right side *future/Karyn and Steve—married*.

EXERCISE 1

ANSWERS: 1. will invite; **2.** will be; **3.** will go; **4.** will have (OR be in); **5.** will choose (OR give OR buy); **6.** will rent; **7.** will help

1. Tell students that this exercise is about Karyn and Steve's wedding plans. Have students read the direction line. Ask: *What do we write on the blanks?* (will + verb) Go over the example.

2. Have students complete Exercise 1 individually. Remind them to review grammar chart **7.1** on page 191 if necessary. Then have them check their answers in pairs. Finally, check the answers as a class.

7.2 Future with *Be Going To*

10-15 mins

1. Have students cover up grammar chart **7.2** on page 192. Then have students find sentences from the reading on page 190 that contain *be going to*. Write a few of the sentences on the board. For example, write: *They're going to graduate from college next year.* Then below that, write: *The wedding cake is going to be very expensive.* Make sure the subject, *be*, *going to*, and the verb line up. Ask: *What do all the sentences have?* (subject + *be* + *going to* + verb) Write these labels above the sentences.

2. Review how to form contractions with *be*. On the board, write: *The bride is going to wear a white dress.* Ask: *How can we make a contraction with the subject and* be? (subject + *'s*) Write: *The bride's going to wear a white dress.*

3. Review how to form the negative. On the board, write: *They are not going to graduate this year.* Ask: *How do we form the negative?* (add *not* after *be*) Then ask: *How can we make a contraction?* (*they're not* or *they aren't*)

4. Demonstrate the use of an adverb in sentences with *be going to*. Say: *Put the adverb between* be *and* going to. On the board, write: *They are probably going to open their gifts at home.*

5. Have students look at grammar chart **7.2**. Review the examples and explanations. Refer students to the Language Note and Pronunciation Notes. Point out that, in informal speech, *going to* in front of another

verb often sounds like *gonna*. Demonstrate the pronunciation of these two sentences:

> *I'm going to have breakfast now.*
> *I'm going to the restaurant now.*

EXERCISE 2

ANSWERS: 1. are going to play (OR perform); **2.** is going to take; **3.** are going to be; **4.** is going to wear; **5.** is going to cost; **6.** is going to be (OR take place); **7.** is going to be

1. Tell students that this exercise is based on the reading on page 190. Have students read the direction line. Ask: *What do we write on the blanks?* (*be going to* + verb) Go over the example in the book.

2. Have students complete Exercise 2 individually. Remind them to review grammar chart **7.2** on page 192 if necessary. Check the answers as a class.

7.3 Choosing *Will* or *Be Going To*

10-15 mins

1. Have students cover up the explanations side of grammar chart **7.3** on page 193. Write the following categories across the board:

   promises

   no previous plans

   predictions

   facts about the future

   previous plans

   offers to help

2. Have students read the sentences in the grammar chart (without looking at the explanations). Say: *Find the sentences that*

match the category. For example, which sentences are promises? Write the sentences on the board under the correct categories. Then have students guess the rules for using *will* or *be going to*. Tell students that sometimes you can use both *will* and *be going to*. Ask: *Do you use* will *or* be going to *for promises?* (*will*)

3. Have students look at the explanations in grammar chart **7.3**. Ask students to compare their work on the board with the chart.

EXERCISE 3

Answers will vary.

 1. Tell students that this exercise is about them and what they're going to be doing. Have students read the direction line. Ask: *Which future tense will we use here?* (*be going to*) Go over the example in the book. Have a volunteer model the example.

5-10 mins

Have students complete Exercise 3 individually. Remind them to review grammar chart **7.2** on page 192 if necessary. Then have pairs compare answers. Monitor pair work. Give help as needed.

Practice Idea: Speaking

Take a class survey. How many people are going to do the same thing? Write the results on the board.

EXERCISE 4

Answers will vary.

 1. Tell students that this exercise is about their predictions for this class. Have students read the direction line. Ask: *Which future tense do we use with predictions?* (*be going to* or *will*) *Which one are we going to use for this exercise?* (*be going to*) Go over the example in the book. Have a volunteer model the example.

10-15 mins

2. Have students complete Exercise 4 individually. Remind them to review grammar chart **7.3** on page 193 if necessary. Then have pairs compare answers. Monitor pair work. Give help as needed.

Practice Idea: Speaking

Take a class survey. How many people predicted the same thing? Write the results on the board.

EXERCISE 5

ANSWERS: 1. are going to give; **2.** 're going to buy; **3.** 're going to send; **4.** 'm going to spend; **5.** 're going to send; **6.** 're going to say, 're going to pay

 1. Tell students that this exercise is about Karyn and Steve's wedding plans. Have students read the direction line. Ask: *What do we write on the blanks?* (*be going to* + verb) Go over the example.

10-15 mins

2. Have students complete Exercise 5 individually. Remind them to review grammar chart **7.1** on page 191 if necessary. Then have them check their answers in pairs. Finally, check the answers as a class.

EXERCISE 6

Answers will vary.

 1. Tell students that this exercise is about their predictions for the next 50 years. Have students read the direction line. Ask: *Which future tense do we use with predictions?* (*be going to* or *will*) *Which one are we going to use for this exercise?* (*will*) Go over the example in the book. Have a volunteer model the example.

10-15 mins

2. Have students complete Exercise 6 in pairs. Remind them to review grammar chart **7.1** on page 191 if necessary. Monitor pair work. Give help as needed.

EXERCISE 7 ★

Answers will vary.

 1. Ask: *What are you going to buy your friends for their birthdays?* Have students read the direction line. Ask: *Which future tense do we use when we don't have a plan?* (*will*) Go over the example in the book. Have a volunteer model the example.

10-15 mins

2. Have students complete Exercise 7 individually. Remind them to review grammar chart **7.1** on page 191 if necessary. Have students compare answers in pairs. Monitor pair work. Give help as needed.

Practice Idea: Writing

Have students write a list of friends and family. Say: *Now write what they like to do or what they need. Then write down what you're going to get them for their birthdays.*

EXERCISE 8

ANSWERS: 1. 'll always love; **2.** 'll do; **3.** 'll work; **4.** 'll have, 'll be; **5.** 'll grow; **6.** 'll be; **7.** won't look

---

10-15 mins

1. Explain that this exercise is about a man proposing to a woman. Have students read the direction line. Ask: *Which future tense do we use for promises?* (*will*) Go over the example.

2. Have students complete Exercise 8 individually. Remind them to review grammar chart **7.1** on page 191 if necessary. Check the answers as a class.

EXERCISE 9

ANSWERS: 1. I'll buy you stamps (OR buy OR get them {for you}); **2.** I'll make the reservation. (OR I'll do it.); **3.** I'll lend you money. **4.** I'll answer (OR get) it. **5.** I'll pay. **6.** I'll call (OR contact) them.

10-15 mins

1. Have students read the direction line. Ask: *Which future tense do we use for offers of help?* (*will*) Go over the example.

2. Have students complete Exercise 9 individually. Remind them to review grammar chart **7.1** on page 191 if necessary. Check the answers as a class.

Practice Idea: Speaking

Create two rings of students. Have half of the students stand in an outer ring around the classroom. Have the other half stand in an inner ring, facing the outer ring. Instruct students to make offers of help using the statements in Exercise 9. Call out *turn* every minute or so. Students in the inner ring should move one space clockwise. Students now offer to help their new partners. Have students say the problems from Exercise 9 in random order. Make sure students look at each other when they're speaking.

Is the Honeymoon Over?
READING

1. Have students look at the photo. Ask: *Who are the people?* (a couple) *Where are they?* (at the beach)

2. Have students look at the title of the reading. Ask: *What is the reading about?* Have students use the title and photo to make predictions.

3. Preteach any vocabulary words students may not know, such as *high season* and *marriage counselor*.

Reading Glossary

high season: the time of year when a lot of people go on vacation

marriage counselor: a person couples can talk with to help them solve problems they are having

BEFORE YOU READ

5-10 mins

1. Have students discuss the questions in pairs. Try to pair students of different cultures together.

2. Ask for a few volunteers to share their answers with the class.

 Reading
CD 1 TR 34

10-15 mins

1. Have students read the text silently. Tell them to pay special attention to questions with the future tense verbs *will* and *be going to*. Then play the audio and have students read along.

2. Check students' comprehension. Ask questions such as: *Where does Steve want to go for their honeymoon?* (Hawaii) *What does Karyn think about this idea?* (expensive, it's going to cost a lot) *What is Steve going to do when they get back from their honeymoon?* (start a new job)

> ## Practice Idea: Listening
>
> To practice listening skills, have students first listen to the audio alone. Ask a few comprehension questions such as: *How much do flights to Hawaii cost?* ($700) *How much does the hotel cost?* ($3,000 for a week). Then have students open their books and read along as they listen to the audio.

7.4 Questions with *Be Going To*

10-15 mins

1. Have students cover up grammar chart **7.4** on page 198. Say: *We're going to review statements, questions, and short answers.* Write on the board: *They are going to spend a lot of money.* Ask a volunteer to write a *yes/no* question for this statement using the words *more than $3,000* (e.g., *Are they going to spend more than $3,000?*). Ask another volunteer to give a short answer (e.g., *Yes, they are.*). Ask a volunteer to write a *wh-* question with *how much* and *honeymoon* (e.g., *How much are they going to spend for the honeymoon?*).

2. Have students look at grammar chart **7.4** and ask them to compare their work on the board with the chart. Go over any errors. Review the other sentences.

3. Review negative questions and statements. Explain that the contraction for the negative statement can be written *you aren't* or *you're not*, but the contraction with the *wh-* question can only be written as *aren't you*.

EXERCISE 10

ANSWERS: 1. Are you going to watch TV? What show are you going to watch? **2.** Are you going to listen to music? Where are you going to listen to

music? **3.** Are you going to read the newspaper? What newspaper are you going to read? **4.** Are you going (to go) shopping? Why are you going (to go) shopping tonight? **5.** Are you going to take a shower? When are you going to take a shower? **6.** Are you going to eat dinner? With whom are you going to eat dinner? (OR Who are you going to eat dinner with?) **7.** Are you going to call someone? Who(m) are you going to call? **8.** Are you going to check your mail? When are you going to check your e-mail (OR it)? **9.** Are you going to do your homework? When are you going to do your homework (OR it)?

10-15 mins

1. Tell students that this exercise is about them. Have students read the direction line. Ask: *What kind of question do you ask first?* (a *yes/no* question) Then ask: *What kind of questions do you ask next?* (a *wh*-question) Go over the example with the class. Model the example with a volunteer.

2. Have students complete the exercise in pairs. Remind them to review grammar chart **7.4** on page 198 if necessary.

> ## Practice Idea: Speaking
>
> Create two rings of students. Have half of the students stand in an outer ring around the classroom. Have the other half stand in an inner ring, facing the outer ring. Instruct students to ask and answer the questions from Exercise 10. Call out "*turn*" every minute or so. Students in the inner ring should move one space clockwise. Students now ask and answer with their new partners. Have students ask questions in random order. Make sure students look at each other when they're speaking.

EXERCISE 11

ANSWERS: 1. Are you going to stay in this city? Why are you going to stay? **2.** Are you going to study something new? What are you going to study? **3.** Are you going to look for a job? When are you going to look for a job? **4.** Are you going to get an A in this course? What grade are you going to get? **5.** Are you going to buy a computer? Why are (OR aren't) you going to buy a computer? What kind of computer are you going to buy (OR get)? **6.** Are you going to visit other American cities? Which cities are you going to visit? **7.** Are you going to transfer to another school? Why are you going to transfer to another school? Which school are you going to transfer to?

10-15 mins

1. Tell students that this exercise is about what they're going to do after this course ends. Have students read the direction line. Ask: *What kind of question do you write first?* (a *yes/no* question) Then ask: *What kind of question do you write?* (a *wh-* question) Go over the example with the class. Model the example with a volunteer.

2. Have students complete the exercise in pairs. Remind them to review grammar chart **7.4** on page 198 if necessary.

Practice Idea: Speaking

Have students write five more *yes/no* questions to ask their partners. Whenever possible, they should also follow up with a *wh-* question.

7.5 Questions with *Will*

10-15 mins

1. Have students cover up grammar chart **7.5** on page 199. Write on the board: *The wedding will cost a lot of money.* Ask a volunteer to write a *yes/no* question for this statement using the words *more than $10,000* (e.g., *Will the wedding cost more than $10,000?*). Ask another volunteer to give an affirmative short answer (e.g., *Yes, it will.*). Ask a volunteer to write a *wh-* question using *how much* (e.g., *How much will it cost?*). Write *more than $10,000* on the board. Then write the last question on the board (*Who will pay?*). Elicit the answer from students (the bride and groom, their parents)

2. Have students look at grammar chart **7.5** and ask them to compare their work on the board with the chart. Go over any errors.

3. Review negative questions and statements. Remind students that the contraction for *will not* is *won't*.

EXERCISE 12

CD 1
TR 35

ANSWERS: 1. will be; **2.** will I do; **3.** 'll help; **4.** won't arrive; **5.** will probably open; **6.** will the wedding start; **7.** 'll start; **8.** will the wedding be; **9.** will you wear; **10.** 'll probably wear; **11.** will not have; **12.** 'll have to; **13.** will attend; **14.** will attend; **15.** will they serve; **16.** will be; **17.** will the wedding last; **18.** will probably last; **19.** will probably stay; **20.** Will the bride and groom leave; **21.** 'll be; **22.** 'll probably leave; **23.** will be; **24.** will be

10-15 mins

1. Have students read the direction line. Go over the example in the book. Explain that sometimes they will have to write negative statements or questions. Remind students to use contractions wherever possible. Do #1 with the class.

2. Have students complete the exercise individually. Remind them to review grammar chart **7.5** on page 199 if necessary. Then play the audio and check the answers as a class.

3. Have students practice the conversations in pairs. Monitor pair work. Give help as needed.

EXERCISE 13

CD 1
TR 36

ANSWERS: 1. 'm going to have (OR will have); **2.** 're going to get (OR will get); **3.** 're going to deliver (OR will deliver); **4.** 'll go; **5.** 'll go; **6.** 'm going to use; **7.** 're going to send (OR will send); **8.** 'll help **9.** 'll pay; **10.** 'll make

1. Have students read the direction line. Say: *In this exercise, you're going to choose* be going to *or* will. Review briefly when to use *will* (promises, no previous plans, and offers of help) and when to use *be going to* (previous plans). Remind students that in all other cases, they can use both *will* or *be going to* (predictions and simple facts about the future). Give examples whenever necessary. Go over the example in the book.

2. Have students complete Exercise 13 individually. Remind them to review grammar chart **7.3** on page 193 if necessary. Then play the audio and check the answers as a class.

3. Have students practice the conversation in pairs.

EXERCISE 14

ANSWERS: 1. is she going to have (OR will she have);
2. are you going to wear (OR will you wear); **3.** 're
going to wear (OR will wear); **4.** Is the wedding
going to be (OR Will the wedding be); **5.** 's going to
be (OR will be); **6.** are they going to wait; **7.** are they
going to live (OR will they live); **8.** 're going to look
(OR will look); **9.** are they going to invite (OR will they
invite); **10.** 's going to be (OR will be); **11.** 're going to
invite; **12.** is going to be (OR will be); **13.** is going to
pay (OR will pay); **14.** are going to pay (OR will pay);
15. 're going to split (OR will split); **16.** are going to
come; **17.** are they going to stay (OR will they stay);
18. will be (OR is going to be); **19.** will have to (OR
are going to have to); **20.** won't come (OR aren't
going to come); **21.** will be (OR going to be)

10-15
mins

1. Have students read the direction line. Say:
   In this exercise, you're going to choose will *or*
   be going to. Review briefly when to use *will*
   (promises, no previous plans, and offers of
   help) and when to use *be going to* (previous
   plans). Remind students that in all other
   cases, they can use both *will* or *be going
   to* (predictions and simple facts about the
   future). Give examples whenever necessary.
   Go over the example in the book.

2. Have students complete Exercise 14
   individually. Remind them to review grammar
   chart **7.3** on page 193 if necessary. Then play
   the audio and check the answers as a class.

Practice Idea: Listening

To provide practice with listening skills, have students
close their books and listen to the audio. Repeat the
audio as needed. Ask comprehension questions, such
as: *Who is getting married next year?* (person A's sister)
How many bridesmaids is her sister going to have? (three)
What are the bridesmaids going to wear? (blue dresses)
Then have students open their books and complete
Exercise 14.

Practice Idea: Speaking

Have students talk about the wedding that is being
discussed in the conversation. Ask questions such as:
*Do you think this is a typical wedding? Why? Have you
been to a wedding like this in the U.S.? What was it like?
Was is very different from weddings in your country? If so,
why? Do you think this wedding is big? Expensive?* Have
students discuss the wedding in groups. Then have
groups report their impressions to the class.

7.6 Future Tense + Time/*If* Clause

10-15
mins

1. Have students go back to the reading on page
   190. Read through the second paragraph and
   draw students' attention to the time clauses
   (e.g., *Before their wedding, they will register for
   gifts.*). Point out that these sentences are made
   up of two clauses: the time clause and the
   main clause. Have students underline the time
   clause and double-underline the main clause.
   Ask: *What tense is used in the time clause?*
   (simple present) *What tense is used in the main
   clause?* (future)

2. Have students look at grammar chart **7.6** on
   page 203. Review all of the examples and
   explanations. Ask students if they know the
   meaning of *if.* Tell students that *if* creates a
   condition. Action *X* will happen if action *Y*
   happens.

3. Direct students to the Punctuation Note. Point
   out that the main clause can come before
   or after the time/*if* clause. Explain that when
   the time/*if* clause goes first, they must use a
   comma. Go over the examples.

4. Direct students to the Usage Note. Go over
   the meaning of the proverb. If possible,
   demonstrate the use of the proverb by
   explaining a difficult decision you will need to
   make in the future.

EXERCISE 15

ANSWERS: 1. come, will (OR are going to) stay; **2.** will (OR are going to) make, return; **3.** will (OR are going to) move, return; **4.** get, will (OR are going to) open; **5.** will (OR are going to) save, have; **6.** will (OR are going to) go, is

10-15 mins

1. Have students read the direction line. Go over the example in the book.

2. Have students complete the exercise individually. Remind them to review grammar chart **7.3** on page 193 if necessary. Have students compare their answers with a partner. Then go over the answers with the class.

EXERCISE 16

Answers will vary.

10-15 mins

1. Tell students that this exercise is about their future plans. Go over the examples in the book. Tell students that they can use *be going to* if they have a plan, or *will* if they did not have a plan and are deciding what to do now. Model the exercise with your own information.

2. Have students complete Exercise 16 individually. Remind them to review grammar chart **7.6** on page 203 if necessary. Then have students compare answers with a partner. Monitor pair work. Give help as needed.

Practice Idea: Speaking

Take a quick class survey. What are everyone's plans?

EXERCISE 17

Answers will vary.

10-15 mins

1. Remind students that *if* introduces a condition. Go over the examples in the book. Model the exercise with your own information.

2. Have students complete Exercise 17 individually. Remind them to review grammar chart **7.6** on page 203 if necessary. Then have students compare answers with a partner. Monitor pair work. Give help as needed.

CD 1
TR 38
EXERCISE 18

ANSWERS: 1. will invite (OR are going to invite); **2.** will the wedding be (OR is the wedding going to be); **3.** will have; **4.** Will you buy (OR Are you going to buy); **5.** will use (OR am going to use); **6.** will wear (OR am going to wear); **7.** will you live (OR are you going to live); **8.** will live (OR are going to live); **9.** finishes; **10.** gets; **11.** will get (OR are going to get); **12.** will not be (OR is not going to be); **13.** will not have (OR are not going to have); **14.** Will your parents come (OR Are your parents going to come); **15.** will take (OR are going to take); **16.** When will you get (OR When are you going to get); **17.** will send; **18.** will be

10-15 mins

1. Tell students that this exercise is a conversation between a young Korean woman and her friend. The Korean woman is planning to get married. Point out the photo of a Korean bride in a traditional wedding dress on page 206. Have students read the direction line. Say: *In this exercise, you're going to choose to use* be going to *or* will. Review briefly when to use *will* (promises, no previous plans, offers of help) and when to use *be going to* (previous plans). Give examples whenever necessary. Go over the example in the book.

2. Have students complete Exercise 18 individually. Remind them to review grammar charts **7.3** on page 193, **7.4** on page 198, **7.5** on page 199, and **7.6** on page 203 if necessary. Then play the audio and check answers as a class.

3. Have students practice the conversation in pairs. Monitor pair work. Give help as needed.

Practice Idea: Listening

To provide practice with listening skills, have students close their books and listen to the audio. Repeat the audio as needed. Ask comprehension questions, such as: *Is the Korean woman going to have a big wedding or a small wedding?* (a small wedding) *How many people is she going to invite?* (about 50) *Where will the wedding be?* (at St. Peter's Church) Then have students open their books and complete Exercise 18.

Practice Idea: Speaking

Have students discuss wedding attire in small groups. Ask students to look at the photo on page 206. Say: *This is a traditional Korean wedding dress. The photo on page 189 shows a couple in traditional Western wedding attire. What is traditional for brides and grooms to wear in your countries?* Try to put students from different countries together.

Jason and Katie—Starting a Married Life READING

1. Have students look at the photo. Ask: *Who are the people?* (a young couple, newlyweds) *Do you think they were married a long time ago or recently?* (recently) *Do they look happy?* (yes)

2. Have students look at the title of the reading. Ask: *What is the reading about?* Have students use the title and the photo to make predictions.

3. Preteach any vocabulary words students may not know such as *newlyweds, attend, loan,* and *suburb.*

Reading Glossary

attend: to be present at
loan: a sum of money borrowed at a rate of interest
newlyweds: people who have just been married
suburb: the general term for an area outside a big city

BEFORE YOU READ

5-10 mins

1. Have students discuss the questions in pairs. Try to pair students of different cultures.

2. Ask for a few volunteers to share their answers with the class.

Reading

CD 1 TR 39

10-15 mins

1. Have students read the reading silently. Tell them to pay special attention to verb tenses: simple present, present continuous, and future. Then play the audio and have students read along.

2. Check students' comprehension. Ask questions such as: *Does Katie work?* (Yes. She's a nurse.) *What does Jason do?* (He's a law student.) *When is he going to graduate?* (next June)

When are they thinking about having children? (in the future; after they are financially stable)

Practice Idea: Listening

To practice listening skills, have students first listen to the audio alone. Ask a few comprehension questions such as: *Does Katie work?* (Yes. She's a nurse.) *What does Jason do?* (He's a law student.) *When is he going to graduate?* (next June) Then have students open their books and read along as they listen to the audio.

7.7 Comparison of Tenses

10-15 mins

1. Have students go back to the reading on page 207. Ask students to find one example for each tense. Say: *Underline the simple present tense, double-underline the present continuous, and circle the future tense.* Ask volunteers to write examples of each tense on the board.

2. Have students look at grammar chart **7.7** on pages 208–209. Ask students to compare their work on the board with the chart. Review all of the examples and explanations of uses.

3. Review the forms of the verb tenses. Go over affirmative and negative statements, *yes/no* questions, short answers, and *wh-* questions (including negative questions and questions about the subject) for each tense. Have students provide other examples for each form.

Presentation Idea

To review the uses of the verb tenses, have students cover up grammar chart **7.7**. Write each example sentence from the chart on a slip of paper, and pass them out to students. On the board, write the headings *simple present tense, present continuous tense, future with* will, and *future with* be going to. Have students read their sentences, decide the tense of the sentence, and write the sentence under the proper heading. Then write the list of explanations (e.g., *with facts, with customs,* etc.) from chart **7.7** next to the sentences on the board. Have students match the example sentences with the explanations.

EXERCISE 19

ANSWERS: 1. 'll (OR is going to) have, graduates; **2.** often studies; **3.** rarely go; **4.** 're saving; **5.** 're thinking; **6.** think

10-15 mins

1. Tell students that this exercise is based on the reading on page 207. Tell them that it is a review of all the tenses they've learned. Have students read the direction line. Go over the example.

2. Have students complete the rest of Exercise 19 individually. Remind them to review grammar chart **7.7** on pages 208–209 if necessary. Then have students practice saying the sentences in pairs. Finally, check the answers as a class.

EXERCISE 20

ANSWERS: 1. don't have; **2.** don't want; **3.** isn't working; **4.** don't depend; **5.** won't graduate

10-15 mins

1. Tell students that this exercise is based on the reading on page 207. Have students read the direction line. Ask: *What do we replace the underlined words with?* (the negative) Go over the example in the book.

2. Have students complete the rest of Exercise 20 individually. Remind them to review grammar chart **7.7** on pages 208–209 if necessary. Check the answers as a class.

EXERCISE 21

ANSWERS: 1. Is Katie a student? No, she isn't. **2.** Is Katie attending college now? No, she's not. **3.** Will Jason have a good job? Yes, he will. **4.** Are they thinking about having children? Yes, they are. **5.** Are they going to have five children? No, they're not.

10-15 mins

1. Tell students that this exercise is based on the reading on page 207. Have students read the direction line. Ask: *What do we write in the blanks?* (a question and a short answer) Go over the example in the book.

2. Have students complete the exercise individually. Remind them to review grammar chart **7.7** on pages 208–209 if necessary. Check the answers as a class.

EXERCISE 22

ANSWERS: 1. Why are they saving their money? **2.** Why don't they want to depend on their parents? **3.** When will Jason (OR he) make good money? **4.** Why does Jason (OR he) want to be a lawyer? **5.** Why isn't Katie (OR she) going to work when her children are small? **6.** When will Jason (OR he) pay back his student loans? **7.** Why don't they go out very much? **8.** What college is Jason (OR he) attending? **9.** When is he going to graduate? **10.** Who is earning money now? **11.** Who wants to help them? **12.** How are they learning about responsibilities?

10-15 mins

1. Have students read the direction line. Ask students what kind of questions they will be writing (*wh-* or information questions). Ask: *Are you going to write answers?* (no) Go over the example in the book.

2. Have students complete Exercise 22 individually. Remind them to review grammar chart **7.7** on pages 208–209 if necessary. Check answers as a class.

Practice Idea: Speaking

Have students ask and answer the questions they wrote for Exercise 22 in pairs. Tell students that the questions are based on the reading on page 207.

Summary of Lesson 7

20-30 mins

1. **Future patterns with *will*** Have students practice forms of *will* in pairs. Say: *One student says, "Affirmative." The other student gives an example, such as, "Sally will wear a white wedding dress."* Instruct students to continue with the other forms of *will*. Then have pairs switch roles and repeat. If necessary, have students review:

   7.1 Future with *Will* (p. 191)
   7.5 Questions with *Will* (p. 199)

2. **Future patterns with *be going to*** Have students practice forms of *be going to* in pairs using the same suggestion above for *will*. If necessary, have students review:

   7.2 Future with *Be Going To* (p. 192)
   7.4 Questions with *Be Going To* (p. 198)

3. **Uses of *be going to* and *will*** Have students close their books. Then read an example from the chart. Have students identify the use. For example, say: *I will help you tomorrow.* Students say: *promise.* On the board, write: *promise.* If necessary, have students review:

   7.3 Choosing *Will* or *Be Going To* (p. 193)

4. **Review and compare the four tenses on pages 208–209** Say examples of the four tenses. Have students identify the tense and use. Then have students practice the tenses and their uses in pairs. (See suggestion for uses of *be going to* and *will* on page 212.) Have students write their sentences before saying them to their partner if needed. If necessary, have students review:

   7.7 Comparison of Tenses (pp. 208–209)

Editing Advice

10-15 mins

Have students close their books. Write the first few sentences without editing marks or corrections on the board. For example:

   1. *I will be go.*
   2. *He will angry.*

Ask students to correct each sentence and provide a rule or explanation for each correction. Then have them turn to page 213. Say: *Now compare your work with the Editing Advice in the book.*

Editing Quiz

ANSWERS: **1.** 'm going to make; **2.** will have; **3.** I get; **4.** 'm going to send; **5.** will you; **6.** 'll send; **7.** I have; **8.** C; **9.** will be nice; **10.** 'll write

10-15 mins

1. Tell students they are going to put the editing advice into practice. Have students read the direction line. Ask: *Do all the shaded words and phrases have mistakes?* (no) Go over the examples with the class. Then do #1 together.

2. Have students complete the quiz individually. Then have them compare answers with a partner before checking answers as a class.

3. For the items students had difficulties with, have them go back and find the relevant grammar chart and review it. Monitor and give help as necessary.

Lesson 7 Test/Review

Use the Assessment CD-ROM with Exam*View*®, Online Workbook, and Web site for additional practice, review, and assessment materials.

PART 1

ANSWERS: **1.** are going to; **2.** is going to (OR will); **3.** 'll; **4.** will (OR are going to); **5.** 'll; **6.** will (OR is going to); **7.** will (OR are going to); **8.** 'll; **9.** 'll (OR is going to)

40-60 mins

1. Part 1 may also be used as an in-class test to assess student performance, in addition to the Assessment CD-ROM with Exam*View*®. Have students read the direction line. Remind students that in some cases, both *will* and *be going to* can be used. Go over the examples with the class.

2. Have students complete Part 1 individually. Collect for assessment.

3. If necessary, have students review:

   7.3 Choosing *Will* or *Be Going To* (p. 193)

PART 2

ANSWERS: **1.** 's not (OR isn't) going to invite;
2. won't wear; **3.** 'm not going to buy; **4.** won't help;
5. 're not (OR aren't) going to meet

1. Part 2 may also be used as an in-class test to assess student performance, in addition to the Assessment CD-ROM with Exam*View*®. Have students read the direction line. Ask: *What will you replace the underlined words with?* (the negative) Go over the example with the class.

2. Have students complete Part 2 individually. Collect for assessment.

3. If necessary, have students review:

   7.1 Future with *Will* (p. 191)
   7.2 Future with *Be Going To* (p. 192)

PART 3

ANSWERS: **1.** Will they send money? No, they won't. **2.** Are you going to invite your relatives? Yes, I am. **3.** Are they going to open the gifts? Yes, they are. **4.** Will they need things for their bathroom? Yes, they will. **5.** Will there be music at the party? Yes, there will.

1. Part 3 may also be used as an in-class test to assess student performance, in addition to the Assessment CD-ROM with Exam*View*®. Have students read the direction line. Point out that students need to write a *yes/no* question as well as a short answer. Go over the example with the class.

2. Have students complete Part 3 individually. Collect for assessment.

3. If necessary, have students review:

   7.4 Questions with *Be Going To* (p. 198)
   7.5 Questions with *Will* (p. 199)

PART 4

ANSWERS: **1.** How will they use the money? **2.** What kind of gift are you going to send? **3.** When will they thank us? **4.** Where are they going to get married? **5.** Why aren't they going to open the gifts at the wedding? **6.** How many people will there be at the wedding? **7.** Who will give money?

1. Part 4 may also be used as an in-class test to assess student performance, in addition to the

Assessment CD-ROM with Exam*View*®. Have students read the direction line. Ask: *What kind of questions will you be writing?* (*wh-* questions) Remind students that an answer is not necessary. Go over the example with the class.

2. Have students complete Part 4 individually. Collect for assessment.

3. If necessary, have students review:

   7.4 Questions with *Be Going To* (p. 198)
   7.5 Questions with *Will* (p. 199)

Test on Comparison of Tenses

PART 1

ANSWERS: **1.** 's working; **2.** 's sleeping; **3.** have;
4. 'm; **5.** go; **6.** is; **7.** walk; **8.** drive; **9.** watches; **10.** 'm studying; **11.** 'm going to take; **12.** think; **13.** will help (OR is going to help; **14.** is; **15.** 're going (to go) (OR will go); **16.** 're going to visit (OR will visit); **17.** lives; **18.** 're going to spend (OR will spend); **19.** get; **20.** 'll send

60-80 mins

1. Part 1 may be used as an in-class test to assess student performance, in addition to the Assessment CD-ROM with Exam*View*®. Have students read the direction line. Point out that this is an email from Barbara to Judy. Go over the example with the class.

2. Have students complete Part 1 individually. Collect for assessment.

3. If necessary, have students review:

   7.7 Comparison of Tenses (pp. 208–209)

PART 2

ANSWERS: **1.** isn't writing; **2.** doesn't take; **3.** aren't going to visit; **4.** doesn't go; **5.** don't live; **6.** won't go

1. Part 2 may be used as an in-class test to assess student performance, in addition to the Assessment CD-ROM with Exam*View*®. Have students read the direction line. Ask: *What will you replace the underlined words with?* (the negative) Go over the example with the class.

2. Have students complete Part 2 individually. Collect for assessment.

3. If necessary, have students review:

   7.7 Comparison of Tenses (pp. 208–209)

PART 3

ANSWERS: 1. Is her husband sleeping? No, he isn't.
2. Does she ever walk to school? Yes, she does. **3.** Is
she going to take a math class? No, she isn't. **4.** Will
she go to Montreal? Yes, she will. **5.** Is she going to
send Judy a letter? No, she isn't. **6.** Is she writing an
e-mail now? Yes, she is. **7.** Does he sister-in-law (OR
she) live in Toronto? No, she doesn't.

1. Part 3 may be used as an in-class test to
   assess student performance, in addition to
   the Assessment CD-ROM with Exam*View*®.
   Tell students that this exercise is based on
   the e-mail in Part 1 on page 217. If necessary,
   review the e-mail before students begin Part 3.

2. Have students read the direction line. Instruct
   students to write a *yes/no* question, as well as a
   short answer that is based on the information
   in the email. Go over the example with the class.

3. Have students complete Part 3 individually.
   Collect for assessment.

4. If necessary, have students review:

   7.7 Comparison of Tenses (pp. 208–209)

PART 4

ANSWERS: 1. A. What is her husband doing? B. He's
working on his car. **2.** A. What courses is she taking
this semester? B. She's taking English and Math. **3.** A.
Who watches her baby? B. Her mother watches her
baby. **4.** A. What course is she going to take next
semester? B. She's going to take a computer course
next semester. **5.** A. Where will they go on vacation
for Christmas? B. They'll go to Canada for Christmas.
6. A. Where does her husband's sister (OR she)
live? B. She lives in Montreal. **7.** A. Why doesn't she
usually drive to school? B. She usually walks to
school.

Part 4 may be used as an in-class test to assess
student performance, in addition to the
Assessment CD-ROM with Exam*View*®. Tell students
that this exercise is based on the email in Part 1
on page 217. If necessary, review the email before
students begin Part 4.

Have students read the direction line. Instruct
students to write a *wh-* question, as well as an
answer that is based on the information in the
letter. Go over the example with the class.

Have students complete Part 4 individually. Collect
for assessment.

If necessary, have students review:

   7.7 Comparison of Tenses (pp. 208–209)

Expansion

These expansion activities provide opportunities for
students to interact with one another and further develop
their speaking and writing skills. Encourage students to
use grammar from this lesson whenever possible.

CLASSROOM ACTIVITIES

10-15
mins
per
activity

1. Tell students that this activity is about future
   plans. Ask: *Do we use* will *or* be going to *when
   we talk about future plans?* (*be going to*) First
   have students check the activities they're
   going to do. Then put students in pairs to ask
   and answer questions.

2. Review the uses of the future tense for each
   item (a. prediction; b. promise; c. plan, promise;
   d. plan, promise; e. promise). Have students work
   in pairs to create dialogs. Then have volunteers
   role-play the dialogs in front of the class.

Practice Idea: Speaking and Writing

Have students role-play an interview between
a news reporter and a famous person. The news
reporter asks questions and takes notes. Then the
reporter writes a news article on the interview.
Have students switch roles and repeat.

3. After students complete their charts, have
   students give their partners advice about their
   concerns. Go over the example with the class.
   Do further examples as necessary. Say: *Listen
   to your friend's concerns about the future. Tell
   your friend what he/she should do. For example,
   if your friend is worried about money, help
   him/her think of ways to save money.*

Practice Idea: Writing

Have students write a future plan based on the advice they get from their partners. Remind them to use *be going to.*

Practice Idea: Writing

Have students exchange first drafts with a partner. Ask students to help their partners edit their drafts. Refer students to the Editing Advice on page 213.

4. After students have completed the activity, survey the class to find out the most popular choices for each situation. Then share with students the type of gifts that Americans would typically get.

TALK ABOUT IT

15-20 mins

1. Model this activity by telling the class about gift-giving customs in the U.S. Use the occasions in Classroom Activity 4 for ideas. Have students discuss the questions in groups and then report back to the class. Put students from different countries together if possible.

2. Have students debate whether a man should support a woman or whether a woman should support a man. Divide the class into two teams. Tell each team to list five reasons supporting their views. Have each team present their arguments. Then give each team an opportunity to respond to the other team's arguments. At the end of the debate, survey the class to see which opinion is more popular.

WRITE ABOUT IT

20-30 mins

Have students read the direction line. Go over the example with them. Brainstorm ideas about possible plans and concerns for the future and write them on the board. Briefly model the activity with the class by beginning a paragraph about your plans and concerns on the board using some of the ideas. Follow the model in the example. Then have students write their own paragraphs. Collect for assessment and/or have students present their paragraphs to a group.

OUTSIDE ACTIVITY

Tell students to interview an American about his or her concerns for the future. Have them use the chart from Classroom Activity 3 on page 221. Students can choose to report their interview to the class or to hand in a written report.

INTERNET ACTIVITY

Tell students to find a wedding or bridal registry on the Internet and answer these questions: What kinds of gifts can a couple register for? What are the prices?

Lesson 8

Lesson Overview

GRAMMAR

Ask: *What did we study in Lesson 7?* (the future tenses: *will* and *be going to*) *What tense are we going to study in this lesson?* (the simple past tense) *Can anyone make a sentence in the simple past tense?* (They dreamed about flying. They designed an airplane.) Have students give examples. Write them on the board.

CONTEXT

1. Ask: *What are we going to learn about in this lesson?* (flying) Activate students' prior knowledge. Ask: *Is anyone here familiar with the history of flying? Who invented the airplane?* (Orville and Wilbur Wright invented the airplane in 1903.)

2. Have students share their knowledge and personal experiences. Ask: *What kinds of airplanes have you flown in? Has anyone here flown in a very small plane? Is anyone a pilot? How old were you when you first flew on a plane?*

Presentation Idea

The topic for this lesson can be enhanced with the following ideas:

1. Books with pictures of the Wright brothers, early airplanes, and famous aviators
2. Books with pictures of early space travel

The Wright Brothers—Men with a Vision READING

1. Have students look at the photo of the Wright brothers. Ask: *Why are the Wright brothers famous?* (They invented the airplane.)

2. Have students look at the title of the reading. Ask: *What is the reading about? How do you know?* Have students use the title and the photos to make predictions about the reading.

3. Preteach any vocabulary words students may not know, such as *aspect, construct, design, crash, fail, fix, invent, investigate,* and *gather.*

Reading Glossary

aspect: point of view, consideration
construct: to build; to put together piece by piece
crash: a violent hit against something, usually with damage; an accident
design: style, form
fail: to not succeed
fix: to repair something
gather: to meet
invent: to create something new
investigate: to look at something carefully; examine

BEFORE YOU READ

5–10 mins

1. Have students discuss the questions in pairs.
2. Ask for a few volunteers to share their answers with the class.

Reading ≡★

CD 2
TR 01

10–15 mins

Have students read the text silently. Tell them to pay special attention to the simple-past-tense verbs. Then play the audio and have students read along silently.

Check students' comprehension. Ask questions such as: *When did the Wright brothers first start thinking about flying?* (as young boys when they received a flying toy from their father) *When did they construct their first flying machine?* (in 1899) *Who was the pilot for their first flight?* (Orville Wright) *Who offered them a contract to build planes?* (President Theodore Roosevelt)

Practice Idea: Listening

To practice listening skills, have students first listen to the audio alone. Ask a few comprehension questions such as: *What business did the Wright brothers have before they got into airplanes?* (bicycle business) *How long was the first flight?* (12 seconds) *Where was the first flight?* (Kitty Hawk, North Carolina) Then have students open their books and read along as they listen to the audio.

Have students read the information. Then tell them that the Wright Brothers National Memorial in North Carolina was designated in 1953 in honor of the Wright Brothers' aviation achievements.

8.1 The Simple Past Tense of Regular Verbs

5-10 mins

1. Have students go back to the reading on page 224. Say: *Find verbs in the past that end in -ed* (*dreamed, changed, received, started,* etc.). Write the verbs on the board. Then ask students to tell you the base form of the verbs. Write them next to the past tense (*dream, change, receive, start,* etc.).

2. Have students look at grammar chart **8.1** on page 225. Explain that to form the simple past tense of regular verbs, you add *-ed*. Review the examples in the chart.

3. Explain that verbs that come after *to* are in the base form, not the past, so their endings do not change. Explain the use of *ago*, which means *before now.*

EXERCISE 1

ANSWERS: 1. worked; **2.** learned; **3.** loved; **4.** opened, repaired; **5.** started; **6.** weighed; **7.** succeeded; **8.** died; **9.** lived

5-10 mins

1. Tell students that this exercise is about the reading on page 224. Have students read the direction line. Ask: *What are you going to underline?* (the past tense verbs) Go over the example in the book.

2. Have students complete the rest of Exercise 1 individually. Remind students to review grammar chart **8.1** on page 225 if necessary. Check the answers as a class.

8.2 Spelling of the Past Tense of Regular Verbs

10-15 mins

1. Copy the lists of verbs (base form and past form) from grammar chart **8.2** on the board. Make sure you separate the eight sets of verbs. For example:

start	*started*
rain	*rained*
die	*died*
live	*lived*

2. Have students cover up grammar chart **8.2** on page 226. Say: *There are eight rules for spelling the past tense of regular verbs. Can you list them?* If students have difficulty, give them hints. For example, say: *Look at the endings of these two verbs*: die *and* live. *What do you add?* (*d*) *So what's the rule?* (When the base form ends in *e*, add *d*.)

3. Have students look at grammar chart **8.2**. Say: *Compare our rules with the rules in the book.* Review the rules in the grammar chart.

Presentation Idea: Writing

Have students cover up the rules in grammar chart **8.2**. Write the rules in random order on the board. Ask students to match the rules on the board with the verbs in the chart.

EXERCISE 2

ANSWERS: 1. played; **2.** studied; **3.** decided; **4.** wanted; **5.** liked; **6.** showed; **7.** looked; **8.** stopped; **9.** happened; **10.** carried; **11.** enjoyed; **12.** dragged; **13.** dropped; **14.** started; **15.** followed; **16.** preferred; **17.** liked; **18.** mixed; **19.** admitted; **20.** propelled

5-10 mins

1. Have students read the direction line. Ask: *What do we write in the blanks?* (the past tense of the regular verbs) Go over the examples in the book. Ask students to tell you what the rules are for the spelling of each verb in the examples (*learned:* add *-ed* to most regular verbs; *loved:* ends in *e*, add *-d*; *clapped:* one syllable, ends in consonant-vowel-consonant, double the final consonant, add *-ed*; *listened:* two-syllable verb, not stressed, don't double final consonant). Point out that the accent marks show which syllable is stressed.

2. Have students complete Exercise 2 individually. Remind students to review grammar chart **8.2** on page 226 if necessary. Check answers as a class.

8.3 Pronunciation of -ed Past Forms

 5-10 mins

Have students cover up grammar chart **8.3** on page 227. Say: *There are three ways to pronounce the -ed ending.* Write the following on the board, and pronounce each sound:

1. /t/
2. /d/
3. /əd/

Give an example of each from the chart. Remind students that this is about pronunciation, not spelling or writing. Then say: *Listen to each word as I say it. Tell me which sound I'm making.* Say words from the grammar chart lists on page 227 in random order. Pronounce each word carefully. Have students guess where the word belongs and write it under the sound they tell you.

Have students look at grammar chart **8.3**. Say: *Compare our lists with the lists in the book.* Go over any errors. Have volunteers pronounce words. If necessary, practice the pronunciation of the past forms chorally as a class.

Presentation Idea

Have students cover up grammar chart **8.3**. Read the past forms of the verbs in the first list in the chart (*jumped, cooked, coughed, kissed, washed*, and *watched*). Ask students to repeat what they think the -ed sound is for that group of words. Then read the verbs from the second list and ask the students to repeat what they think the -ed sound is for that group of words, and so on. After the last group of verbs, ask students to look at the chart. Go over the rules for pronunciation. If necessary, practice the pronunciation of the past forms chorally as a class.

EXERCISE 3

 5-10 mins

Have students read the direction line. Turn to Exercise 2 on page 226. Ask: *What are we going to pronounce?* (the base form and the past form) Have a volunteer pronounce #1. Have students finish the exercise in pairs. Circulate to help with pronunciation.

EXERCISE 4

ANSWERS: 1. played; **2.** dreamed; **3.** studied; **4.** started; **5.** used; **6.** tried; **7.** crashed; **8.** fixed; **9.** stayed; **10.** offered; **11.** decided; **12.** died; **13.** lived; **14.** changed

 5-10 mins

1. Have students read the direction line. Go over the example in the book. Then do #1 with the class. Ask a volunteer to give an answer.

2. Have students complete Exercise 4 individually. Then have students practice saying the sentences in pairs. Circulate to listen to students practice their pronunciation. Remind them to review grammar chart **8.3** on page 227 if necessary. Finally, check the answers as a class.

Charles Lindbergh and Amelia Earhart READING

1. Have students look at the title of the reading and the photos. Ask: *What is the reading about?* Have students use the title and the photos to make predictions about the reading.

2. Preteach any vocabulary words students may not know, such as: *brave, adventurous, historic*, and *disappear*.

Reading Glossary

adventurous: daring; bold
brave: unafraid of danger
disappear: to go out of sight
historic: important in history; famous

BEFORE YOU READ

 5-10 mins

1. Have students discuss the questions in pairs.
2. Ask for a few volunteers to share their answers with the class.

Reading

CD 2 TR 02
 5-10 mins

1. Have students read the text silently. Tell them to pay special attention to the past tense forms of *be*. Then play the audio and have students read along silently.

2. Check students' comprehension. Ask questions such as: *What kind of people flew in airplanes at*

the beginning of the twentieth century? (brave and adventurous people) *Whom did Charles Lindbergh work for?* (the U.S. Mail Service) *Why did he become famous?* (He was the first person to fly alone across the Atlantic Ocean.) *How old was Earhart when she flew across the Atlantic alone?* (34 years old) *Where did she disappear?* (somewhere over the Pacific Ocean)

Presentation Idea

The topic for this reading can be enhanced with the following ideas:

1. Books with photos of Lindbergh and Earhart
2. A world map

Practice Idea: Listening

To practice listening skills, have students first listen to the audio alone. Ask a few comprehension questions such as: *How long was Charles Lindbergh's flight from New York to Paris?* (33 hours) *How did Amelia Earhart become famous?* (She was the first woman to fly across the Atlantic Ocean alone.) Then have students open their books and read along as they listen to the audio.

8.4 Past Tense of *Be*

10-15 mins

1. Have students go back to the reading on page 228. Say: *Find all of the past forms of* be (*was, were*). Write students' responses on the board.
2. Have students look at grammar chart **8.4** on page 229. Explain that, as they just discovered, there are only two past forms of *be*. Go through the example sentences.
3. Explain that with *there*, we use *was* for singular and *were* for plural.
4. Explain that the negative is formed by putting *not* after *was* or *were*.
5. Write the contractions for *was not* (*wasn't*) and *were not* (*weren't*) on the board.

EXERCISE 5

ANSWERS: 1. were; **2.** was; **3.** were; **4.** were; **5.** was; **6.** was; **7.** Were; **8.** was; **9.** were; **10.** was; **11.** were

5-10 mins

1. Have students read the direction line. Ask: *When do we use* was? (with *I*, *he*, *she*, *it*, singular subject) *When do we use* were? (with *we*, *you*, *they*, plural subject) Go over the example in the book.
2. Have students complete Exercise 5 individually. Remind them to review grammar chart **8.4** on page 229 if necessary. Check the answers as a class.

Practice Idea: Writing

Have students write sentences about a famous historical person from their country. Instruct students to use the past form of *be*. If possible, have students from the same country work together in pairs or groups. Ask volunteers to share their information with the class.

8.5 Uses of *Be*

10-15 mins

1. Have students cover up grammar chart **8.5** on page 230. Make a matching exercise on the board. Write the example sentences from grammar chart **8.5** in random order on the board. Then write the explanations in random order on the board. Ask students to match the example sentences to the appropriate explanations.
2. Have students look at grammar chart **8.5**. Say: *Now check your work against the grammar chart*. Go over any errors.
3. Go over each example and each explanation.

EXERCISE 6

ANSWERS: 1. The airplane wasn't common transportation in the early 1900s. **2.** Lindbergh wasn't from Kansas. **3.** Earhart's last flight wasn't successful. **4.** The Wright brothers' first plane wasn't in the air for many hours. **5.** Earhart wasn't an inventor. **6.** There weren't a lot of planes 100 years ago. **7.** The Wright brothers weren't born in the twentieth century. **8.** The 2003 flight at Kitty Hawk wasn't successful.

1. Have students read the direction line. Ask: *What kind of statement are we going to write?* (a negative statement) Quickly review the contractions for *was not* and *were not* on the board. Go over the example in the book.

2. Have students complete Exercise 6 individually. Remind them to review grammar chart **8.5** on page 230 if necessary. Check the answers as a class.

8.6 Questions with *Was/Were* ≡★

1. Have students cover up grammar chart **8.6** on page 231. Write the following statements on the board:

The first flight was long.

The first flight was successful.

The Wright brothers were inventors.

There were a lot of people at the 100-year celebration.

There was a lot of rain that day.

Say: *Write a* yes/no *question and a short answer for each statement.*

2. Write the following statements on the board:

The first flight was 12 seconds.

The first flight was in Kitty Hawk, North Carolina.

Say: *Write a* wh- *question for each statement.*

3. Write the following statements on the board:

She wasn't successful because her plane disappeared somewhere over the Pacific Ocean.

I wasn't there because I missed the plane.

Say: *Write a negative* wh- *question for each statement.*

4. Write the following statements on the board:
No one was with Earhart when she disappeared.

There was one person in the airplane.

Say: *Write a subject question for each statement.*

5. Have students look at grammar chart **8.6** on page 231. Say: *Check your work against the chart in the book.* Go over the examples and explanations.

6. Review the comparison of statements and questions. Have students cover the chart with a piece of paper. Ask students to look only at the first statement (*Amelia was born before 1903.*). Then say: *Ask a* yes/no *question about*

the country she was born in (Was she born in the U.S.?). Then have students reveal the answer by moving their papers down one line. Use this method for the whole chart.

EXERCISE 7

ANSWERS: 1. Was the telephone an important invention? Yes, it was. **2.** Were the Wright brothers inventors? Yes, they were. **3.** Was Lindbergh American? Yes, he was. **4.** Was travel by plane common 100 years ago? No, it wasn't. **5.** Were there airplanes 100 years ago? Yes, there were. **6.** Were you in class yesterday? (Answers will vary.) **7.** Were you interested in the story about the aviators? (Answers will vary.) **8.** Were you born in the U.S.? (Answers will vary.)

1. Have students read the direction line. Ask: *What do we write?* (a yes/no question and a short answer) Go over the example in the book.

2. Have students complete the exercise individually. Remind them to review grammar chart **8.6** on page 231 if necessary. Check the answers as a class.

EXERCISE 8

Answers will vary.

1. Tell students that they will be interviewing their partners about leaving his or her country and coming to the U.S. Have students read the direction line. Say: *Write down your partner's information.* Model #1 with a student.

2. Have students complete the exercise in pairs. Monitor pair work. Give help as needed. Remind them to review grammar chart **8.6** on page 231 if necessary.

> ### Practice Idea: Speaking
>
> Do a survey with the class. Have students report the results of their interviews in small groups. Then have the groups report their results to the class (e.g., *Three students were born in Ecuador, one was born in Egypt, and one was born in Japan.*). Record the results on the board.

ANSWERS: 1. A: Why was Lindbergh (OR he) a hero? B: He was the first person to fly across the Atlantic Ocean. **2.** A: What nationality was Earhart? B: She was American. **3.** A: How old was Lindbergh when he crossed the ocean? B: He was 25 years old. **4.** A: Who were the Wright brothers? B: They were (famous) inventors. **5.** A: When was Earhart born? B: She was born in 1897. **6.** A: Why were the Wright brothers (OR they) famous? B: They invented the first airplane. **7.** A: Why wasn't the flight in 2003 at Kitty Hawk (OR it) successful? B: It rained hard and the plane failed to get off the ground.

10-15 mins

1. Have students read the direction line. Ask: *What kind of questions will we write?* (wh- or information questions) Say: *Write the question with the information in the parentheses.* Go over the example. Then say: *If the parentheses contain a different subject, write the question with the new subject.* Point out that #2 has a different subject in parentheses. Do #2 as a class.

2. Have students complete the exercise individually. Then have them practice asking and answering the questions in pairs. Monitor pair work. Give help as needed. Remind them to review grammar chart **8.6** on page 231 if necessary. Check the questions and answers as a class.

◀)) EXERCISE 10

CD 2
TR 03

ANSWERS: 1. was not; **2.** was; **3.** were you; **4.** Were you; **5.** wasn't; **6.** Was your trip; **7.** wasn't it; **8.** was; **9.** were; **10.** Were there; **11.** was; **12.** was; **13.** was; **14.** weren't; **15.** was; **16.** was; **17.** was; **18.** were

10-15 mins

1. Have students read the direction line. Go over the example with the class. Remind students that they might need to use other words in the blanks.

2. Have students complete Exercise 10 individually. Remind them to review grammar chart **8.6** on page 231 if necessary. Play the audio and check answers as a class.

Practice Idea: Listening

To provide practice with listening skills, have students close their books and listen to the audio. Repeat the audio as needed. Ask comprehension questions, such as: *Where was person B last week?* (out of town; in Washington, D.C.) *Was the trip expensive?* (no) *How did person B get to Washington, D.C.?* (by plane) Then have students open their books and complete Exercise 10.

Practice Idea: Speaking

Have students create their own conversations in pairs. Say: *Use Exercise 10 as a model.* Then have volunteers role-play all or part of their conversations in front of the class.

8.7 Simple Past Tense of Irregular Verbs—An Overview

10-15 mins

1. Have students cover up grammar chart **8.7** on page 234. Write the following sentences on the board:

   I (come) to the U.S. by plane.

   My flight (take) six hours.

   I (feel) happy when I arrived.

   Explain that some verbs are irregular and have irregular past tense endings. Say: *You already learned at least one important irregular verb in the past.* Elicit a response (*be = was/were*). Elicit any prior knowledge students may have. Ask: *Do you know the past tense of the irregular verbs in parentheses?* Have volunteers write them on the board.

2. Then have students look at grammar chart **8.7.** Review the example sentences in the grammar chart.

Robert Goddard READING

1. Have students look at the photos. Ask: *Why is Robert Goddard famous?* (He invented the rocket.)

2. Have students look at the title of the reading. Ask: *What is the reading about? How do you know?* Have students use the title and the photos to make predictions about the reading.

3. Preteach any vocabulary words students may not know such as *firecracker, prove, light, last,* and *grow.*

Reading Glossary

firecracker: a bright, colorful light explosive intended for celebration
grow: to develop; mature
last: to continue to exist
light: to set on fire
prove: to show that something is true or genuine

BEFORE YOU READ

1. Have students discuss the questions in pairs.
2. Ask for a few volunteers to share their answers with the class.

5-10 mins

Reading ≡★

CD 2
TR 04

10-15 mins

1. Have students read the text silently. Tell them to pay special attention to the past tense verbs. Then play the audio and have students read along silently.

2. Check students' comprehension. Ask questions such as: *What did Goddard teach at the university?* (physics) *Where did Goddard think people could travel to with rockets?* (the moon) *How long did the first rocket flight last?* (2½ seconds)

Practice Idea: Listening

To practice listening skills, have students first listen to the audio alone. Ask a few comprehension questions such as: *What did the* New York Times *say about Goddard?* (that Goddard had less knowledge about science than a high school student) *What did the* New York Times *say in 1969, when the American rocket Apollo 11 landed on the moon?* (that they regret the error) Then have students open their books and read along as they listen to the audio.

Did you know?

Have students read the information. Tell them that after her flight into space, Valentina Tereshkova was honored with the title Hero of the Soviet Union.

8.8 List of Irregular Past Tense Verbs ≡★

10-15 mins

1. Have students cover up grammar chart **8.8** on page 236. Ask students to go back to the reading on page 235. Ask: *How many of these verbs do you know? Write the base form above or next to the past tense form.* Ask for volunteers to tell you the base form of the verbs in the reading.

2. Tell students to look at grammar chart **8.8**. Say: *Check your work with the grammar chart.* Point out any errors.

3. Explain that some irregular verbs don't have any changes in the past; they're spelled the same and they're pronounced the same. Quickly go through the first list in the chart to demonstrate the pronunciation. Elicit a response. Ask: *If the spelling and the pronunciation don't change, how do we know which one is in the past, and which one is in the present or base form?* (by the context of the rest of the sentence)

4. Review the verbs with vowel changes. Explain that the verbs are grouped according to vowel change similarities. Say: *English language learners must memorize the past form of irregular verbs.* Point out that there is an alphabetical list of irregular verbs in Appendix D. Demonstrate the pronunciation of the base form and the past form of each verb. Have students repeat after you.

5. The last chart shows irregular verbs with miscellaneous changes. Review those verbs and demonstrate their pronunciation. Have students repeat after you. Point out that past tense verbs only have one form, except for *be,* which has two (*was/were*).

EXERCISE 11

ANSWERS: 1. built – I, flew – I; **2.** used – R; **3.** launched – R; **4.** sent – I; **5.** became – I; **6.** went – I; **7.** put – I; **8.** transmitted – R

1. Have students read the direction line. Ask: *What do we underline?* (the verbs) Go over the example in the book.

2. Have students complete Exercise 11 individually. Remind them to review grammar charts **8.1** on page 225 and **8.8** on page 236 if necessary. Check the answers as a class.

EXERCISE 12

ANSWERS: 1. was; **2.** thought; **3.** put, drove; **4.** flew, fell; **5.** saw; **6.** wrote

1. Have students read the direction line. Ask: *What do we write in the blanks?* (the past tense of one of the verbs from the box) Go over the example.

2. Have students complete the exercise individually. Remind them to review grammar chart **8.8** on page 236 if necessary. Go over the answers with the class.

EXERCISE 13

ANSWERS: 1. had; **2.** became; **3.** read; **4.** sold; **5.** built; **6.** had; **7.** made; **8.** flew; **9.** saw; **10.** heard; **11.** brought; **12.** went

1. Have students read the direction line. Ask: *What do we write in the blanks?* (the past tense of the verbs in parentheses) Go over the example.

2. Have students complete the exercise individually. Remind them to review grammar chart **8.8** on page 236 if necessary. Go over the answers with the class.

Practice Idea: Speaking

Have students practice telling another student the stories of the Wright brothers or Goddard. Have them practice in pairs. Then have volunteers tell their stories to the class.

8.9 Negative Forms of Past Tense Verbs ≡★

1. Have students cover up grammar chart **8.9** on page 238. Ask students to go back to the

reading on page 235. Say: *Circle the negative verbs in the past tense.* Write students' examples on the board (*didn't fly* and *did not stop*).

2. Tell students to look at grammar chart **8.9**. Write on the board: *didn't + base form.* Explain that this is how the negative is formed for all verbs—regular and irregular.

3. Review all of the example sentences in the chart.

EXERCISE 14

ANSWERS: 1. didn't dream; **2.** didn't sell; **3.** didn't have; **4.** didn't want; **5.** didn't build; **6.** didn't think; **7.** didn't want; **8.** didn't write; **9.** didn't fly; **10.** didn't stay; **11.** didn't see; **12.** didn't put; **13.** didn't walk; **14.** didn't go

1. Have students read the direction line. Ask: *What do we write in the blanks?* (the negative form of the underlined verb) Go over the example in the book.

2. Have students complete Exercise 14 individually. Remind them to review grammar chart **8.9** on page 238 if necessary. Check the answers as a class.

EXERCISE 15
Answers will vary.

1. Tell students that this exercise is about their experiences before coming to the U.S. Have students read the direction line. Ask: *What do we write in the blanks?* (the affirmative or negative of the verb) Say: *Make sure the information is true for you.* Instruct students to add specific information for each item whenever possible. Go over the examples in the book.

2. Have students complete Exercise 15 individually. Remind them to review grammar chart **8.9** on page 238 if necessary. Then have students compare answers in pairs. If possible, have students from different countries work together. Monitor pair work. Give help as needed.

Practice Idea: Writing

Have students write three more sentences in the past tense about their lives before coming to the U.S. Have students compare their new statements with a partner.

EXERCISE 16

Answers will vary.

10-15 mins

1. Tell students that this exercise is about their experiences after coming to this city or country. Have students read the direction line. Say: *Make the sentences affirmative or negative, according to what's true for you.* Go over the examples in the book. Have a student model #1.

2. Have students complete Exercise 16 individually. Remind them to review grammar chart **8.9** on page 238 if necessary. Then have students compare answers with their partners. If possible, have students from different countries work together. Monitor pair work. Give help as needed.

EXERCISE 17

Answers will vary.

10-15 mins

1. Tell students that this exercise is about their experiences this week. Have students read the direction line. Say: *Make the sentences affirmative or negative, according to what's true for you.* Go over the examples in the book. Have a student model #1.

2. Have students complete Exercise 17 in pairs. Remind them to review grammar chart **8.9** on page 238 if necessary. If possible, have students from different countries work together. Monitor pair work. Give help as needed.

Practice Idea: Speaking

Have students write a time line based on either Exercise 16 or 17. Then have students practice telling their partners the events that happened to them. Ask volunteers to present their time lines to the class.

Hero Pilot READING

1. Have students look at the photo. Ask: *Who is this man?* (Chesley Sullenberger, a pilot)

2. Have students look at the title of the reading. Ask: *What is the reading about? How do you know?* Have students use the title and the photo to make predictions about the reading.

3. Preteach any vocabulary words students may not know, such as *emergency landing, takeoff, passengers,* and *scared.*

Reading Glossary

emergency landing: when a plane has to land quickly because of a problem
passengers: the people travelling on a plane/train/boat
scared: afraid, frightened
takeoff: when a plane goes up into the air

BEFORE YOU READ

5-10 mins

1. Have students discuss the questions in pairs.
2. Ask for a few volunteers to share their answers with the class.

CD 2
TR 05
10-15 mins

Reading =★

1. Have students read the text silently. Tell them to pay special attention to past-tense questions. Then play the audio and have students read along silently.

2. Check students' comprehension. Ask questions such as: *Why is Sully a hero?* (he saved the lives of more than 150 people) *Where did Sully land the plane?* (the Hudson River) *What did President Obama do?* (invited Sully and his crew to the inauguration)

Practice Idea: Listening

To practice listening skills, have students first listen to the audio alone. Ask a few comprehension questions such as: *What is Chesley Sullenberger's nickname?* (Sully) *What did he do?* (made an emergency landing in the Hudson River) *Why did his plan lose power?* (A flock of birds flew into the engine.) Then have students open their books and read along as they listen to the audio.

8.10 Questions with Past-Tense Verbs

 10-15 mins

1. Have students cover up grammar chart **8.10** on page 243. Write the following sentences on the board:

   The pilot landed the plane.
   The plane lost power.

   Say: *Write yes/no questions and short answers for these two sentences.*

2. Write on the board: *Where* and *How. Have students write a wh- question for each of the two sentences.*

3. Write the following sentence on the board:

   The pilot didn't go to the airport.

   Have students write a negative question for this sentence. Then say: *Write a negative wh- question for this sentence with* why.

4. Have students look at grammar chart **8.10**. Say: *Now compare your sentences with the sentences in the grammar chart.* Write on the board: Did + *subject + base form ... ?* Explain that this is how questions are formed in the simple past for all verbs—regular and irregular. Review negative and affirmative short answers. Then write on the board: Wh- *word* + did + *subject + base form ... ?* Explain that this is how *wh-* questions are formed in the simple past for all verbs— regular and irregular. Finally, write: Didn't + *subject + base form ... ?* and Wh- *word* + didn't + *subject + base form ... ?* Explain that this is how negative questions are formed in the simple past for all verbs—regular and irregular.

5. Quickly review the comparison of affirmative statements and questions.

EXERCISE 18

ANSWERS: 1. No, he didn't. **2.** Yes, he did. **3.** No, they didn't. **4.** Yes, it did. **5.** Yes, he was.

 10-15 mins

1. Have students read the direction line. *What do we write in the blanks?* (a short answer) Go over the example with the class.

2. Have students complete Exercise 18 in pairs. Remind them to review grammar chart **8.10** on page 243 if necessary. Then have them ask and answer the questions with their partners.

If possible, have students from different countries work together. Monitor pair work. Give help as needed.

EXERCISE 19

Answers will vary.

 10-15 mins

1. Tell students that they will be interviewing a partner about his or her life before coming to the U.S. Have students read the direction line. Model #1 with a student.

2. Have students complete Exercise 19 in pairs. Remind them to review grammar chart **8.10** on page 243 if necessary. If possible, have students from different countries work together. Monitor pair work. Give help as needed.

> ### Practice Idea: Speaking
>
> Create two rings of students. Have half of the students stand in an outer ring around the classroom. Have the other half stand in an inner ring, facing the outer ring. Instruct students to ask and answer the questions from Exercise 19. Call out *turn* every minute or so. Students in the inner ring should move one space clockwise. Students now ask and answer with their new partners. Have students ask questions in random order. Make sure students look at each other when they're speaking.

EXERCISE 20

ANSWERS: 1. Did his brother die in 1912? No, he didn't. **2.** Did Goddard build an airplane? No, he didn't. **3.** Did Lindbergh love to fly? Yes, he did. **4.** Did Earhart cross the ocean? Yes, she did. **5.** Did Earhart work for the U.S. Mail Service? No, she didn't. **6.** Did Earhart become famous? Yes, she did. **7.** Did Lindbergh disappear? No, he didn't. **8.** Was Earhart born in the twentieth century? No, she wasn't. **9.** Did the Wright brothers win money for their first flight? No, they didn't. **10.** Did people believe Goddard at first? No, they didn't. **11.** Did Goddard dream about flight? Yes, he did. **12.** Did Sully (OR he) make a safe landing? Yes, he did. **13.** Did birds fly into both engines? No, they didn't. **14.** Were the passengers safe? Yes, they were.

1. Have students read the direction line. Ask: *What do we write?* (a yes/no question and a short answer) Go over the example in the book.

2. Have students complete the exercise individually. Remind them to review grammar chart **8.10** on page 243 if necessary. Check the answers as a class.

EXERCISE 21

ANSWERS: 1. did the Wright brothers build their plane; **2.** did the first plane crash; **3.** didn't newspapers report; **4.** did Lindbergh work; **5.** did he cross the ocean; **6.** did he win; **7.** was Lindbergh; **8.** was Earhart born; **9.** did she disappear; **10.** didn't Earhart return; **11.** did the first man walk on the moon; **12.** didn't Goddard see; **13.** was Sully a hero; **14.** lives did he save; **15.** didn't he return to the airport

1. Have students read the direction line. Say: *Complete the questions.* Ask: *What kind of questions are they?* (wh- or information questions) Go over the example in the book.

2. Have students complete the exercise individually. Remind them to review grammar chart **8.10** on page 243 if necessary. Check the answers as a class.

> ### Practice Idea: Speaking
>
> Have students practice asking and answering the questions in pairs.

EXERCISE 22 =★

ANSWERS: 1. When was Lindbergh born? He was born in 1902. **2.** What kind of toy did their father (OR he) give them? He gave them a flying toy. **3.** What kind of shop did they have? They had a bicycle shop. **4.** Where did they design airplanes? They designed airplanes in their bicycle shop. **5.** When did they fly their first plane? They flew their first plane in 1903. **6.** How many seconds did it stay in the air? It stayed in the air for 12 seconds. **7.** Why didn't the U.S. government want to see the airplane at first? They didn't believe it. **8.** What did Goddard invent? He invented the rocket. **9.** Why did Goddard (OR he) take his rocket to his aunt's farm? He took his rocket (OR it) to his aunt's farm to see if it would fly. **10.** Why did people laugh at Goddard (OR him)? People laughed at Goddard (OR him) because they didn't believe him (OR they thought he was a fool). **11.** Where did Sully (OR he) land his plane? He landed it in the Hudson River in New York City. **12.** When did Sully (OR he) receive an invitation from the president? He received the invitation in January 2009. **13.** Where did the president thank him? He thanked him at the inauguration.

1. Have students read the direction line. Ask: *What kind of questions are we going to write?* (wh- or information questions) Go over the example in the book. Tell students to try to answer the questions without looking at the answers.

2. Have students complete the exercise individually. Remind them to review grammar chart **8.10** on page 243 if necessary. Check the answers as a class.

> ### Practice Idea: Speaking
>
> Have students practice asking and answering the questions in pairs.

EXERCISE 23
Answers will vary.

1. Tell students that this activity is about them. Have students read the direction line. Ask: *What do we check?* (events that happened to them) Go over the examples with the class. Then have volunteers model the examples.

2. Have students check the statements individually. Remind them to review grammar chart **8.10** on page 243 if necessary. Then have students ask and answer questions in pairs. Monitor pair work.

Answers will vary.

1. Tell students that this activity is about things they did when they were children. Have students read the direction line. Ask: *What do we check?* (things that happened when we were young) Go over the example with the class. Then have volunteers model the example.

2. Have students check the statements individually. Remind them to review grammar chart **8.10** on page 243 if necessary. Then have students ask and answer questions in pairs. Monitor pair work.

Practice Idea: Speaking

Create two rings of students. Have half of the students stand in an outer ring around the classroom. Have the other half stand in an inner ring, facing the outer ring. Instruct students to make statements from Exercise 24 and ask and answer questions. Call out *turn* every minute or so. Students in the inner ring should move one space clockwise. Students now make a statement and ask and answer with their new partners. Have students say the statements in random order. Make sure students look at each other when they're speaking.

8.11 Questions About the Subject ━★

1. Have students cover up grammar chart **8.11** on page 249. Write the following sentences on the board: *Someone saved the passengers. Something happened to Sully's plane. A president invited Sully.*

   Say: *Write questions about the subjects of these three sentences.* Elicit the pattern for questions about the subject (subject + verb + complement). Ask: *Is this pattern the same as or different from the pattern for statements?* (the same)

2. Have students look at grammar chart **8.11**. Tell students to check their questions. Go over any errors. Remind students that with questions about the subject, the past tense form is used,

not the base form. Also point out that we don't use *did* in questions about the subject. Go over the examples for comparison.

EXERCISE 25

ANSWERS: 1. Russia; **2.** an American; **3.** Goddard; **4.** Earhart; **5.** Lindbergh; **6.** T. Roosevelt; **7.** the *New York Times*; **8.** no one

1. Tell students to cover up the answers at the bottom of page 249. Have students read the direction line. Ask: *How much have you learned about the history of flight? Let's take a quiz.* Go over the example with the class.

2. Have students complete the exercise individually. Remind them to review grammar chart **8.11** on page 249 if necessary. Have students check answers in pairs.

Practice Idea: Speaking

Tell students to write three more questions to ask their group members. Remind students to write questions about the subject. Have students take turns asking and answering their new questions.

EXERCISE 26

Answers will vary.

1. Have students read the direction line. Say: *You're going to ask your classmates questions.* Ask: *What kind of question is the first one?* (a question about the subject) Say: *Remember, questions about the subject don't use* did. Go over the example with the class. Have volunteers model the example.

2. Have students complete the exercise in groups. Remind them to review grammar chart **8.11** on page 249 if necessary. Monitor group work. Give help as needed.

EXERCISE 27

ANSWERS: 1. came; **2.** were you; **3.** moved; **4.** was; **5.** did you move; **6.** lost; **7.** happened; **8.** hit; **9.** destroyed; **10.** went; **11.** did you stay; **12.** came; **13.** Did they come; **14.** waited **15.** found; **16.** saved;

17. brought; **18.** didn't come; **19.** started; **20.** arrived; **21.** supported; **22.** did **23.** didn't go; **24.** had; **25.** got; **26.** started; **27.** did you choose

---

1. Have students read the direction line. Ask: *What tense are we going to use in this exercise?* (the past) Say: *Right. The past of* be *and the simple past of other verbs.* Go over the example in the book. Do #1 and 2 with the class.

2. Have students complete Exercise 27 individually. Remind them to review the grammar charts from **Lesson 8** if necessary. Check answers as a class.

10-15 mins

Practice Idea: Speaking

Have students create their own dialogs. Say: *Use Exercise 27 as a model.* Ask volunteers to role-play all or part of their dialogs in front of the class.

Summary of Lesson 8

20-30 mins

1. *Be* Review the forms of the simple past tense of *be.* Have students cover up the sentences in the chart on page 252. Then have students work in pairs to make sentences with *was* and *were.*

Write on the board: *was   were*

affirmative
negative
yes/no *question*
short answer
wh- *question*
negative question
subject question

Say: *Write statements and questions for both* was *and* were. Then have students open their books and compare their sentences with the sentences in the chart. If necessary, have students review:

8.4 Past Tense of *Be* (p. 229)
8.5 Uses of *Be* (p. 230)
8.6 Questions with *Was/Were* (p. 231)

2. Other Verbs Review the simple past tense of other verbs—regular and irregular. Have students cover up the sentences in the chart on page 252. Then have students work in pairs

to make sentences with *work* and *buy.* Write on the board: *regular* (work)   *irregular* (buy)

affirmative
negative
yes/no *question*
short answer
wh- *question*
negative question
subject question

Say: *Write statements and questions for* work *and* buy. Then have students compare their sentences with the sentences in the chart. If necessary, have students review:

8.1 The Simple Past Tense of Regular Verbs (p. 225)
8.2 Spelling of the Past Tense of Regular Verbs (p. 226)
8.3 Pronunciation of –ed Past Forms (p. 227)
8.7 Simple Past Tense of Irregular Verbs— An Overview (p. 234)
8.8 List of Irregular Past Tense Verbs (p. 236)
8.9 Negative Forms of Past Tense Verbs (p. 238)
8.10 Questions with Past-Tense Verbs (p. 243)
8.11 Questions About the Subject (p. 249)

Editing Advice

10-15 mins

Have students close their books. Write the first few sentences without editing marks or corrections on the board. For example:

1. *I wanted to bought a new car.*
2. *I studied for the last test.*
He droped his pencil.

Ask students to correct each sentence and provide a rule or explanation for each correction. This activity can be done individually, in pairs, or as a class. After students have corrected each sentence, tell them to turn to pages 253–254. Say: *Now compare your work with the Editing Advice in the book.*

Editing Quiz

ANSWERS: 1. write; **2.** did you write; **3.** C; **4.** Was he; **5.** C; **6.** did he go; **7.** Did he go; **8.** C; **9.** were; **10.** C;

11. died; **12.** was he born; **13.** was born; **14.** was; **15.** C; **16.** saw; **17.** happened; **18.** C; **19.** walked; **20.** forgot; **21.** die; **22.** was; **23.** C

10-15 mins

1. Tell students they are going to put the editing advice into practice. Have students read the direction line. Ask: *Do all the shaded words and phrases have mistakes?* (no) Go over the examples with the class. Then do #1 together.

2. Have students complete the quiz individually. Then have them compare answers with a partner before checking answers as a class.

3. For the items students had difficulties with, have them go back and find the relevant grammar chart and review it. Monitor and give help as necessary.

Lesson 8 Test/Review

40-60 mins

Use the Assessment CD-ROM with Exam *View®*, Online Workbook, and Web site for additional practice, review, and assessment materials.

PART 1

ANSWERS: **1.** ate; **2.** saw; **3.** got; **4.** sat; **5.** hit; **6.** made; **7.** took; **8.** found; **9.** said; **10.** read; **11.** drank; **12.** built; **13.** stopped; **14.** left; **15.** bought; **16.** thought; **17.** ran; **18.** carried; **19.** sold; **20.** stood

1. Part 1 may be used in addition to the Assessment CD-ROM with ExamView® as an in-class test to assess student performance. Say: *Some of these verbs are regular and some are irregular.* Go over the example with the class.

2. Have students complete Part 1 individually. Collect for assessment.

3. If necessary, have students review:
   8.2 Spelling of the Past Tense of Regular Verbs (p. 226)
   8.8 List of Irregular Past-Tense Verbs (p. 236)

PART 2

ANSWERS: **1.** weren't; **2.** didn't fly; **3.** wasn't; **4.** didn't invent; **5.** didn't die; **6.** didn't go; **7.** didn't come; **8.** wasn't born; **9.** didn't build; **10.** didn't lose

1. Part 2 may be used in addition to the Assessment CD-ROM with ExamView® as an in-class test to assess student performance. Have students read the direction line. Ask: *What do we write on the blanks?* (the negative) Go over the example with the class.

2. Have students complete Part 2 individually. Collect for assessment.

3. If necessary, have students review:
   8.4 Past Tense of *Be* (p. 229)
   8.9 Negative Forms of Past Tense Verbs (p. 238)

PART 3

ANSWERS: **1.** Did Orville Wright become famous? Yes, he did. **2.** Was Goddard an aviator? No, he wasn't. **3.** Did Earhart fly across the Atlantic Ocean? Yes she did. **4.** Was Goddard born in the U.S.? Yes, he was. **5.** Did the Wright brothers write about rockets? No, they didn't. **6.** Did the Americans send a man into space? Yes, they did. **7.** Did Wilbur Wright die in 1945? No, he didn't. **8.** Did Russia put men on the moon in 1969? No, they didn't. **9.** Did they laugh at his ideas in 1969? No, they didn't. **10.** Did Sully (OR he) land the airplane safely? Yes, he did.

1. Part 3 may be used in addition to the Assessment CD-ROM with ExamView® as an in-class test to assess student performance. Have students read the direction line. Ask: *Do we use wh- words in these questions?* (no; we write yes/no questions) Go over the example as a class.

2. Have students complete Part 3 individually. Collect for assessment.

3. If necessary, have students review:
   8.6 Questions with *Was/Were* (p. 231)
   8.10 Questions with Past-Tense Verbs (p. 243)

PART 4

ANSWERS: **1.** When was Lindbergh born? **2.** When did Earhart cross the ocean? **3.** How much money did Lindbergh (OR he) get for his flight? **4.** Why did Earhart (OR she) want to fly around the world? **5.** How many people saw Lindbergh (OR him) in Paris? **6.** Why didn't Goddard's colleagues (OR they) believe his ideas? **7.** When did Orville Wright die? **8.** Which president examined Goddard's (OR his) ideas? **9.** How did Sully (OR he) lose an engine? **10.** Who made an emergency landing?

1. Part 4 may be used in addition to the Assessment CD-ROM with Exam*View*® as an in-class test to assess student performance. Have students read the direction line. Go over the example with the class. Remind students not to answer the questions.

2. Have students complete Part 4 individually. Collect for assessment.

3. If necessary, have students review:

   8.6 Questions with *Was/Were* (p. 231)
   8.10 Questions with Past-Tense Verbs (p. 243)
   8.11 Questions About the Subject (p. 249)

Expansion

These expansion activities provide opportunities for students to interact with one another and further develop their speaking and writing skills. Encourage students to use grammar from this lesson whenever possible.

CLASSROOM ACTIVITIES

10-15 mins per activity

1. Have students work in groups. Say: *Choose a member of the group to interview about his or her first experiences here in the U.S. Take turns asking questions. Then report the results of the interview to the class* (e.g., *When Lina arrived, she lived in Minneapolis. Her cousin, Felipe, picked her up at the airport.*). If necessary, brainstorm more questions for the interview and write them on the board.

2. Tell students that they will interview their partners about their experiences before and after they came to the U.S. Go over the sample interview. Have students review the example in Exercise 26 on page 250 before beginning this activity.

3. Have students complete the sentences individually. Then have them compare their sentences with a partner. Ask volunteers to talk about their experiences.

TALK ABOUT IT

15-20 mins

Write on the board: *space exploration* and elicit from students any ideas they have about the topic. Ask: *What do you think of when you see "space exploration"?* Write their ideas on the board. Put students in small groups or pairs to discuss their opinions about space exploration. Monitor group work. Give help as needed. Have volunteers share their opinions with the class.

WRITE ABOUT IT

20-30 mins

Have students read the direction line. Review the model with the students. Have students help you begin writing a paragraph on the board about a famous person you admire following the model. Then have students write their two paragraphs. Encourage students to add more information. Collect for assessment and/or have students present their paragraphs to a group.

Practice Idea: Writing

Have students exchange first drafts with a partner. Ask students to help their partners edit their drafts. Refer students to the Editing Advice on pages 253–254.

OUTSIDE ACTIVITIES

1. Tell students to interview an American about a vacation he or she took. Tell them to find out where he or she went, with whom, for how long, and other related information. Brainstorm the questions they can ask in class beforehand. Students can report their interviews to the class or hand in a written report.

2. Tell students to interview an American about a famous person he or she admires. Tell them to find out what this famous person did. Brainstorm the questions they can ask in class beforehand. Students can report their interviews to the class or hand in a written report.

1. Tell students to use the Internet to find out
    something about one of the following famous
    people (or have students research a famous person
    from their countries). They should answer these
    questions: What did he or she do? When did he or
    she do it? When was he or she born? Is he or she still
    alive? If not, when did he or she die?

    a. Marie Curie
    b. Alexander Fleming
    c. Thomas Edison
    d. Alexander Graham Bell
    e. Bill Gates
    f. Henry Ford
    g. Jonas Salk
    h. Edwin Hubble
    i. Enrico Fermi
    j. John Von Neumann
    k. Leo Baekeland
    l. Ian Wilmut

    Ask volunteers to make a brief presentation in front
    of the class. Encourage students to include time
    lines and photos.

2. Tell students to find a Web site with information
    about the 2004 landing on Mars. Find a picture of
    Mars. Have volunteers present their information to
    the class.

3. Tell students to find a Web site with information
    about the 2003 anniversary of the Wright brothers'
    first flight. Have them find out what events took place.
    Have volunteers present their information to the class.

Lesson 9

Lesson Overview

GRAMMAR

Ask: *What did we study in Lesson 8?* (the simple past tense) *What are we going to study in this lesson?* (infinitives, modals, and imperatives) *Can anyone give me examples of infinitives* (to go, to buy), *modals* (can, could, will, would), *or imperatives* (stand, walk, stop)? Have students give examples. Write them on the board.

CONTEXT

1. Ask: *What will we learn about in this lesson?* (smart shopping) Activate students' prior knowledge. Ask: *What is "smart shopping"? Are you a smart shopper? Where do you like to shop? In your opinion, where can you get the best bargains?*

2. Have students share their knowledge and personal experiences.

Presentation Idea

The topic for this lesson can be enhanced with the following ideas:

1. Store flyers
2. Store coupons, rebates, and rain checks

9.1 Infinitives—An Overview

5-10 mins

Have students look at grammar chart **9.1** on page 262. Say: *The infinitive of the verb is* to + *the base form.* Explain that an infinitive never has an ending and that it never shows tense. Read the example sentences from the chart.

Getting the Best Price   READING

1. Have students look at the photo. Ask: *Where is the man in the photo?* (a store) *What does he want to buy?* (a television)

2. Have students look at the title of the reading. Ask: *What is the reading about? How do you know?* Have students use the title and the photo to make predictions about the reading.

3. Preteach any vocabulary words students may not know, such as *prove* and *receipt*.

Reading Glossary

prove: to show that something is true or genuine
receipt: a piece of paper showing that a bill is paid

BEFORE YOU READ

5-10 mins

1. Have students discuss the questions in pairs.

2. Ask for a few volunteers to share their answers with the class.

🔊 Reading ═★

CD 2
TR 06

10-15 mins

1. Have students read the text silently. Tell them to pay special attention to infinitives. Then play the audio and have students read along silently.

2. Check students' comprehension. Ask questions such as: *If you find a lower price, what do some stores do?* (match the price) *How can you prove that another store has a cheaper price?* (by showing an advertisement) *What does the salesperson want to do?* (He wants to help his store make money.) *What do you need to keep to prove that you bought an item?* (the receipt)

Practice Idea: Listening

To practice listening skills, have students first listen to the audio alone. Ask a few comprehension questions such as: *If you find a lower price in another store, what do some stores do?* (match the price) *What can the salesperson do if you don't have an advertisement?* (the salesperson can call the other store to check the price) Then have students open their books and read along as they listen to the audio.

9.2 Verbs Followed by an Infinitive

1. Have students go back to the reading on page 262. Say: *Circle all the verbs (other than be) that come before the infinitives (want, go, try, etc.).* Have volunteers give you examples. Go over any errors.

2. Have students look at grammar chart **9.2** on page 263. Say: *There are some verbs that are often followed by an infinitive, for example* plan, want, need, *and* like. Go over the examples. Point out the list of other verbs that are often followed by an infinitive. Ask students to go back to the reading to see if they circled any of the verbs from the chart.

3. Review the sentences in the different tenses. Say: *An infinitive can follow a verb that's in the past, present, and future. But notice that the infinitive itself does not show tense or whether the subject is singular or plural.*

4. Direct students to the Pronunciation Notes. Demonstrate the informal pronunciation of *want to* ("wanna"). Explain that most native speakers say *wanna*—but it's never written that way. Have students practice the pronunciation chorally as a class.

5. Explain that often the *to* in infinitives is pronounced "ta" or "da" (after a vowel sound as in *try "ta" get*) or "a" (after a "d" sound as in *decided "a" buy*). Demonstrate the pronunciation. Go over the example sentences. Read the sentences in the top part of the chart as well. Have students practice the pronunciation chorally as a class.

EXERCISE 1

Answers: 1. to save (OR to spend); **2.** to spend; **3.** to get; **4.** to check; **5.** to be; **6.** to shop (OR to compare prices)

1. Have students read the direction line. Ask: *What are you going to write?* (a verb in the infinitive) Go over the example in the book.

2. Have students complete the rest of Exercise 1 individually. Remind students to review grammar chart **9.2** if necessary. Have students share their answers with the class.

EXERCISE 2

Answers will vary.

1. Have students read the direction line. Say: *Write a sentence using the verbs given. You can write a sentence in the present or the past. Remember, these verbs are used with infinitives.* Go over the examples in the book. Ask volunteers to model the examples.

2. Have students complete Exercise 2 individually. Remind students to review grammar chart **9.2** on page 263 if necessary. Then have students compare answers in pairs. Monitor pair work. Give help as needed.

> ### Practice Idea: Writing
>
> Have students write a short paragraph about their partners. Use some of the information from Exercise 2. Say: *Tell the class about your classmate. Write a paragraph about him or her. Be sure to include interesting information.*

EXERCISE 3

Answers: 1. Do you try to compare prices? **2.** Do you plan to buy something new? **3.** Do you like to shop alone? **4.** Do you like to shop online? **5.** Do you like to use coupons? **6.** Do you like to get the best price?

1. Have students read the direction line. Say: *Find out more information about your classmate.* Remind students that they should use different tenses. Go over the example in the book. Ask volunteers to model the example.

2. Have students complete Exercise 3 in pairs. Remind students to review grammar chart **9.2** on page 263 if necessary. Monitor pair work. Give help as needed.

EXERCISE 4

Answers: 1. Do you want (OR plan) to take a computer course next semester? Why do (OR don't) you want (OR plan) to take a computer course next semester? **2.** Do you want (OR plan) to move? Why do you want (OR plan) to move? When do you want (OR plan) to move? **3.** Do you want (OR plan) to leave this country? Why do (OR don't) you want (OR plan) to leave this country? When do you want (OR plan) to leave this country? **4.** Do you want (OR plan) to get (another) job? What kind of job do you want (OR plan) to get? **5.** Do you want (OR plan) to become an American citizen? Why do (OR don't) you want (OR plan) to become an American citizen? **6.** Do you want (OR plan) to transfer to a different school? Why do (OR don't) you want (OR plan) to transfer to a different school? **7.** Do you want (OR plan) to take another English course next semester? Which course do you want (OR plan) to take? **8.** Do you want (OR plan) to learn another language? Which language do you want (OR plan) to learn? **9.** Do you want (OR plan) to review the last lesson? Why do (OR don't) you want (OR plan) to review the last lesson?

10-15 mins

1. Have students read the direction line. Ask: *How are we going to begin the first question?* (with *Do you want to …*) *What kind of question is the second question?* (a *wh-* question) Go over the example in the book. Ask a volunteer to model the example with you. Answer the example question with a negative answer.

2. Have students complete Exercise 4 in pairs. Remind students to review grammar chart **9.2** on page 263 if necessary. Monitor pair work. Give help as needed.

> ### Practice Idea: Speaking
>
> Have students write five more questions to ask a partner. Have students take turns asking and answering. Ask volunteers to share some questions and answers with the class.

9.3 *It + Be +* Adjective + Infinitive

5-10 mins

1. Have students go back to the reading on page 265. Say: *There are two phrases in the reading that begin with the impersonal* it (*it is necessary to go* and *it's important to keep*). *Underline them.* Write on the board: It + be + adjective + infinitive. Have volunteers give you examples. Go over any errors.

2. Have students look at grammar chart **9.3**. Say: *We often use an infinitive with sentences beginning with an impersonal* it. Go over the examples. Point out the list of adjectives that are often followed by an infinitive.

EXERCISE 5
Answers will vary.

5-10 mins

1. Tell students that this exercise is about their opinions. Have students read the direction line. Go over the example in the book. Have a volunteer model the example.

2. Have students complete Exercise 5 individually. Remind them to review grammar chart **9.3** on page 265 if necessary. Quickly go around the class to have students share their answers.

EXERCISE 6
Answers will vary.

5-10 mins

1. Tell students that this exercise is about their opinions. Have students read the direction line. Go over the example in the book. Have a volunteer model the example.

2. Have students complete Exercise 6 individually. Remind them to review grammar chart **9.3** on page 265 if necessary. Quickly go around the class to have students share their answers.

EXERCISE 7
Answers will vary.

10-15 mins

1. Tell students that this exercise is about their opinions. Have students read the direction line. Do #1 as a class.

2. Have students ask and answer the questions in pairs. Remind them to review grammar chart **9.3** on page 265 if necessary. Have volunteers share their answers with the class.

> ### Practice Idea: Speaking
>
> Have students discuss their ideas in groups. Ask: *Did anyone have the same ideas you had? Do you agree or disagree with what your groups members wrote?*

9.4 *Be* + Adjective + Infinitive

 5-10 mins Have students look at grammar chart **9.4** on page 267. Say: *We often use an infinitive after certain adjectives.* Go over the examples. Point out the list of adjectives that are often followed by an infinitive.

EXERCISE 8
Answers will vary.

5-10 mins
1. Tell students that this exercise is about them. Have students read the direction line. Go over the example in the book. Have a volunteer model the example.

2. Have students complete Exercise 8 individually. Remind students to review grammar chart **9.4** on page 267 if necessary. Quickly go around the class to have students share their answers.

EXERCISE 9
ANSWERS: Answers will vary.

10-15 mins
1. Tell students that they'll first answer the questions themselves and then they'll interview a partner. Have students read the direction line. Tell students to answer the questions with complete sentences.

2. Have students first answer the questions individually. Remind students to review grammar charts **9.3** on page 265 and **9.4** on page 267 if necessary. Then have students ask and answer questions in pairs. Monitor pair work. Give help as needed.

Practice Idea: Speaking

Create two rings of students. Have half of the students stand in an outer ring around the classroom. Have the other half stand in an inner ring, facing the outer ring. Instruct students to ask and answer the questions from Exercise 9. Call out *turn* every minute or so. Students in the inner ring should move one space clockwise. Students now ask and answer with their new partners. Have students ask questions in random order. Make sure students look at each other when they're speaking.

9.5 Using an Infinitive to Show Purpose

 5-10 mins
1. Have students cover up grammar chart **9.5** on page 268. Say: *We often use an infinitive to show purpose or to show why we're doing something. For example,* I went to the store to buy milk. *The infinitive (*to buy*) shows that the purpose of going to the store was to buy milk.* Have students go back to the reading on page 262. Say: *Double-underline the infinitives that show purpose or why something is being done.* Have volunteers give you examples. Go over any errors.

2. Have students look at grammar chart **9.5**. Go over the examples. Point out that some people make the mistake of using *for* to show purpose.

3. Explain that the use of *to* in order to show purpose is a short form of *in order to*. Read through the example sentences. Then go back to the top of the chart and ask volunteers to substitute *in order to* for *to* in the other example sentences.

EXERCISE 10
Answers will vary.

10-15 mins
1. Have students read the direction line. Go over the example in the book. Have a volunteer do #1.

2. Have students complete Exercise 10 individually. Remind them to review grammar chart **9.5** on page 268 if necessary. Check the answers as a class.

Practice Idea: Speaking

Have students practice asking and answering questions based on each item in Exercise 10. Instruct students to use this pattern:

A: Why did you buy a phone card?
B: To call my friends.

Tell students that some questions will be in the present:

A: Why do you use a dictionary?
B: To look up words.

EXERCISE 11

ANSWERS: 1. (in order) to check (OR compare);
2. (in order) to get; **3.** (in order) to make; **4.** (in
order) to learn; **5.** (in order) to change (OR to
lighten); **6.** (in order) to make

10-15
mins

1. Have students read the direction line. Ask:
What kind of verb do we write on the blanks?
(infinitives) Go over the example in the book.
Ask: *What does the infinitive show here?* (It
shows purpose—it shows what person A uses
the camera for.)

2. Have students complete Exercise 11
individually. Remind them to review grammar
chart **9.5** on page 268 if necessary. Check the
answers as a class. Then have students practice
the conversation in pairs.

Practice Idea: Listening

To provide practice with listening skills, have
students close their books and listen to the audio.
Ask comprehension questions such as: *What kind of
camera does person A have?* (a digital camera) *Is the
digital camera big or small?* (small) *Why did person
A go to several stores?* (to find the best price) Then
have students open their books and complete
Exercise 11.

Practice Idea: Speaking

Have students write a similar conversation about
another new electronic device, such as an MP3 player.
Have students work in pairs. Then ask volunteers to
role-play their conversations in front of the class.

Getting A Customer's Attention READING

1. Have students look at the photo. Ask: *Where does the
woman work?* (in a restaurant or food store) *What's
she doing?* (offering samples of food to customers)

2. Have students look at the title of the reading. Ask:
What is the reading about? How do you know? Have

students use the title and photo to make predictions
about the reading.

3. Preteach any vocabulary words students may not
know, such as *technique, encourage, service,* and
competition.

Reading Glossary

competition: the people, as a group, that one is trying
to do better than, especially in business
encourage: to give strength or hope to someone; urge
service: general attention to customers' needs in a
business
technique: a method, procedure by which something is
performed

BEFORE YOU READ

5-10
mins

1. Have students discuss the questions in pairs.

2. Ask for a few volunteers to share their answers
with the class.

Reading

10-15
mins

1. Have students read the text silently. Tell them
to pay special attention to objects before an
infinitive. Show them an example of this by
writing the first sentence on the board and
underlining *several techniques.* Then play the
audio and have students read along silently.

2. Check students' comprehension. Ask questions
such as: *What are two techniques stores use to
get you to buy their products?* (free samples
and getting two for the price of one) *What do
movie theaters do to get more customers?* (offer
lower prices at early hours)

Practice Idea: Listening

To practice listening skills, have students first listen
to the audio alone. Ask a few comprehension
questions such as: *What is an example of good
service?* (a salesperson might offer to carry your
purchase to the car for you) *Why do owners
and managers of businesses have to use many
techniques to get our attention?* (because of so
much competition between businesses) Then have
students open their books and read along as they
listen to the audio.

9.6 Object Before an Infinitive

5-10 mins

1. Have students cover up grammar chart **9.6** on page 270. Then ask them to look at the reading. Ask them to study the verb phrases that are highlighted in the text. Ask: *Can you find a pattern?* (verb + object + infinitive) Then ask: *What verbs are followed by an object?* (*encourage* and *want*)

2. Have students look at grammar chart **9.6**. Say: *After* like, want, need, expect, *and* encourage, *we can use a noun or object pronoun + infinitive.* If necessary, briefly review object pronouns (see grammar chart **5.6** on pages 138–139). Go over the examples and explanations.

 EXERCISE **12**

CD 2 TR 09

ANSWERS: Conversation 1: 1. to help; **2.** us; **3.** to buy; **4.** her to use; **5.** you to consider; **6.** her
Conversation 2: 1. you to; **2.** me to
Conversation 3: 1. me to get; **2.** us
Conversation 4: 1. me; **2.** to help; **3.** him; **4.** to help; **5.** him to; **6.** to give

5-10 mins

1. Have students read the direction line. Tell students that they need to circle the correct answer to complete the conversations.

2. Have students complete Exercise 12 individually. Remind them to review grammar chart **9.6** on page 270 if necessary. Play the audio and check answers as a class.

Practice Idea: Speaking

Have students practice the conversations in pairs. Have volunteers role-play the conversations in front of the class.

Practice Idea: Listening

To provide practice with listening skills, have students close their books and listen to the audio. Say: *You will hear four short conversations.* Ask comprehension questions, such as: *In Conversation 1, does the mother need the salesman's help?* (yes) *What does the daughter want her parents to do?* (buy her a new cell phone) *What does the mother need help with?* (choosing a plan to buy) Then have students open their books and complete Exercise 12 on page 271.

EXERCISE **13**

ANSWERS: 1. them to leave; **2.** wanted them to buy; **3.** want you to talk; **4.** encourage you to be; **5.** expected her to buy; **6.** wanted him to buy; **7.** expect you to graduate

10-15 mins

1. Have students read the direction line. Ask: *What do we write on the blanks?* (the first verb in parentheses, an object pronoun, and the infinitive of the second verb in parentheses) Go over the example in the book.

2. Have students complete the exercise individually. Remind them to review grammar chart **9.6** on page 270 if necessary. Then have students compare answers and practice the conversation in pairs. Monitor pair work. Give help as needed.

9.7 Overview of Modals

10-15 mins

1. Have students cover up grammar chart **9.7** on page 273. Write on the board: *can, could, should, will, would, may, might,* and *must.* Activate prior knowledge. Ask: *Does anyone know any of these words?* Then write on the board: *He can sleep late every day.* Ask: *Do you notice anything different about the word* can? *How is it different from other verbs?* (It doesn't have an *-s* form. You don't use the infinitive after *can*.)

2. Then have students look at grammar chart **9.7**. Say: *Modals are different from other verbs in the following ways.* Review the facts about modals.

3. Quickly go over the meanings of the modals in the chart. (*Can* means ability, possibility, and permission. *Should* is used to give or ask for advice. *Must* is a very formal way of expressing necessity. It's used to talk about rules and laws. *Have to* is another way of saying *must*, but it's less formal. *Might* and *may* mean the same thing. They are used to show possibility.) Explain, though, that you will go over each modal in depth later in the lesson.

4. Review the comparison of affirmative and negative statements and questions.

Smart Shopping: Coupons, Rain Checks, and Rebates READING

1. Have students look at the illustrations. Ask: *What kind of coupon is this?* (a manufacturer's coupon) *What does "do not double" mean?* (the store can't double the value of the coupon) *Have you ever used a rain check?*

2. Have students look at the title of the reading. Ask: *What is the reading about? How do you know?* Have students use the title and the pictures to make predictions about the reading.

3. Preteach any vocabulary words students may not know such as *manufacturer*, *expiration*, and *limit*.

Reading Glossary

expiration: a date at which something is no longer valid
limit: the greatest amount or extent allowed
manufacturer: a business that makes things

BEFORE YOU READ

5-10 mins

1. Have students discuss the questions in pairs.

2. Ask for a few volunteers to share their answers with the class.

CD 2
TR 10
Reading =★

10-15 mins

1. Have students read the text silently. Tell them to pay special attention to modals and related expressions. Then play the audio and have students read along silently.

2. Check students' comprehension. Ask questions such as: *Why do manufacturers send coupons to customers?* (to get you to try their products) *What should you do if you can't find a sale item on the shelf?* (ask for a rain check) *When you fill out a rebate form, what does the manufacturer send you?* (some money)

9.8 *Can* =★

5-10 mins

1. Have students cover up grammar chart **9.8** on page 275. Make a matching exercise on the board. Write on one side of the board:

   I can't afford to eat in a restaurant every day.

   You can return an item within 30 days.

   If you use coupons, you can save money.

   I can find many ways to save money.

   On the other side of the board write:

   ability

   possibility

   permission

   have enough money to buy something

   Say: *Match the examples with the explanations.*

2. Tell students to look at grammar chart **9.8**. Say: *Check your work with the grammar chart.* Point out any errors. Go over all of the example sentences.

3. Explain that the negative of *can* is *cannot* and the contraction is *can't*.

4. Direct students to the Pronunciation Notes. Go over the pronunciation of *can* and *cannot*. Tell students that they must listen for the sound

of the vowel and not the ending because the final *t* in *can't* is difficult to hear. Tell students that this is often confusing for native speakers as well. Point out that in short answers *can* may sound like /kæn/. But tell students that in a short answer they can easily distinguish between the two by listening for *yes* or *no*.

5. Demonstrate the pronunciation with the sentences in the grammar chart. Then read the sentences in Exercise 14 (say some of them as negatives). Ask students to hold up their hands if they hear *can* and to keep their hands down if they hear *can't*. Then have students practice the pronunciation chorally as a class.

EXERCISE 14
Answers will vary.

5-10 mins

1. Have students read the direction line. Say: *Check what's true for supermarkets in your native country or a country you lived in for a long time.* Point out that these statements are true for American supermarkets.

2. Have students complete the activity individually. Remind them to review grammar chart **9.8** on page 275 if necessary. Then have students compare answers in pairs or groups. If possible, put students from different countries together.

EXERCISE 15
Answers will vary.

5-10 mins

1. Have students read the direction line. Go over the examples. Point out that in this exercise, *can* is being used to express ability.

2. Have students complete the exercise individually. Remind them to review grammar chart **9.8** on page 275 if necessary. Then have students practice pronouncing *can* and *can't* in pairs. Monitor pair work. Give help as needed.

Practice Idea: Speaking

Take a quick survey of the class. How many students can or can't do the activities in the exercise?

EXERCISE 16

ANSWERS: 1. Can you write with your left hand? **2.** Can you type without looking at the keyboard? **3.** Can you run fast? **4.** Can you play chess? **5.** Can you ski? **6.** Can you play the piano? **7.** Can you speak French? **8.** Can you bake a cake? **9.** Can you play the guitar? **10.** Can you sew?

10-15 mins

1. Tell students that they will interview a partner. Have students read the direction line. Ask: *What kind of questions are we asking?* (yes/no questions) Go over the example. Have volunteers model the example. Point out that in this exercise, *can* is being used to express ability.

2. Have students complete the exercise in pairs. Remind them to review grammar chart **9.8** on page 275 if necessary. Monitor pair work. Give help as needed.

EXERCISE 17
Answers will vary.

5-10 mins

1. Have students read the direction line. Write a model sentence on the board: *I can _____ (really) well.* Complete it about yourself.

2. Have students complete their sentence individually. Remind them to review grammar chart **9.8** on page 275 if necessary. Have students share what they do well with a partner. Ask volunteers to tell the class what their partners can do well.

Practice Idea: Speaking

Have students write what they do well on a small piece of paper. Tell students not to write their names. Ask students to pick a paper from the hat, and then try to find the person who wrote it. Say: *Go around the class and ask* yes/no *questions* (e.g., *Can you swim well? Can you ride a bike well?*).

9.9 *Should*

5-10 mins

1. Have students look at grammar chart **9.9** on page 277. Say: *We use* should *to give or ask for advice.* Read the examples in the chart.

2. Go over the negative and the contraction *shouldn't*. Point out that the negative is used to give advice or a warning.

EXERCISE 18
Answers will vary.

10-15 mins

1. Have students read the direction line. Ask: *What do we write in the blanks?* (advice about shopping in the U.S.) Go over the examples in the book.

2. Have students complete Exercise 18 in pairs. Remind students to review grammar chart **9.9** on page 277 if necessary. Monitor pair work. Give help as needed.

> ## Practice Idea: Speaking
>
> Have students compare advice in groups. Then have them compile the best advice from the group and present it to the class.

EXERCISE 19
Answers will vary.

10-15 mins

1. Have students read the direction line. Go over the example in the book. Ask a volunteer to do #1.

2. Have students complete Exercise 19 individually. Remind students to review grammar chart **9.9** on page 277 if necessary. Then have students compare answers in pairs. Tell them to take turns saying one of the statements and their partner gives advice. Monitor pair work. Give help as needed.

EXERCISE 20

CD 2 TR 11

ANSWERS: 1. shouldn't do (OR buy OR get); **2.** should we buy (OR get); **3.** should buy (OR get); **4.** shouldn't eat; **5.** should use; **6.** should be; **7.** should look; **8.** should buy (OR get); **9.** should come (OR shop); **10.** should bring; **11.** Should we pay

1. Tell students that this is a conversation between a husband and wife at the supermarket. Have students read the direction line. Say: *You can use a negative or an affirmative statement.* Go over the example in the book.

2. Have students complete Exercise 20 individually. Remind students to review grammar chart **9.9** on page 277 if necessary. Then have students compare answers in pairs. Play the audio and check answers as a class.

EXERCISE 21
Answers will vary.

10-15 mins

1. Tell students that this exercise is about their opinions on raising children. Have students read the direction line.

2. Have students complete Exercise 21 individually. Remind students to review grammar chart **9.9** on page 277 if necessary. Then have students compare answers in groups. If possible, have students from different countries work together. Monitor group work. Give help as needed.

> ## Practice Ideas: Speaking
>
> 1. What else do students think children shouldn't do? Have students discuss other ideas in their groups. Then have groups report to the class.
>
> 2. What should parents do or not do? Have groups write a list of 5–10 statements. Then have groups exchange lists and say whether they agree or disagree with the statements.

EXERCISE 22

ANSWERS: 1. Why should they study the lessons? **2.** When should the teacher (OR he OR she) take attendance? **3.** What else should the students (OR they) bring to class? **4.** Why should I study modals? **5.** Why should we register for classes early? **6.** Why should the teacher (OR he OR she) speak clearly? **7.** Why shouldn't the students (OR they) talk during a test? **8.** Where should we do homework? **9.** Why should the teacher (OR he OR she) announce a test ahead of time?

---

1. Have students read the direction line. Say: *Make questions out of the statements.* Go over the example. Have volunteers model #1.

2. Have students complete the rest of Exercise 22 in pairs. Remind students to review grammar chart **9.9** on page 277 if necessary. Make sure students take turns asking and answering. Monitor pair work. Give help as needed.

Practice Idea: Writing

Have students write their own "I should" lists. Say: *What do you think you should do? Make a list:* I should exercise more, I should eat more vegetables, *etc.*

9.10 *Must*

1. Have students look at grammar chart **9.10** on page 280. Say: *We use* must *to talk about rules or advice.* Then read the examples in the chart. Have students go back to the reading on page 274. Ask: *How is* must *used in the text?* (It's used to talk about the rules for buying an item with a rain check.)

2. Go over the negative and the contraction *mustn't.* Explain that *must not* and *cannot* mean the same thing. Point out the picture of the handicapped parking space.

Context Note

Only people with a special permit can park in handicapped parking spaces. Permits are obtained through the state's department/registry of motor vehicles and are only granted to those with certain physical limitations. A car parked in a handicapped space without a permit may be ticketed.

EXERCISE 23

ANSWERS: 1. must; **2.** must not; **3.** must; **4.** must not; **5.** must not

 1. Say: *These are some rules in a supermarket.* Have students read the direction line. Point out the photos of the man making a sandwich

at the deli counter and the expiration date on the gallon of juice.

2. Have students complete Exercise 23 individually. Remind them to review grammar chart **9.10** on page 280 if necessary. Go over the answers as a class.

Practice Idea: Writing

Have students write rules for other work situations (e.g., hospital, restaurant, school). Students can work alone or in pairs or groups.

EXERCISE 24
Answers will vary.

 1. Say: *In this exercise, you have to name something you* must have *or do* in a certain situation. Go over the example in the book. Ask a volunteer what else you need to drive (a car, the keys, gas, etc.).

2. Have students complete the exercise individually. Remind them to review grammar chart **9.10** on page 280 if necessary. Then have students compare answers in groups. Monitor group work. Give help as needed.

Practice Idea: Speaking

Survey the class. Have groups report their answers to the class (e.g., *Everyone in our group said you must have a passport if you want to leave the country.*).

9.11 *Have To*

1. Have students look at grammar chart **9.11** on page 282. Say: Have to *is similar to* must. Have to *is less formal.* Then read the examples in the chart. Have students go back to the reading on page 274. Say: *See how* have to *is used in the text. It means:* it's necessary.

2. Explain that *don't have to* means *it's not necessary.* Go over the examples in the chart.

EXERCISE 25
Answers will vary.

10-15 mins

1. Ask: *What do you have to do in this class? What don't you have to do in this class?* Have students read the direction line. Go over the example with the class.

2. Have students complete the exercise individually. Remind them to review grammar chart **9.11** on page 282 if necessary. Go over the answers as a class.

Practice Idea: Writing

Have students write about what they had to do in their last school. Briefly review the past tense (*I had to . . . I didn't have to . . .*). Collect for assessment or have students exchange papers to compare.

EXERCISE 26

ANSWERS: 1. Do you have to take attendance? **2.** Do you have to give students grades? **3.** Do you have to call students by their last names? **4.** Do you have to wear a suit? **5.** Do you have to work in the summer? **6.** Do you have to have a master's degree? **7.** Do you have to work on Saturdays? **8.** Do you have to come to school every day?

5-10 mins

1. Say: *Now you're going to interview me.* Have students read the direction line. Model the example with a student.

2. Have students interview you. Remind them to review grammar chart **9.11** on page 282 if necessary.

EXERCISE 27
Answers will vary.

10-15 mins

1. Ask: *What do students and teachers have to or don't have to do in your country?* Have students read the direction line. Go over the example with the class. Tell them they can use the ideas from Exercise 25 to help them.

2. Have students complete the exercise individually. Remind them to review grammar chart **9.11** on page 282 if necessary. Then

have students compare answers in groups. If possible, put students from different countries together.

Practice Idea: Writing and Speaking

Have students make a poster with things you have to or don't have to do in their countries. If possible, have pairs or groups from the same country work together. Display the posters around the classroom. Have a class discussion comparing the posters.

EXERCISE 28

ANSWERS: 1. buy 2; **2.** buy (OR get); **3.** put back (OR pay full price for); **4.** send; **5.** show her driver's license; **6.** go to (OR use)

10-15 mins

1. Have students read the direction line. Go over the example with the class.

2. Have students complete the exercise individually. Remind them to review grammar chart **9.11** on page 282 if necessary. Go over the answers as a class.

Practice Idea: Speaking

Have students change the statements about what Judy has to or doesn't have to do into the first person (e.g., *I have to use it by tomorrow or I won't get the discount.*). Then have students practice saying the statements in pairs.

9.12 *Must* and *Have To*

5-10 mins

1. Have students look at grammar chart **9.12** on page 284. Point out that the affirmative *must* and *have to* have similar meanings, but the negatives *mustn't* and *don't have to* are very different. Go over the examples. *Must* and *have to* can both be used for rules, although *must* sounds much more formal. *Have to* can also be used for personal obligation.

2. Say: Must not *means that something is prohibited or against the law.* Don't have to

simply means that something is not necessary.
Go over the example sentences.

EXERCISE 29

ANSWERS: 1. don't have to; **2.** don't have to; **3.** must not; **4.** must not; **5.** don't have to

10-15 mins

1. Say: *In this exercise, you have to decide when to use* have to, don't have to, must, *or* must not. Have students read the direction line. Say: *Remember that* have to *and* must *are similar in meaning, but* don't have to *and* must not *are different.* Go over the examples with the class.

2. Have students complete the exercise individually. Remind them to review grammar chart **9.12** on page 284 if necessary. Go over the answers with the class.

Practice Idea: Writing

Have students write about rules and regulations at their workplace. Make sure students use *have to/ don't have to* and *must/must not*.

9.13 *Might/May* and *Will*

10-15 mins

1. Have students look at grammar chart **9.13** on page 285. Have students read the example sentences. Explain that *might* and *may* have the same meaning. Both show possibility. The adverb *maybe* also has the same meaning. All three mean *it's possible.* Tell students not to confuse *maybe* (the adverb) and *may be* (the verb—e.g., *I may be free tomorrow night.*).

2. Have students go back to the reading on page 274. Have them substitute *may* for *might* and *might* for *may* in the text.

3. Explain that the negative of *may* is *may not* and the negative of *might* is *might not,* and that there are no contractions for *may not* or *might not.*

4. *Will* expresses certainty of something happening in the future. Point out the *if* clauses in the two example sentences: *If the price is 3 for $1.00, you will pay 34¢ for one. If the sign says "Two for one," the store will give you one item for free.*

EXERCISE 30

ANSWERS: 1. be; **2.** get (OR receive); **3.** have (OR get); **4.** go down; **5.** not be fresh (OR be spoiled); **6.** buy (OR try) a different brand

10-15 mins

1. Have students read the direction line. Ask: *What do you write after* may *or* might? (a verb in the base form) Go over the example with the class.

2. Have students complete the exercise individually. Remind them to review grammar chart **9.13** on page 285 if necessary. Go over the answers with the class.

EXERCISE 31
Answers will vary.

10-15 mins

1. Say: *This time you have to write* may, might, *or* will. *Remember, you can use* may *and* might *interchangeably: they mean the same thing.* Have students read the direction line. Go over the examples with the class.

2. Have students complete the exercise individually. Remind them to review grammar chart **9.13** on page 285 if necessary. Then have students compare statements in pairs. Monitor pair work. Have volunteers share some of their statements with the class.

9.14 Making Requests

5-10 mins

1. Have students cover up grammar chart **9.14** on page 286. Tell one student: *Stand up.* Then say to another student: *Could you stand up?* Explain that imperatives like *stand up, sit down, don't run,* etc., can be used to make a request, but that modals can also be used for requests. They sound softer and more polite. Say: *Could you stand up? Could you sit down?*

2. Have students look at grammar chart **9.14**. Explain that the imperative is the base form of the verb. The subject is *you,* but it's not spoken. For negative, put *don't* in front of the verb. Go over the example sentences.

3. *May* and *could* are both used for requests. Go over the two example sentences.

The Customer Service Counter READING

1. Have students look at the title of the reading. Ask: *What is the reading about?* Have students make predictions.

2. Preteach any vocabulary words students may not know such as *cash, fill out,* and *approval.*

Reading Glossary

approval: permission; consent
cash: to exchange a check for currency
fill out: to complete

BEFORE YOU READ

1. Have students discuss the questions in pairs.
2. Ask for a few volunteers to share their answers with the class.

 Reading

CD 2
TR 12

1. Before reading, have students fill out the check-cashing application on page 288.

10-15 mins

2. Have students read the text silently. Tell them to pay special attention to requests. Then play the audio and have students read along silently.

3. Check students' comprehension. Ask questions such as: *Where is there a check-cashing service?* (at the customer service counter at Nick's) *What does person A need to cash a check?* (a check-cashing card) *What does person A have to fill out to get a check-cashing card?* (an application) *What mistakes did person A make in filling out the application?* (wrote in the gray box; wrote the date incorrectly) *When will person A get the check-cashing card?* (in a week to ten days)

> ### Practice Idea: Listening
>
> To practice listening skills, have students first listen to the audio alone. Ask a few comprehension questions such as: *What does person A need to do?* (cash a check) *Does person A have a check-cashing card?* (no) *What else does person A do at the customer service counter?* (buy stamps). Then have students open their books and read along as they listen to the audio.

9.15 Imperatives

10-15 mins

1. Have students cover up grammar chart **9.15** on page 289. Remind students that modals can make requests sound more polite. Go over the examples.

2. Have students cover up grammar chart **9.15**. Make a matching exercise on the board. Write the following sentences on one side of the board:

   1. *Please sign your name at the bottom.*
   2. *Stand up!*
   3. *Watch out! There's a car coming.*
   4. *Always do your best.*
   5. *Have a nice day.*
   6. *Go away.*

   On the other side of the board, write:

   a. *to give a warning*
   b. *in some impolite expressions*
   c. *to give a command*
   d. *to give instructions*
   e. *to give encouragement*
   f. *in certain conversational expressions*

   Say: *Match the examples with the explanations.*

3. Tell students to look at grammar chart **9.15**. Say: *Check your work with the grammar chart.* Point out any errors. Go over all the example sentences.

4. Explain that *let's (let us)* + the base form of a verb is used to make a suggestion. Go over the examples.

EXERCISE 32 ≡★

ANSWERS: 1. Fill; **2.** Don't use; **3.** Write (OR Print); **4.** write (OR include); **5.** Don't write (OR put); **6.** don't fill; **7.** give (OR include); **8.** Write (OR Put); **9.** Give

---

1. Have students read the direction line. Go over the example with the class. Point out that students need to choose either an affirmative or negative imperative verb.

2. Have students complete the exercise individually. Remind them to review grammar chart **9.15** on page 289 if necessary. Then have students compare statements in pairs. Monitor pair work.

EXERCISE 33

Answers will vary.

 10-15 mins

1. Tell students that they will be giving instructions for one of the activities listed. Have students read the direction line. Go over the example with the class.

2. Have students complete the exercise in pairs. Remind them to review grammar chart **9.15** on page 289 if necessary. Monitor pair work. If possible, have pairs who wrote about the same activity compare their instructions.

Practice Idea: Writing

Have pairs write each line of their instructions on strips of paper. Then have them exchange strips with another pair. The pairs should try to put the instructions in the correct order, and then guess what the instructions are for.

EXERCISE 34

Answers will vary.

10-15 mins

1. Say: *Think about the things I always ask you to do in class. Think about the instructions, commands, and requests I give you. You're going to write some of them down.* Have students read the direction line. Go over the examples with the class.

2. Have students complete the exercise individually. Remind them to review grammar chart **9.15** on page 289 if necessary. Then have students read their sentences to the class.

EXERCISE 35

ANSWERS: 1. walk; **2.** bring (OR take); **3.** go (OR hurry); **4.** buy (OR get); **5.** walk; **6.** drive (OR take the car)

10-15 mins

1. Say: *In this exercise, we're going to practice* let's. Have students read the direction line. Go over the example with the class.

2. Have students complete Exercise 35 individually. Remind them to review grammar chart **9.15** on page 289 if necessary. Check answers as a class. Then have students practice the conversation in pairs. Monitor pair work.

Practice Idea: Speaking

Have students write dialogs in pairs. Make sure students use *let's* in the dialogs. Tell students to use the dialog in Exercise 35 as a model. Have students practice their dialogs. Have volunteers role play their dialogs for the class.

EXERCISE 36

Answers will vary.

10-15 mins

1. Say: *What things would you like to do or would you like me to do in class?* Have students read the direction line. Go over the examples with the class.

2. Have students complete the exercise in pairs. Remind them to review grammar chart **9.15** on page 289 if necessary. Then have students compare their suggestions in groups. Have groups report to the class.

9.16 Using Modals to Make Requests and Ask Permission

5-10 mins

1. Have students cover up grammar chart **9.16** on page 292. Tell one student: *Raise your hand.* Then say to another student: *Could you raise your hand?* Write the two requests on the board. Ask: *Are both of these requests?* (yes) *Which one is more polite?* (*Could you raise your hand?*) Explain that both imperatives and modals can be used to make a request or ask permission, but that modals sound softer and more polite.

2. Make a matching exercise on the board. Write the examples and explanations from the grammar chart on the board in random order. On one side of the board, write:

1. *May/Can I help you?*
2. *Why don't you fill out another form?*
3. *Would/Could you cash my check, please?*
4. *I would like to cash a check.*
5. *May/Could/Can I use your pen, please?*

On the other side of the board, write the following explanations:

a. *Use these modals to make a request.*
b. *Use these modals to ask permission.*
c. *This modal means "want."*
d. *Use this phrase to offer a suggestion.*
e. *Use these expressions to offer help.*

Say: *Match the examples with the explanations.*

3. Tell students to look at grammar chart **9.16**. Say: *Check your work with the grammar chart.* Point out any errors. Go over all the example sentences.

Presentation Idea

Have students go back to the reading on pages 287–288. Have students read through for modals and imperatives. Ask students to identify the use for the modal or imperative (making a request, offer help, etc.). Have students work in pairs.

EXERCISE 37

ANSWERS: 1. I'd like to buy a new computer. **2.** Could (OR Would) you show me your latest models? **3.** Would you like to see the laptops or the desktops? **4.** Could (OR Would) you show me the desktops? **5.** Could (OR Would) you turn it on? **6.** Why don't you buy this computer? **7.** Could (OR Would) you tell me the price? **8.** May (OR Can OR Could) I take it home and try it out? **9.** Would you like to buy a service contract? **10.** Can (OR May OR Could) I see the service contract?

10-15 mins

1. Say: *This is a conversation between a salesperson and a customer in an electronics store. We're going to make the conversation more polite by using modals.* Have students

read the direction line. Go over the example with the class.

2. Have students complete the exercise individually. Remind them to review grammar chart **9.16** on page 292 if necessary. Go over the answers with the class.

Practice Idea: Speaking

Have students practice the conversation or create similar conversations in pairs. Ask volunteers to role-play the conversation in front of the class.

Summary of Lesson 9

30-40 mins

1. Imperatives. Remind students that for an imperative, you use the base form of the verb. In groups, have students take turns giving each other commands (e.g., *Sit down. Write your name.*). If necessary, have students review:

9.15 Imperatives (p. 289)

2. *Let's.* Remind students that *let's* is the contraction of *let us* and that it is used for making suggestions. Have students make a list of things to do and places to go in their countries. Then have students work in pairs to plan a trip and itinerary to each country (e.g., *Let's go to Bogotá. Let's visit the Museum of Gold. Then let's see a bullfight.*). If necessary, have students review:

9.15 Imperatives (p. 289)

3. Infinitive patterns. Review infinitive patterns. Have students write a sentence for each infinitive pattern:

Sentence 1: verb followed by an infinitive
Sentence 2: *it* + *be* + adjective + infinitive
Sentence 3: *be* + adjective + infinitive
Sentence 4: using an infinitive to show purpose
Sentence 5: object before an infinitive

If necessary, have students review:

9.2 Verbs Followed by an Infinitive (p. 263)
9.3 *It* + *Be* + Adjective + Infinitive (p. 265)
9.4 *Be* + Adjective + Infinitive (p. 267)

9.5 Using an Infinitive to Show Purpose (p. 268)

9.6 Object Before an Infinitive (p. 270)

4. **Modals.** Review modals. Go over examples and explanations in the chart. Have students work in pairs to write sentences for each modal. Monitor pair work. Give help as needed. If necessary, have students review:

9.7 Overview of Modals (p. 273)

9.8 *Can* (p. 275)

9.9 *Should* (p. 277)

9.10 *Must* (p. 280)

9.11 *Have To* (p. 282)

9.12 *Must* and *Have To* (p. 284)

9.13 *Might/May* and *Will* (p. 285)

9.14 Making Requests (p. 286)

9.16 Using Modals to Make Requests and Ask Permission (p. 292)

Editing Advice

10-15 mins

Have students close their books. Write the first few sentences without editing marks or corrections on the board. For example:

1. *I must to go.*

2. *They like play.*

Ask students to correct each sentence and provide a rule or explanation for each correction. This activity can be done individually, in pairs, or as a class. After students have corrected each sentence, tell them to turn to page 295. Say: *Now compare your work with the Editing Advice in the book.*

Editing Quiz

ANSWERS: 1. me to help you; **2.** want you to be; **3.** It is important to compare; **4.** (in order) to; **5.** can look; **6.** have to pay (OR must pay); **7.** try to use; **8.** C; **9.** C; **10.** easy to make; **11.** C; **12.** happy to help; **13.** can you; **14.** C

10-15 mins

1. Tell students they are going to put the editing advice into practice. Have students read the direction line. Ask: *Do all the shaded words and phrases have mistakes?* (no) Go over the examples with the class. Then do #1 together.

2. Have students complete the quiz individually. Then have them compare answers with a partner before checking answers as a class.

3. For the items students had difficulties with, have them go back and find the relevant grammar chart and review it. Monitor and give help as necessary.

Lesson 9 Test/Review

60-80 mins

Use the Assessment CD-ROM with Exam*View*®, Online Workbook, and Web site for additional practice, review, and assessment materials.

PART 1

ANSWERS: 1. to, don't need to learn; **2.** Ø, must not stop; **3.** to, doesn't expect to pass; **4.** to, don't want to study; **5.** to, doesn't have to give; **6.** Ø, might not have; **7.** to, isn't important to practice; **8.** to, isn't easy to learn; **9.** Ø, Let's not speak; **10.** Ø, don't be

1. Part 1 may also be used in addition to the Assessment CD-ROM with Exam*View*® as an in-class test to assess student performance. Have students read the direction line. Say: *In this exercise, you have to decide if the sentence needs a* to. *Then write the negative form.* Go over the examples with the class.

2. Have students complete Part 1 individually. Collect for assessment.

3. If necessary, have students review:

9.1 Infinitives—An Overview (p. 262)

9.2 Verbs Followed by an Infinitive (p. 263)

9.3 *It + Be + Adjective + Infinitive* (p. 265)

9.4 *Be + Adjective + Infinitive* (p. 267)

9.5 Using an Infinitive to Show Purpose (p. 268)

PART 2

ANSWERS: 1. should I wear a seat belt? **2.** do you want to buy some grapes? **3.** must he fill out the application? **4.** does she need to drive to New York? **5.** can't I park at a bus stop? **6.** is it necessary to eat vegetables? **7.** does she have to buy a car? **8.** would they like to see me?

1. Part 2 may also be used in addition to the Assessment CD-ROM with Exam*View*® as an in-class test to assess student performance. Have students read the direction line. Remind students that questions without modals or the verb *be* will need *do* or *does*. Go over the examples with the class.

2. Have students complete Part 2 individually. Collect for assessment.

3. If necessary, have students review:

   9.7 Overview of Modals (p. 273)
   9.8 *Can* (p. 275)
   9.9 *Should* (p. 277)
   9.10 *Must* (p. 280)
   9.11 *Have To* (p. 282)
   9.12 *Must* and *Have To* (p. 284)
   9.13 *Might/May* and *Will* (p. 285)

PART 3

ANSWERS: 1. Could; **2.** can; **3.** Can; **4.** may; **5.** should; **6.** Do I have to; **7.** don't have to; **8.** should; **9.** may; **10.** will; **11.** would; **12.** Can; **13.** should

1. Part 3 may also be used in addition to the Assessment CD-ROM with Exam*View*® as an in-class test to assess student performance. Have students read the direction line. Say: *This is a phone conversation between a woman and her mechanic. The mechanic is fixing her car. In this exercise, you have to choose the correct modal.* Go over the example as a class.

2. Have students complete Part 3 individually. Collect for assessment.

3. If necessary, have students review:

   9.8 *Can* (p. 275)
   9.9 *Should* (p. 277)
   9.10 *Must* (p. 280)
   9.11 *Have To* (p. 282)
   9.12 *Must* and *Have To* (p. 284)
   9.13 *Might/May* and *Will* (p. 285)

PART 4

ANSWERS: 1. D; **2.** D; **3.** S; **4.** D; **5.** S; **6.** D; **7.** D; **8.** D; **9.** S; **10.** S; **11.** D; **12.** D

1. Part 4 may also be used in addition to the Assessment CD-ROM with Exam*View*® as an

in-class test to assess student performance. Have students read the direction line. Go over the examples with the class.

2. Have students complete Part 4 individually. Collect for assessment.

3. If necessary, have students review:

   9.8 *Can* (p. 275)
   9.9 *Should* (p. 277)
   9.10 *Must* (p. 280)
   9.11 *Have To* (p. 282)
   9.12 *Must* and *Have To* (p. 284)
   9.13 *Might/May* and *Will* (p. 285)

PART 5

ANSWERS: 1. don't have to; **2.** don't have to, can; **3.** should; **4.** don't have to; **5.** May; **6.** should; **7.** don't have to; **8.** might; **9.** can't; **10.** must not

1. Part 5 may also be used in addition to the Assessment CD-ROM with Exam*View*® as an in-class test to assess student performance. Have students read the direction line.

2. Have students complete Part 5 individually. Collect for assessment.

3. If necessary, have students review:

   9.8 *Can* (p. 275)
   9.9 *Should* (p. 277)
   9.10 *Must* (p. 280)
   9.11 *Have To* (p. 282)
   9.12 *Must* and *Have To* (p. 284)
   9.13 *Might/May* and *Will* (p. 285)

Expansion

These expansion activities provide opportunities for students to interact with one another and further develop their speaking and writing skills. Encourage students to use grammar from this lesson whenever possible.

CLASSROOM ACTIVITIES

1. Have students do the activity in pairs. They can either complete the chart together or complete individually and then compare. If possible, have students from different countries work together.

10-15 mins per activity

Practice Idea: Writing

Ask: *What other structures can we use to give advice, suggestions, or warnings to people who are getting married? (should, have to/don't have to,* imperatives*) Add more advice to your charts using these structures or modals.*

2. Have students work individually to fill out the chart. Then put students in pairs to compare charts.

Practice Idea: Speaking

For Activities 1 and 2, have students create a dialog based on the advice they give. Ask volunteers to role-play their dialogs in front of the class.

3. Have students work in groups to fill out the chart. Then have each group compare their chart with another group's.

Practice Idea: Writing

Have students write a letter or e-mail to a friend who is planning to come to the U.S. to study. Tell students to use the information they wrote in the chart to write the letter.

4. Have students work in pairs to write instructions for any one of the three situations listed in the book.

5. Ask students ahead of time to bring in any kind of application. If possible, have several applications on hand in case students forget theirs. Have students work in pairs: one gives instructions, the other fills out the application. Monitor pair work and give help as needed.

6. Ask students ahead of time to bring in circulars from stores. If possible, have several store circulars on hand in case students forget theirs. Have students compare their ads in pairs.

TALK ABOUT IT

 10-15 mins Elicit from the students ways to save money when you shop and write their ideas on the board. Then have students discuss the questions in groups. Have groups report to the class.

WRITE ABOUT IT

 20-30 mins

1. Model an example for the class. Write on the board, for example: *In my country, we don't use rebate checks, and there aren't very many coupons. Most of the time, especially in the small stores, you have to pay in cash.* Then have students write their own paragraph in pairs following your model. If possible, have students from the same country work together.

2. Have students read the start of the composition. Then have them brainstorm ideas with a partner (e.g., *look on the Internet; go to several stores, etc.*). Then have them work on their own to write a composition giving advice about shopping in the U.S. Tell them to use the model to help them.

Practice Idea: Writing

Have students exchange first drafts with a partner. Ask students to help their partners edit their drafts. Refer students to the Editing Advice on page 295.

INTERNET ACTIVITIES

1. Tell students: *You're going to comparison shop for electronics on the Internet.* Suggest products such as a DVD player, TV, digital camera, or computer. Ask students to find prices for two items. Have students make a chart of the products they looked for and the prices they found. Survey the class. Who found the best prices?

2. Tell students to use the Internet to find application forms. (Examples: change-of-address form from the post office; application for a checking account from a bank; application for a credit card; application for a frequent flyer program from an airline; motor vehicle registration form in your state). Have them look for an application on the Internet and ask them to print out the application and bring it in to class to fill out.

Lesson 10

Lesson Overview

GRAMMAR

Ask: *What did we study in Lesson 9?* (infinitives, modals, and imperatives) *What will we study in this lesson?* (count and noncount nouns, quantity words) *Give me examples of count* (eggs, apples) *and noncount* (milk, coffee) *nouns. What's a quantity word?* (a word that describes how much there is of a count or noncount noun) Have students give examples. Write them on the board.

CONTEXT

1. Ask: *What are we going to learn about in this lesson?* (nutrition and health) Activate students' prior knowledge. Ask: *Are you a healthy eater? What foods are healthy? What foods are unhealthy?*

2. Have students share their knowledge and personal experiences.

Presentation Idea

The topic for this lesson can be enhanced with the following ideas:

1. Pictures of food talked about in the lesson
2. Food packages with nutritional information
3. The food pyramid

10.1 Count and Noncount Nouns—An Overview

5-10 mins

1. Write on one side of the board: *one apple— two apples, one egg—twelve eggs, one bean— three beans.* On the other side of the board, write: *bread, milk, cheese.* Ask: *What's the difference between these two groups of nouns?* (The first group has both singular and plural forms. The second group does not have a plural form.) Say: *Nouns can be divided into two*

groups: count and noncount nouns. Ask: *Which one is the first group here on the board?* (count) *Which is the second group?* (noncount)

2. Have students look at grammar chart **10.1** on page 306. Go over the examples and explanations.

A Healthy Diet READING

1. Have students look at the photo. Ask: *What is this woman doing?* (reading the label on a box of food) *Why is she doing it?* (to look at the nutritional information)

2. Have students look at the title of the reading. Ask: *What is the reading about?* Have students use the title and the pictures to make predictions about the reading.

3. Preteach any vocabulary words students may not know, such as *carbohydrate, supplement, package,* and *ingredient.*

Reading Glossary

carbohydrate: any of a group of nutrients, such as sugar and starch, that provides the body with energy

ingredient: a part of something

package: a container, especially one wrapped up and sealed

supplement: something added to an existing thing to complete or improve it

BEFORE YOU READ

1. Have students discuss the questions in pairs.

2. Ask for a few volunteers to share their answers with the class.

 Reading

CD 2 TR 13

10-15 mins

1. Have students read the text silently. Tell them to pay special attention to count and noncount nouns. Then play the audio and have students read along silently.

2. Check students' comprehension. Ask questions such as: *What is the best kind of carbohydrate?*

(whole grains) *Name some good vegetables to eat.* (broccoli, carrots, peas, and corn) *What kinds of problems can a diet with a lot of red meat cause?* (heart disease, diabetes, and cancer) *Is all fat bad?* (No; fat from olive oil and nuts is very good, for example.)

Practice Idea: Listening

To practice listening skills, have students first listen to the audio alone. Ask a few comprehension questions such as: *Why is it important to eat well?* (to maintain good health) *Is brown rice or white rice healthier?* (brown rice) *What is cholesterol?* (cholesterol is a substance found in animal foods) Then have students open their books and read along as they listen to the audio.

10.2 Noncount Nouns

 10-15 mins

1. Have students cover up grammar chart **10.2** on pages 307–308. Write these four categories across the board:

   a. *Nouns that have no distinct, separate parts. We look at the whole.*

   b. *Nouns that have parts that are too small or insignificant to count.*

   c. *Nouns that are classes or categories of things. The members of the category are not the same.*

   d. *Nouns that are abstractions.*

2. Have students go back to the reading on pages 306–307. Ask: *Which group do the nouns in the reading belong to? Write them in your notebooks under the correct group.* Have volunteers write the words on the board.

3. Then have students look at grammar chart **10.2**. Say: *Now compare your work with the chart.* Go over any errors.

4. Remind students that noncount nouns do not have a plural. Write on the board: *air.* Say: *You can't write* airs.

EXERCISE 1

ANSWERS: 1. milk; **2.** cholesterol; **3.** candy; **4.** nutrition; **5.** milk (OR cream OR sugar); **6.** Olive oil, Butter; **7.** Coffee; **8.** salt; **9.** sugar

5-10 mins

1. Have students read the direction line. Ask: *What are you going to write on the blanks?* (noncount nouns) Go over the example in the book.

2. Have students complete Exercise 1 individually. Remind them to review grammar chart **10.2** on pages 307–308 if necessary. Check the answers as a class.

EXERCISE 2

ANSWERS: 1. mail; **2.** snow; **3.** popcorn; **4.** homework; **5.** sand; **6.** happiness; **7.** advice; **8.** unemployment

5-10 mins

1. Have students read the direction line. Remind students that the noncount nouns for this exercise are in grammar chart **10.2** on pages 307–308. Go over the example in the book.

2. Have students complete Exercise 2 individually. Remind them to review grammar chart **10.2** on pages 307–308 if necessary. Then have students compare answers in pairs. Check answers as a class.

Practice Idea: Speaking

Have students work in pairs to identify the group from grammar chart **10.2** that each noncount noun in Exercise 2 belongs to (group A, B, C, or D).

10.3 Count and Noncount Nouns

5-10 mins

1. Write on the board:

   rice

   beans

   fruit

   food

   candy

Ask: *Are these count or noncount nouns?* Say: *Sometimes things in grammar are not logical. Rice is noncount but beans are count. You have to learn the exceptions. Fruit, food, and candy are noncount nouns when they are used as a general term. For example: The food at this hotel is good. But if you mean kinds of food or kinds of fruit, they can be count nouns. For example: Oranges and lemons are fruits that contain a lot of Vitamin C. Candy is generally noncount, but if you are talking about pieces of candy, then you can use the plural form. For example: There are three candies on the table.*

2. Review the example sentences in the chart.

EXERCISE 3

ANSWERS: 1. fruit; **2.** fruits; **3.** candy; **4.** food; **5.** foods; **6.** rice, beans

5-10 mins

1. Remind students that some noncount nouns have a plural form when the meaning is different (e.g., *fruit/fruits, candy/candies*). Have students read the direction line. Go over the example in the book.

2. Have students complete Exercise 3 individually. Remind them to review grammar chart **10.3** on page 309 if necessary. Go over the answers as a class.

10.4 Describing Quantities of Count and Noncount Nouns

10-15 mins

1. Have students cover up grammar chart **10.4** on page 310. Say: *We can use numbers with count nouns, but we can't use numbers with noncount nouns. With noncount nouns, we use units of measure, such as* a bottle, a glass, a can, *etc.*

2. Write the following categories across the board in chart form:

   container

   portion

   measurement

shape or whole piece

other

Then write a list of ten phrases on one side of the board:

a bag of flour

a pound of meat

a work of art

a slice of pizza

a carton of milk

a piece of meat

a quart of oil

a piece of information

a roll of film

an ear of corn

Say: *Try to guess where these nouns and units of measure go.* Have volunteers fill in the chart on the board with the ten phrases.

3. Have students look at grammar chart **10.4**. Say: *Now compare your work with the chart.* Go over any errors. Review the example sentences and the units of measure in the chart.

EXERCISE 4

Answers will vary.

10-15 mins

1. Have students read the direction line. Ask: *What do we write on the blanks?* (a logical quantity/unit of measure) Go over the examples in the book.

2. Have students complete the exercise individually. Remind them to review grammar chart **10.4** on page 310 if necessary. Go over the answers with the class.

> ### Practice Idea: Writing
>
> Have students write about the food they bought or ate over the last week (e.g., *On Monday, I ate two slices of pizza. I also drank a can of soda and half a gallon of milk.*).

Practice Idea: Speaking

Bring in a ball (such as a soccer ball). Have students sit in a circle or have groups sit in a circle. Say: *The person who has the ball throws the ball to someone else and says a unit of measure such as* a piece. *The person who catches it must say the unit of measure plus a noncount noun that can be used with it. For example,* a piece of cake. *Then that person throws the ball to someone and calls out another unit of measure, and so on.*

10.5 *A Lot Of, Much, Many*

5-10 mins

1. Have students go back to the reading on pages 306–307. Say: Many, a lot of, *and* much *mean a large number of something. Scan quickly through the article. Circle* a lot of, much, *and* many *and the nouns that follow.* Ask: *What kind of nouns follow* a lot of? (count and noncount) *Much?* (noncount) *Many?* (count)

2. Have students look at grammar chart **10.5** on page 311. Say: *Use* many *for count nouns and* a lot of *for count and noncount nouns. Use* much *in negative sentences and questions with noncount nouns.* Go over the examples.

3. Direct students to the Language Notes. Explain that when the noun is omitted, use *a lot*, not *a lot of*.

EXERCISE 5

ANSWERS: 1. a lot of; **2.** a lot of; **3.** Many (OR A lot of); **4.** much; **5.** many (OR a lot of); **6.** a lot of; **7.** many; **8.** much; **9.** much; **10.** a lot of; **11.** a lot of

5-10 mins
1. Have students read the direction line. Remind them that sometimes more than one answer is possible. Go over the examples in the book.

2. Have students complete Exercise 5 individually. Remind them to review grammar chart **10.5** on page 311 if necessary. Go over the answers with the class.

10.6 *A Few, A Little*

5-10 mins
Have students look at grammar chart **10.6** on page 312. Say: *A few* and *a little mean small quantities. We use* a few *with count nouns and* a little *with noncount nouns.* Go over the examples.

EXERCISE 6

ANSWERS: 1. a little; **2.** a few (OR several; **3.** a little; **4.** a few (OR several); **5.** A few (OR Several); **6.** a little; **7.** a few (OR several); **8.** a little; **9.** a little; **10.** a few (OR several)

5-10 mins
1. Have students read the direction line. Go over the examples in the book.

2. Have students complete Exercise 6 individually. Remind them to review grammar chart **10.6** on page 312 if necessary. Go over the answers with the class.

10.7 *Some, Any, No, and A/An*

5-10 mins
1. Have students look at grammar chart **10.7** on page 313. Say: *We are going to look at the use of* some, any, no, *and* a/an *in affirmative and negative sentences and in questions.* Point out the top of the chart. Read through the categories (singular count, plural count, and noncount).

2. Say: *For affirmative sentences, we use* a/an *with singular nouns,* some *with plural nouns, and* some *with noncount nouns.* Go over all of the sentences.

3. Say: *For questions, you can use* some *or* any *with plural and noncount nouns. With singular nouns we use* a/an. Go over the sentences.

4. Say: *Finally, in the negative, we use* a/an *with singular nouns,* any *after negative verbs with plural nouns, and* any *after negative verbs with noncount nouns.* Go over all of the sentences. Explain that if they use an affirmative verb, they can use *no* before a plural noun and a noncount noun.

EXERCISE 7

ANSWERS: 1. some; **2.** any; **3.** some (OR any); **4.** any; **5.** some; **6.** any; **7.** an; **8.** some (OR any); **9.** a; **10.** any

5-10 mins
1. Have students read the direction line. Ask: *When do we use* an? (*An* is used before a vowel sound.) Go over the example in the book.

2. Have students complete Exercise 7 individually. Remind them to review grammar chart **10.7** on page 313 if necessary. Go over the answers with the class.

EXERCISE 8

Answers will vary.

10-15 mins

1. Have students read the direction line. Go over the examples. Ask: *How do we say:* no Cuban students in the class? (*There aren't any Cuban students in the class* or *There are no Cuban students in the class.*)

2. Have students answer the questions individually. Remind them to review grammar chart **10.7** on page 313 if necessary. Quickly go over the answers as a class.

EXERCISE 9 =★

ANSWERS: 1. a lot of; **2.** no; **3.** any; **4.** some (OR a little); **5.** a lot of; **6.** some (OR a little); **7.** a lot of (OR much); **8.** some (OR a little); **9.** any (OR a little OR some); **10.** any, any

10-15 mins

1. Have students read the direction line. Remind them that more than one answer may be possible. Say: *For example, sometimes* much *and a lot of can be used for the same noun.* Go over the example. Ask: *What are some other expressions of quantity?* (*much, many, a little, a few,* etc.)

2. Have students answer the questions individually. Remind them to review grammar charts **10.4** on page 310, **10.5** on page 311, **10.6** on page 312, and **10.7** on page 313 if necessary. Then have students compare answers in pairs. Circulate to give help as needed.

Practice Idea: Speaking

Have students discuss their countries' food and diet in groups. If possible, put students from different countries together. Have groups report interesting information to the class.

EXERCISE 10

ANSWERS: 1. Do you eat much rice? **2.** Do you eat much fish? **3.** Do you eat much chicken? **4.** Do you eat much pork? **5.** Do you eat much bread? **6.** Do you eat much cheese? **7.** Do you drink much apple juice? **8.** Do you drink much lemonade? **9.** Do you drink much milk? **10.** Do you drink

much tea? **11.** Do you drink much coffee? **12.** Do you drink much soda or pop?

10-15 mins

1. Have students read the direction line. Say: *Remember,* much *is used with questions and with the negative for noncount nouns.* Go over the examples in the book. Model the examples with volunteers.

2. Have students complete Exercise 10 in pairs. Remind them to review grammar chart **10.5** on page 311 if necessary. Have students take turns asking and answering questions. Monitor pair work. Give help as needed.

EXERCISE 11

Answers will vary.

10-15 mins

1. Have students read the direction line. Ask: *What kind of questions are we asking?* (yes/no questions) *Make sure to answer with a complete answer.* Go over the examples in the book. Model the examples with volunteers.

2. Have students complete Exercise 11 in pairs. Remind them to review grammar charts **10.5** on page 311, **10.6** on page 312, and **10.7** on page 313 if necessary. Have them take turns asking and answering questions. Circulate to observe pair work. Give help as needed.

Practice Idea: Speaking

Create two rings of students. Have half of the students stand in an outer ring around the classroom. Have the other half stand in an inner ring, facing the outer ring. Instruct students to ask and answer the questions from Exercise 10 or 11. Call out *turn* every minute or so. Students in the inner ring should move one space clockwise. Students now ask and answer with their new partners. Have students ask questions in random order. Make sure students look at each other when they're speaking.

EXERCISE 12

CD 2 TR 14

ANSWERS: 1. a few; **2.** a lot of; **3.** any; **4.** much; **5.** a lot of; **6.** many; **7.** a lot of; **8.** a lot of; **9.** much; **10.** much; **11.** a lot of; **12.** a lot

1. Have students read the direction line. Go over the example. Explain that this is a conversation between a husband and a wife. Point out the photo of the husband and wife.

2. Have students complete Exercise 12 individually. Remind them to review grammar charts **10.5** on page 311, **10.6** on page 312, and **10.7** on page 313 if necessary. Check answers as a class. Then have students practice the conversations in pairs.

Practice Idea: Listening

To provide practice with listening skills, have students close their books and listen to the audio. Repeat the audio as needed. Ask comprehension questions, such as: *Where did the husband call from?* (work) *How many times did he call?* (many times) *Did the wife answer the phone?* (no) Then have students open their books and complete Exercise 12.

Practice Idea: Speaking

Have students role-play all or part of the conversation in front of the class.

 EXERCISE 13

CD 2
TR 15
ANSWERS: **1.** some (OR a little); **2.** any; **3.** glass; **4.** slices; **5.** some (OR any); **6.** many (OR a few OR several); **7.** some (OR a little); **8.** some (OR any); **9.** piece of (OR slice of); **10.** some (OR a little); **11.** some (OR a little); **12.** any (OR much OR a lot of)

1. Explain that this is a conversation at a restaurant between a waitress and a customer. Direct students' attention to the picture of the waitress and customer. Have students read the direction line. Go over the example. Remind students that more than one answer may be possible.

2. Have students complete Exercise 13 individually. Remind them to review grammar charts **10.5** on page 311, **10.6** on page 312, and **10.7** on page 313 if necessary. Check answers as a class. Then have students practice the conversations in pairs.

Practice Idea: Listening

To provide practice with listening skills, have students close their books and listen to the audio. Repeat the audio as needed. Ask comprehension questions, such as: *What does the customer want to drink?* (coffee with cream and orange juice) *What kind of eggs does the customer want?* (scrambled) *Does the customer want pancakes?* (yes) Then have students open their books and complete Exercise 13.

Practice Idea: Speaking

Have students create similar conversations. Then have volunteers role-play their conversations in front of the class.

Eat Less, Live Longer READING

1. Have students look at the title of the reading. Ask: *What is the reading about? How do you know?* Have students use the title and photo to make predictions about the reading.

2. Preteach any vocabulary words students may not know, such as *overweight* and *consume*.

Reading Glossary

consume: to eat and drink
overweight: heavier than the normal or permitted weight

BEFORE YOU READ

1. Have students discuss the questions in pairs.

2. Ask for a few volunteers to share their answers with the class.

 Reading ═★

CD 2
TR 16
1. Have students read the text silently. Tell them to pay special attention to *too much*, *too many*, and *a lot of*. Then play the audio and have students read along silently.

2. Check students' comprehension. Ask questions such as: *What percentage of Americans are overweight?* (66 percent) *Why are so many*

Americans overweight? (They consume too much and exercise too little.) *What does the Okinawa diet consist of?* (fruit, fish, water, and green tea)

Practice Idea: Listening

To practice listening skills, have students first listen to the audio alone. Ask a few comprehension questions such as: *Why are many Americans overweight?* (they spend too much time in front of the TV and not enough time exercising) *What percent of commercials during children's programs are for food products?* (50 percent) Then have students open their books and read along as they listen to the audio.

Context Note

About 127 million adults in the U.S. are overweight, 60 million are obese, and 9 million are severely obese. Currently, 64.5 percent of U.S. adults are overweight and 30.5 percent are obese. Obesity is the second leading cause of preventable death in the U.S.

10.8 *A Lot Of* vs. *Too Much/ Too Many* ≡★

⏲ 5-10 mins

1. Have students cover up grammar chart **10.8** on page 318. Then have them turn to the reading on page 317. Say: *Find* too many, too much, *and* a lot of. *Pay attention to how they're used. Does the usage feel negative or neutral?*

2. Tell students to look at grammar chart **10.8**. Say: *A lot of is used to describe a large quantity. It is a neutral term. But* too much *and* too many *show that something is excessive.* We use *too much* with noncount nouns and *too many* with count nouns. Go over all the example sentences. Point out that *too much* is also used after verbs.

🔊 CD 2 TR 17

EXERCISE 14 ≡★

ANSWERS: **1.** much; **2.** a lot of; **3.** a lot; **4.** a lot of; **5.** many; **6.** a lot of; **7.** a lot of; **8.** a lot of; **9.** a lot; **10.** a lot of; **11.** a lot of; **12.** too much

⏲ 10-15 mins

1. Explain that this is a conversation between a mother and her 12-year-old son. Have students read the direction line. Go over the example.

2. Have students complete Exercise 14 individually. Remind them to review grammar chart **10.8** on page 318 if necessary. Play the audio and check answers as a class. Then have students practice the conversations in pairs.

Practice Idea: Listening

To provide practice with listening skills, have students close their books and listen to the audio. Ask comprehension questions, such as: *Why is the mother worried about her son?* (She thinks he watches too much TV, eats too much junk food, and doesn't get enough exercise.) *What's the new rule?* (The son can't watch TV until he finishes his homework.) Then have students open their books and complete Exercise 14.

Practice Idea: Speaking

Have students create their own dialogs in pairs. Say: *Use Exercise 14 as a model.* Then have volunteers role-play their conversations in front of the class.

EXERCISE 15

Answers: First part of sentence: 1. much; **2.** many; **3.** much; **4.** many

⏲ 10-15 mins

1. Have students read the direction line. Say: *What tense do we use in the main clause after an* if *clause?* (the future) Go over the example in the book. Have a volunteer model the example.

2. Have students complete the exercise individually. Remind them to review grammar chart **10.8** on page 318 if necessary. Then have students compare answers in pairs. Monitor pair work. Give help as needed.

10.9 *Too Much/ Too Many* vs. *Too* ≡★

⏲ 5-10 mins

1. Have students look at grammar chart **10.9** on page 320. Say: *We use too with adjectives and adverbs.* Too much *and* too many *are used with nouns.* Too much *is used with noncount nouns, and* too many *is used with count nouns.*

2. Go over the examples and explanations in the grammar chart.

EXERCISE 16

ANSWERS: Situation A: 1. too; **2.** too many; **3.** too; **4.** too; **5.** too much

Situation B: 1. too; **2.** too much; **3.** too many; **4.** too much; **5.** too many

1. Say: *There are two situations in this exercise. Situation A is about students who are complaining about the cafeteria. Situation B is about students who are complaining about their class and their school.* Have students read the direction line. Ask: *What do we write in the blanks?* (*too, too much,* or *too many*) Go over the example.

2. Have students complete the exercise individually. Remind them to review grammar chart **10.9** on page 320 if necessary. Go over the answers as a class.

EXERCISE 17
Answers will vary.

1. Say: *Now it's your turn to complain!* Have students read the direction line. Go over the example. Model the exercise for the students with your own complaints.

2. Have students complete the exercise individually. Remind them to review grammar chart **10.9** on page 320 if necessary. Then have students compare answers in pairs.

EXERCISE 18

ANSWERS: 1. a lot of; **2.** too; **3.** too; **4.** a lot of; **5.** too much; **6.** a lot of; **7.** a lot of; **8.** too many, too much; **9.** a lot of; **10.** too much

1. Have students read the direction line. Say: *Remember, we use* too, too much, *and* too many *if there is a problem or something is excessive. We use* a lot of *when we want to show a large quantity.* Go over the example. Model the exercise for the students with your own complaints.

2. Have students complete the exercise individually. Remind them to review grammar chart **10.9** on page 320 if necessary. Then have students compare answers in pairs.

EXERCISE 19
CD 2
TR 18

ANSWERS: 1. a lot of (OR any); **2.** a lot of; **3.** a cup of (OR some); **4.** much (OR any OR a lot of); **5.** a few (OR some OR a lot of); **6.** some (OR a can of); **7.** no; **8.** much; **9.** any; **10.** a lot of; **11.** piece of; **12.** too; **13.** too; **14.** some (OR a lot of)

1. Explain that this is a conversation between a doctor and patient. Have students read the direction line. Remind students that in some cases more than one answer is possible. Go over the example.

2. Have students complete Exercise 19 individually. Remind them to review grammar charts **10.4** on page 310, **10.5** on page 311, **10.6** on page 312, **10.7** on page 313, **10.8** on page 318, and **10.9** on page 320 if necessary. Then have students practice the conversation in pairs.

Practice Idea: Speaking

Have pairs of students create a dialog out of one or both of the lists of complaints. Then ask volunteers to role-play their dialogs in front of the class.

Practice Idea: Writing

Have students write a letter of complaint to someone, such as a local government representative, based on the sentences they wrote in Exercise 17.

Practice Idea: Listening

To provide practice with listening skills, have students close their books and listen to the audio. Ask comprehension questions, such as: *How is the patient's cholesterol level?* (too high) *How is the patient's blood pressure?* (too high) *Does the patient eat a lot of salt?* (yes) Then have students open their books and complete Exercise 19.

Practice Idea: Speaking

Have volunteers role-play all or part of the conversation.

Summary of Lesson 10

10-15 mins

Words that we use before count and noncount nouns. Have students cover up the singular count, plural count, and noncount noun columns in the chart. Then go through each word, beginning with *the*, and ask if singular count nouns (such as *book*), plural count nouns (such as *books*), and noncount nouns (such as *tea*) can be used with the word. For an extra challenge, have students write a sentence using the word with a noun. If necessary, have students review Lesson 10.

Editing Advice

10-15 mins

Have students close their books. Write the first few sentences without editing marks or corrections on the board. For example:

1. *I want to give you an advice.*
2. *My mother gave me many advices.*
   He received three mails today.

Ask students to correct each sentence and provide a rule or explanation for each correction. This activity can be done individually, in pairs, or as a class. After students have corrected each sentence, tell them to turn to pages 323–324. Say: *Now compare your work with the Editing Advice in the book.*

Editing Quiz

ANSWERS: 1. Ø (OR very); **2.** advice; **3.** any (OR much); **4.** a lot; **5.** cup of coffee; **6.** little sugar; **7.** two pieces of toast; **8.** a lot of friends; **9.** a fast food place (OR fast food places); **10.** too; **11.** too

10-15 mins

1. Tell students they are going to put the editing advice into practice. Have students read the direction line. Ask: *Do all the shaded words and phrases have mistakes?* (no) Go over the examples with the class. Then do #1 together.

2. Have students complete the quiz individually. Then have them compare answers with a partner before checking answers as a class.

3. For the items students had difficulties with, have them go back and find the relevant grammar chart and review it. Monitor and give help as necessary.

Lesson 10 Test/Review

15-20 mins

Use the Assessment CD-ROM with Exam*View*®, Online Workbook, and Web site for additional practice, review, and assessment materials.

PART 1

ANSWERS: 1. glass; **2.** teaspoon; **3.** gallon; **4.** piece; **5.** bowl; **6.** piece; **7.** piece; **8.** gallon; **9.** sheet; **10.** tube

1. Part 1 may also be used in addition to the Assessment CD-ROM with Exam*View*® as an in-class test to assess student performance. Have students read the direction line. Go over the example with the class.

2. Have students complete Part 1 individually. Collect for assessment.

3. If necessary, have students review:
   10.4 Describing Quantities of Count and Noncount Nouns (p. 310)

PART 2

ANSWERS: 1. much; **2.** A few; **3.** some; **4.** an; **5.** some; **6.** any; **7.** several; **8.** a; **9.** much; **10.** much

1. Part 2 may also be used in addition to the Assessment CD-ROM with Exam*View*® as an in-class test to assess student performance. Have students read the direction line. Go over the example with the class.

2. Have students complete Part 2 individually. Collect for assessment.

3. If necessary, have students review:
   10.5 *A Lot Of, Much, Many* (p. 311)
   10.6 *A Few, A Little* (p. 312)
   10.7 *Some, Any, No,* and *A/An* (p. 313)
   10.8 *A Lot Of* vs. *Too Much/Too Many* (p. 318)

Expansion

These expansion activities provide opportunities for students to interact with one another and further develop their speaking and writing skills. Encourage students to use grammar from this lesson whenever possible.

CLASSROOM ACTIVITIES

10-15 mins per activity

1. Have students work individually to fill out the chart. Then put students in pairs to compare charts. If possible, have students from different countries work together. Then have students compare charts in groups. Ask: *Who is the healthiest person in your group?* Have groups report to the class.

2. Have students work individually to complete the chart. Point out the pictures of the submarine sandwich, tortilla chips, and pretzel. Then have students compare charts in groups. Ask: *What foods are the most popular?* Have groups report to the class.

Practice Idea: Speaking

Have students make a chart with five to ten food items commonly eaten in their native countries. Then have students exchange charts with a partner. Have the pairs fill out each others' charts. Have students discuss interesting food items with the class.

3. Have students work individually to make true statements. Then have students compare answers in pairs.

TALK ABOUT IT

10-15 mins

Have students discuss each question in pairs or in groups and then report to the class. Try to put students from different countries together.

Practice Idea: Speaking

Have students make presentations about food, eating habits, and shopping customs in their countries. Encourage students to make posters, create skits, or even prepare food.

WRITE ABOUT IT

20-30 mins

1. Have students read the direction line. Brainstorm other information to include. Have students help you write the start of a paragraph about shopping for food on the board. Then have students complete the assignment individually. Collect for assessment and/or have students present their paragraphs to a group.

2. Have students read the direction line and the example paragraph. In pairs, have them write a list of ideas about eating in their country. Ask: *What do you eat a lot of? What do you have for breakfast?* to help them with their brainstorming. Then have them write their paragraphs individually. Collect for assessment and/or have students present their paragraphs to a group.

Practice Idea: Writing

Have students exchange first drafts with a partner. Ask students to help their partners edit their drafts. Refer students to the Editing Advice on pages 323–324.

OUTSIDE ACTIVITIES

1. Have students bring to class a package of a food or drink that they enjoy. Have them read the label for "Nutrition Facts" and find out about the calories, grams of fat, cholesterol, sodium, protein, vitamins, and minerals. Tell them to decide if it is a nutritious food. Why or why not? Have students discuss their food in groups. Then do a quick survey. Which food do students think is the least healthy? Which food do they think is the most healthy?

2. Have students bring a favorite recipe to class and explain how to prepare this recipe. Then have them discuss if their recipes are healthy or not.

INTERNET ACTIVITIES

1. Tell students that they are going to find an article on nutrition on the Internet. Have students note any interesting information on nutrition from the article. Then have them compare the information against their own diets. Ask a few volunteers to share their information with the class.

2. Brainstorm names of foods that students like to eat. Check for correct spelling. Tell them to use the Internet to find a recipe for something they like and bring it to class. As an extra challenge, have students find, print out, and bring pictures of the foods to go along with their recipes.

Lesson 11

Lesson Overview

GRAMMAR

Ask: *What did we study in Lesson 10?* (count and noncount nouns, quantity words) *What are we going to study in this lesson?* (adjectives, noun modifiers, and adverbs) *What is an example of an adjective?* (healthy, intelligent, blind) *What is an example of an adverb?* (patiently, quickly) Have students give examples. Write them on the board.

CONTEXT

1. Ask: *What will we learn about in this lesson?* (great women) Activate students' prior knowledge. Ask: *Who is Helen Keller?* (A blind and deaf woman who learned to speak and read Braille. She worked to raise money to build schools for blind people.) *Who is Grandma Moses?* (A woman who became an artist in her seventies. Her paintings hang in famous museums.)

2. Have students share their knowledge and personal experiences. Ask students to name some great women from their countries.

Presentation Idea

The topic for this lesson can be enhanced with the following ideas:

1. A sample of something in Braille
2. A book by Helen Keller; a book about Helen Keller with photos
3. A book on Grandma Moses; prints of Grandma Moses's paintings

Helen Keller   READING

1. Have students look at the photo. Ask: *What's this person doing?* (reading with her fingers) *Does anyone know what this type of reading material is called in English?* (Braille)

2. Have students look at the title of the reading. Ask: *What is the reading about?* Have students use the title and photo to make predictions about the reading.

3. Preteach any vocabulary words students may not know, such as *remarkable, wild, patient, extensive,* and *tireless.*

Reading Glossary

extensive: great in amount or area, considerable
patient: having or showing patience, calm, or being undisturbed
remarkable: worthy of attention, noticeable
tireless: dedicated
wild: unruly, uncontrolled

BEFORE YOU READ

5-10 mins

1. Have students discuss the questions in pairs.
2. Ask for a few volunteers to share their answers with the class.

Reading ═★

CD 2
TR 19

10-15 mins

1. Have students read the text silently. Tell them to pay special attention to adjectives and adverbs. Then play the audio and have students read along silently.

2. Check students' comprehension. Ask questions such as: *Was Helen Keller deaf and blind at birth?* (No, she became deaf and blind after an illness at 19 months.) *What happened when she couldn't understand anything?* (She became frustrated and angry.) *Who taught Helen to communicate?* (Anne Sullivan) *How old was Helen when she graduated from college?* (24)

Practice Idea: Listening

To practice listening skills, have students first listen to the audio alone. Ask a few comprehension questions such as: *How old was Helen when Anne Sullivan became her teacher?* (7) *How old was Helen when she learned to speak?* (10) Then have students open their books and read along as they listen to the audio.

Have students read the information. Ask them if there are similar colleges in their countries.

11.1 Adjectives and Adverbs

5-10 mins

1. Have students cover up grammar chart **11.1** on page 331. Write the sentences from the grammar chart on the board in random order. Underline the adverb or adjective. For example, write:

   Helen learned <u>quickly</u>.

   She became <u>blind</u>.

   Helen was a <u>healthy</u> baby.

   Tell students: *Adjectives describe nouns. We can use adjectives before nouns or after the verbs* be, become, look, seem, *and other sense-perception verbs.* Then say: *Adverbs of manner tell how or in what way we do things. They usually follow the verb phrase.* Ask students which words are adjectives and which words are adverbs. Tell them to pay attention to the verbs they follow.

2. Have students look at grammar chart **11.1**. Say: *Now compare your work with the chart.*

3. Quickly go over the examples and explanations in the chart.

EXERCISE 1

ANSWERS: 1. adj. **2.** adj., adj., adj. **3.** adj. **4.** adv. **5.** adj. **6.** adv. **7.** adv. **8.** adj. **9.** adj. **10.** adv.

5-10 mins

1. Have students read the direction line. Say: *The abbreviation for adjective is* adj. *The abbreviation for adverb is* adv. Go over the examples in the book.

2. Have students complete Exercise 1 individually. Remind them to review grammar chart **11.1** on page 331 if necessary. Check the answers as a class.

11.2 Adjectives

5-10 mins

1. Have students cover up grammar chart **11.2** on page 332. Activate prior knowledge. Say: *I'm going to read you some statements about adjectives; tell me if they are true or false.* Read these statements:

   Adjectives describe verbs. (false)

Adjectives are always singular. (true)

Some words that end in -ed are adjectives— for example, married. *(true)*

We can never put two adjectives before a noun. (false)

2. Then have students look at grammar chart **11.2**. Say: *Let's look at these examples and see if we were wrong or right.* Go over the examples and explanations.

3. Point out that after an adjective, we can substitute a singular noun with *one* and a plural noun with *ones.*

4. Explain that you can only use an article before an adjective if the adjective is in front of a noun.

EXERCISE 2

ANSWERS: 1. normal (OR healthy); **2.** frustrated; **3.** full (OR interesting); **4.** fair (OR equal); **5.** patient (OR good); **6.** intelligent (OR educated OR interesting); **7.** interesting (OR fascinating); **8.** Blind

5-10 mins

1. Have students read the direction line. Ask: *What are we going to write in the blanks?* (an adjective and sometimes an article—*a* or *an*) Go over the examples in the book.

2. Have students complete Exercise 2 individually. Remind them to review grammar chart **11.2** on page 332 if necessary. Go over the answers as a class.

> **Practice Idea: Writing**
>
> Have students write a few sentences about a remarkable person from their countries. Ask them to use adjectives. Have students compare their writing in pairs. Ask volunteers to share their information with the class.

EXERCISE 3

Answers will vary.

5-10 mins

1. Tell students that this exercise is about their class. Have students read the direction line. Ask: *What are we going to write in the blanks?* (an adjective and sometimes an article—*a* or *an*) Go over the examples in the book.

2. Have students complete Exercise 3 individually. Remind them to review grammar chart **11.2** on page 332 if necessary. Have students compare answers in pairs. Monitor pair work. Give help as needed.

EXERCISE 4

ANSWERS: 1. Do you prefer a big city or a small one? **2.** Do you prefer an old house or a new one? **3.** Do you prefer a cold climate or a warm one? **4.** Do you prefer a small car or a big one? **5.** Do you prefer a soft mattress or a hard one? **6.** Do you prefer green grapes or red ones? **7.** Do you prefer red apples or yellow ones? **8.** Do you prefer strict teachers or easy ones? **9.** Do you prefer noisy children or quiet ones? **10.** Do you prefer used textbooks or new ones?

10-15 mins

1. Say: *You're going to learn what things your partner prefers.* Have students read the direction line. Go over the examples in the book. Have volunteers model the examples.

2. Have students complete the exercise in pairs. Remind them to review grammar chart **11.2** on page 332 if necessary. Monitor pair work. Give help as needed.

Practice Idea: Writing

Have students write four more questions to ask their partners. Then do a quick survey of the class to find out what students prefer.

A Special Athlete READING

1. Have students look at the photo. Ask: *What is this woman wearing around her neck?* (a silver medal) *How do you think she won the medal?*

2. Have students look at the title of the reading. Ask: *What is the reading about?* Have students use the title and photo to make predictions about the reading.

3. Preteach any vocabulary words students may not know, such as *compete* and *wheelchair*.

Reading Glossary

compete: participate in a competition or contest
wheelchair: a special chair with wheels that moves so that people who can't walk can be mobile

BEFORE YOU READ

5-10 mins

1. Have students discuss the questions in pairs.

2. Ask for a few volunteers to share their answers with the class.

Reading

CD 2 TR 20

10-15 mins

1. Have students read the text silently. Tell them to pay special attention to nouns that describe nouns. Then play the audio and have students read along silently.

2. Check students' comprehension. Ask questions such as: *How did Gina lose part of her leg?* (in a car accident) *Where did she win a silver medal?* (2008 Paralympic Games in China) *What's her job?* (sports director)

Practice Idea: Listening

To practice listening skills, have students first listen to the audio alone. Ask a few comprehension questions such as: *Which sports could Gina play in a wheelchair?* (waterskiing, basketball, and volleyball) *Which medal did she win at the 2008 Paralympic Games?* (silver) Then have students open their books and read along as they listen to the audio.

11.3 Noun Modifiers

10-15 mins

1. Have students look at grammar chart **11.3** on page 335. Say: *We can use a noun to describe another noun.* Point out that when two nouns come together, the second noun is more general. The first noun describes the second noun.

2. Explain that when two nouns come together, the first noun is always singular. Go over the examples in the chart.

EXERCISE 5

ANSWERS: **1.** book store; **2.** department store;
3. shoe store; **4.** sign language; **5.** eyeglasses;
6. flower pot; **7.** rose garden; **8.** five-dollar bill;
9. six-year-old child; **10.** two-week vacation;
11. toothbrush; **12.** six-foot-tall man

5–10 mins

1. Have students read the direction line. Ask:
   *Which goes first: the general noun or the specific
   noun?* (the specific noun) Go over the example
   in the book.

2. Have students complete Exercise 5
   individually. Remind them to review grammar
   chart **11.3** on page 335 if necessary. Go over
   the answers with the class.

EXERCISE 6

ANSWERS: **1.** wheelchair; **2.** basketball player;
3. ten-year-old child; **4.** college team;
5. bachelor's degree; **6.** community health;
7. gold medal

5–10 mins

1. Have students read the direction line. Say:
   *Remember, when nouns are combined together,
   the first noun is singular.* Go over the example
   in the book.

2. Have students complete Exercise 6
   individually. Remind them to review grammar
   chart **11.3** on page 335 if necessary. Have
   students compare answers in pairs. Monitor
   pair work.

EXERCISE 7

ANSWERS: **1.** college education; **2.** car accident;
3. volleyball player; **4.** eyesight, 19-month-old
baby; **5.** college degree

10–15 mins

1. Have students read the direction line. Say:
   *Remember, when nouns are combined together,
   the first noun is singular.* Go over the example
   in the book.

2. Have students complete Exercise 7
   individually. Remind them to review grammar
   chart **11.3** on page 335 if necessary. Go over
   the answers as a class.

EXERCISE 8

Answers will vary.

10–15 mins

1. Have students read the direction line. Tell
   them they are going to ask and answer
   questions. Go over the example in the book.

2. Have students complete Exercise 8 in pairs.
   Remind them to review grammar chart **11.3**
   on page 335 if necessary. Monitor pair work.

11.4 Comparing Adverbs of Manner and Adjectives ≡★

1. Have students cover up grammar chart **11.4**
   on page 337. Write the following two columns,
   side by side on the board (underline the
   adjectives and adverbs):

   ADJECTIVES

   Anne was a <u>patient</u> teacher.

   Helen was a <u>quick</u> learner.

   This is a <u>fast</u> car.

   We had a <u>hard</u> test.

   Helen was a <u>good</u> student.

   ADVERBS

   She taught <u>patiently</u>.

   She learned <u>quickly</u>.

   He drives <u>fast</u>.

   I studied <u>hard</u>.

   She did <u>well</u> in school.

   Say: *Study the adjectives and adverbs. What's
   different about them? What's the same?* Write
   students' ideas on the board.

2. Have students look at grammar chart **11.4**.
   Say: *Now compare your work with the chart.*
   Point out that adverbs of manner tell *how*
   we do something, while adjectives describe
   nouns. Go over any errors. Review the example
   sentences in the chart.

3. Direct students' attention to the bottom section
   of the chart. Point out the position of the adverb
   in the example sentences. Explain that an adverb
   comes before the verb or after the verb phrase.
   An adverb cannot come between the verb and
   the object. Point out that you can use *very* before
   an adverb of manner.

EXERCISE 9

ANSWERS: 1. True; **2.** True; **3.** False; **4.** False; **5.** False

1. Say: *This is a comprehension exercise based on the reading about Helen Keller on page 330.* Have students read the direction line. Go over the example in the book.

2. Have students complete Exercise 9 individually. Remind them to review grammar chart **11.4** on page 337 if necessary. Go over the answers with the class.

11.5 Spelling of -*ly* Adverbs

1. Have students cover up grammar chart **11.5** on page 338. Copy the lists of adjectives and adverbs from grammar chart **11.5** on the board. Make sure to separate the four sets of adjectives and adverbs. For example:

easy	*easily*
lucky	*luckily*
happy	*happily*
simple	*simply*
double	*doubly*
comfortable	*comfortably*
full	*fully*
nice	*nicely*
free	*freely*
brave	*bravely*

Say: *There are four rules for spelling -ly adverbs. Can you guess what they are?* If students have difficulty, give them hints.

2. Have students look at grammar chart **11.5**. Say: *Compare our rules with the rules in the book.* Review the rules in the grammar chart. Make sure to point out that the spelling of *truly* is an exception to the last rule.

EXERCISE 10

ANSWERS: 1. badly; **2.** well; **3.** lazily; **4.** truly; **5.** nicely; **6.** fully; **7.** responsibly; **8.** politely; **9.** fast; **10.** constantly; **11.** terribly; **12.** beautifully

1. Have students read the direction line. Have a volunteer do #1.

2. Have students complete Exercise 10 individually. Remind them to review grammar chart **11.5** on page 338 if necessary. Go over the answers with the class.

EXERCISE 11

ANSWERS: 1. beautifully; **2.** responsibly; **3.** neatly; **4.** well; **5.** cheerfully; **6.** fluently; **7.** politely; **8.** hard; **9.** sadly; **10.** patiently; **11.** correctly

1. Have students read the direction line. Ask: *What do we write on the blanks?* (the adverb form of the underlined adjective) Go over the example.

2. Have students complete the exercise individually. Remind them to review grammar chart **11.5** on page 338 if necessary. Then have students compare answers in pairs. Circulate to give help as needed.

EXERCISE 12

Answers will vary.

1. Have students read the direction line. Say: *Write a sentence that's true for you. Use adverbs of manner to tell how you do these things.* Go over the example in the book. Say: *Don't forget to change pronouns.* Have a volunteer model #1.

2. Have students complete Exercise 12 individually. Remind them to review grammar chart **11.5** on page 338 if necessary. Then have students compare answers with a partner. Monitor pair work. Give help as needed.

Practice Idea: Speaking

Have students make questions from the items in Exercise 12. Have students take turns asking and answering questions. Say: *Answer the questions with an adverb. For example:* Do you speak English? Yes. I speak English well. *Or:* How do you speak English? I speak English well.

EXERCISE 13

ANSWERS: 1. C; **2.** wildly; **3.** year; **4.** C; **5.** poor; **6.** C; **7.** small child; **8.** C; **9.** clearly; **10.** elementary school; **11.** very bright student; **12.** C; **13.** C; **14.** patiently; **15.** sign language; **16.** C; **17.** college classes; **18.** married; **19.** C; **20.** eyesight

1. Say: *Now we're going to learn a little more about Helen Keller's teacher, Anne Sullivan.* Have students read the direction line. Go over the examples in the book.

2. Have students complete Exercise 13 individually. Remind them to review grammar charts **11.1** on page 331, **11.2** on page 332, **11.3** on page 335, **11.4** on page 337, and **11.5** on page 338. Then have students compare answers in pairs. Monitor pair work. Give help as needed. Go over the answers as a class.

EXERCISE 14
CD 2
TR 21

ANSWERS: 1. healthy; **2.** happy; **3.** impolite; **4.** rudely; **5.** crazy; **6.** easily; **7.** new; **8.** nice;

9. positive; **10.** active; **11.** well; **12.** fluently; **13.** quickly; **14.** curious; **15.** frequently

1. Have students read the direction line. Say: *You must decide whether to use an adjective or an adverb.* Go over the example.

2. Have students complete Exercise 14 individually. Remind them to review grammar chart **11.4** on page 337, if necessary. Point out the picture of the wheelchair on page 341. Play the audio and then check answers as a class.

Practice Idea: Listening

To provide practice with listening skills, have students close their books and listen to the audio. Ask comprehension questions, such as: *Are the two friends similar?* (No. They are complete opposites.) *What does Paula constantly do?* (complain about everything) *Is Paula happy?* (no) Then have students open their books and complete Exercise 14.

Practice Idea: Writing

Have students write about two of their friends. Tell students to use the composition in Exercise 14 as a model. Then have students exchange their writing with a partner.

Grandma Moses READING

1. Have students look at the photos. Ask: *What is the woman in the top photo doing?* (embroidery)

2. Have students look at the title of the reading. Ask: *What is the reading about?* Have students use the title and photos to make predictions.

3. Preteach any vocabulary words students may not know, such as *elderly* and *embroidery*.

Reading Glossary

elderly: old, aged
embroidery: fine needlework

5-10 mins

1. Have students discuss the questions in pairs.

2. Ask for a few volunteers to share their answers with the class.

Reading ≡★

CD 2 TR 22

1. Have students first read the text silently. Tell them to pay special attention to *very* and *too*. Then play the audio and have students read along silently.

10-15 mins

2. Check students' comprehension. Ask questions such as: *What does* "You can't teach an old dog new tricks" *mean?* (It's hard for older people to learn something new.) *What did Grandma Moses do before she became a painter?* (She was a farmer's wife.) *Why didn't she start painting earlier?* (She was too busy.) *What kind of pictures did she paint?* (pictures of farm life) *Are her paintings well known?* (Yes, some hang in major art museums.)

Practice Idea: Listening

To practice listening skills, have students first listen to the audio alone. Ask a few comprehension questions such as: *When was Grandma Moses born?* (1860) *How old was she when she started painting?* (in her seventies) Then have students open their books and read along as they listen to the audio.

11.6 *Too* vs. *Very* ≡★

5-10 mins

1. Have students read through the first half of the second paragraph of the reading on page 342 again. Ask them to pay special attention to the use of *too* and *very*. Ask: *Which shows that there's a problem:* too *or* very? (too)

2. Have students look at grammar chart **11.6** on page 343. Read through the examples and explanations. Point out that we often use an infinitive after *too*.

EXERCISE 15 ≡★

ANSWERS: 1. too; **2.** very; **3.** very; **4.** too; **5.** very; **6.** too; **7.** very; **8.** too; **9.** too; **10.** very; **11.** very; **12.** very; **13.** too; **14.** very; **15.** too

---

5-10 mins

1. Have students read the direction line. Go over the examples.

2. Have students complete Exercise 15 individually. Remind them to review grammar chart **11.6** on page 343 if necessary. Go over the answers as a class.

11.7 *Too* and *Enough* ≡★

5-10 mins

1. Have students cover up grammar chart **11.7** on page 344. Write the following sentences from the grammar chart on the board:

   In her 70s, Grandma Moses was too weak to do farm work.

   When she was younger, she worked too hard to have time for painting.

   She was talented enough to get the attention of an art collector.

   She painted skillfully enough to get her pictures in art museums.

   When she was younger, she didn't have enough time to paint.

   Say: *Look at the first two sentences. What do you notice about adjectives and adverbs and* too? (*Too* is used before adjectives and adverbs.) To help students, write on the board: *too* + adjective/adverb.

2. Then say: *Look at the next sentences. What do you notice about adjectives and adverbs and* enough? (*Enough* is used after adjectives and adverbs.)

3. Say: *Now what do you notice about the use of* enough *in the last sentence? What does it come before in the sentence?* (*Enough* is used before nouns.)

4. Have students look at grammar chart **11.7**. Go over the examples and explanations.

EXERCISE 16

ANSWERS: **1.** too hard; **2.** old enough; **3.** too sick; **4.** enough money; **5.** enough experience; **6.** strong enough; **7.** too heavy; **8.** enough exercise

5–10 mins

1. Have students read the direction line. Go over the examples. Ask: *In the first example, is the boy going to go to first grade?* (No, he's too young.) *In the second example, can she get a driver's license?* (Yes, she's old enough.)

2. Have students complete Exercise 16 individually. Remind them to review grammar chart **11.7** on page 344 if necessary. Then have students compare work in pairs. Monitor pair work. Give help as needed.

EXERCISE 17

CD 2
TR 23

ANSWERS: **1.** C; **2.** quickly; **3.** C; **4.** enough time; **5.** busy; **6.** C; **7.** old enough; **8.** C; **9.** proud; **10.** (very) well; **11.** very; **12.** C; **13.** C; **14.** too; **15.** hard; **16.** very; **17.** good; **18.** new

10–15 mins

1. Have students read the direction line. Ask: *Does every underlined word have a mistake?* (no) Go over the example in the book.

2. Have students complete Exercise 17 individually. Remind them to review grammar charts **11.1** on page 331, **11.2** on page 332, **11.3** on page 335, **11.4** on page 337, **11.5** on page 338, **11.6** on page 342, and **11.7** on page 344 if necessary. Then play the audio and check answers as a class.

Practice Idea: Listening

To provide practice with listening skills, have students close their books and listen to the audio. Ask comprehension questions, such as: *What did this person learn from the story about Grandma Moses?* (that you're never too old to learn something new) *Where is this person now?* (in the U.S.) *Is this person the same age as the other students in the class?* (no) Then have students open their books and complete Exercise 17.

Summary of Lesson 11

20–30 mins

1. **Adjectives and adverbs.** Have students cover up the Summary on page 346. On the board, write:

beautiful
careful
late
good

Say: *Write eight sentences with these words. Use each word as an adjective and as an adverb.*

Then have students compare their sentences with the ones in the Summary. If necessary, have students review:

11.1 Adjectives and Adverbs (p. 331)

2. **Adjective modifiers and noun modifiers.** Have students cover up the Summary on page 346. Create an exercise on the board. Write:

clean
driver's
new
winter
warm
shoe
store
new

Then write the following in two columns:

Adjective modifier
a _____ window
a _____ store
a _____ coat
a _____ license

Noun modifier
a _____ window
a _____ store
a _____ coat
a _____ license

Say: *Fill in the blanks with the appropriate word.* Then have students compare their work with the summary. If necessary, have students review:

11.2 Adjectives (p. 332)
11.3 Noun Modifiers (p. 335)

3. ***Very/Too/Enough.*** Have students cover up the Summary on page 346. Create an exercise on the board.

Write:

> He's _____ healthy.
> He's _____ young to retire. He's only 55.
> He's old _____ to understand life.
> He has _____ money to take a vacation.

Say: *Complete these sentences with* very, too, *or* enough.

Then have students compare their work with the Summary. If necessary, have students review:

> **11.6** *Too* vs. *Very* (p. 342)
> **11.7** *Too* and *Enough* (p. 344)

Editing Advice

 Have students close their books. Write the first few sentences without editing marks or corrections on the board. For example:

1. *Those are importants ideas.*
2. *He is a driver truck.*

Ask students to correct each sentence and provide a rule or explanation for each correction. This activity can be done individually, in pairs, or as a class. After students have corrected each sentence, tell them to turn to pages 346–347. Say: *Now compare your work with the Editing Advice in the book.*

Editing Quiz

ANSWERS: 1. is married; **2.** C; **3.** old enough; **4.** computer programming; **5.** (much) too; **6.** C; **7.** flower shop; **8.** a very interesting job; **9.** interesting; **10.** very nice; **11.** C; **12.** kindly; **13.** C; **14.** C; **15.** English quickly; **16.** well; **17.** C

1. Tell students that they are going to put the editing advice into practice. Have students read the direction line. Ask: *Do all the shaded words and phrases have mistakes?* (no) Go over the examples with the class. Then do #1 together.

2. Have students complete the quiz individually. Then have them compare answers with a partner before checking answers as a class.

3. For the items students had difficulties with, have them go back and find the relevant grammar chart and review it. Monitor and give help as necessary.

Lesson 11 Test/Review

 Use the Assessment CD-ROM with Exam*View®*, Online Workbook, and Web site for additional practice, review, and assessment materials.

20-30 mins

PART 1

ANSWERS: 1. very beautiful pictures; **2.** too old; **3.** nineteen-month-old baby; **4.** sign language; **5.** car accident; **6.** volleyball team; **7.** wheelchair; **8.** well enough

1. Part 1 may be used in addition to the Assessment CD-ROM with Exam*View®* as an in-class test to assess student performance. Have students read the direction line. Go over the example with the class.

2. Have students complete Part 1 individually. Collect for assessment.

3. If necessary, have students review:

> **11.3** Noun Modifiers (p. 335)

PART 2

ANSWERS: 1. neat, sloppily; **2.** calmly, fast; **3.** fluently, hard; **4.** easily, difficult; **5.** accurately, carefully; **6.** soft, loudly; **7.** beautifully, sick; **8.** responsible, childishly; **9.** carefully, foolishly; **10.** regularly, lazy

Part 2 may also be used as an in-class test to assess student performance, in addition to the Assessment CD-ROM with Exam*View®*. Have students read the direction line. Go over the examples with the class.

Have students complete Part 2 individually. Collect for assessment. If necessary, have students review:

> **11.1** Adjectives and Adverbs (p. 331)
> **11.4** Comparing Adverbs of Manner and Adjectives (p. 337)

Expansion

These expansion activities provide opportunities for students to interact with one another and further develop their speaking and writing skills. Encourage students to use grammar from this lesson whenever possible.

CLASSROOM ACTIVITIES

10-15 mins per activity

1. Have students work individually to complete the personality survey. Check whether students know the meaning of all the adverbs. Then put students in pairs to compare. If possible, have students from different countries work together.

Practice Idea: Speaking

Do a quick survey of the class. Write the results for each item on the board. How do the students rate the "personality" of the class?

2. Have students work in pairs. Partners take turns naming things. One partner says: *Name some things you do well.* The other partner names three to five things that he or she does well. Have volunteers tell the class what their partners can do.

TALK ABOUT IT

15-20 mins

Have students discuss each question in groups or with the class. Try to put students from different countries together.

WRITE ABOUT IT

20-30 mins

1. If students have difficulty thinking of anyone to write about, brainstorm famous people who have accomplished things in spite of a disability or age. Have students help you write the beginning of a paragraph about one of the famous people they come up with as an example on the board. Then have students write their own paragraph following the model.

2. Have students think of a woman they admire and make a list of things they could write about that woman. Have them tell a partner about the person they are thinking of. Say: *You can write about anyone whom you admire—the woman can be famous or just someone you know.* Then have them write their paragraphs individually. Collect for assessment and/or have students present their paragraphs to a group.

Practice Idea: Writing

Have students exchange first drafts with a partner. Ask students to help their partners edit their drafts. Refer students to the Editing Advice on pages 346–347.

OUTSIDE ACTIVITIES

Ask students to rent the movie *The Miracle Worker.* Tell them it's the story of Helen Keller and Anne Sullivan. Tell them to watch it at home and then be prepared to talk about the movie in class.

INTERNET ACTIVITIES

1. Tell students to use the Internet to find information about the following people. They should find out who they are and what extraordinary things they did.
   a. Erik Weihenmayer
   b. Sherman Bull
   c. Enrique Oliu
   d. Lance Armstrong

2. Tell students to use the Internet to find the American Sign Language finger alphabet and find out how to spell their names.

3. Tell students to use the Internet to find some paintings by Grandma Moses. Have them bring a picture of one to class; have volunteers describe the painting they chose.

Lesson 12

Lesson Overview

GRAMMAR

1. Ask: *What did we study in Lesson 11?* (adjectives, adverbs, and noun modifiers)

2. Ask: *What are we going to study in this lesson?* (comparatives and superlatives) *What are some examples of comparatives and superlatives?* (comparatives: taller, faster; superlatives: tallest, fastest) Have students give examples. Write them on the board.

CONTEXT

1. Ask: *What will we learn about in this lesson?* (U.S. geography) Activate students' prior knowledge. Ask: *Does anyone know a lot about U.S. geography? How many states can you name? What are some famous cities?* (New York, Los Angeles, Chicago, Boston)

2. Have students share their knowledge and personal experiences. Ask students to talk about places they've visited around the world.

Presentation Idea

The topic for this lesson can be enhanced with the following ideas:

1. Pictures, postcards, and books about different states

2. A large, colorful map of the U.S.

3. A yearbook with class superlatives (funniest student, best-looking student, etc.)

Context Notes

The Willis Tower (formerly the Sears Tower) Built in 1973, it was the tallest building in the world until 1998. It is 1,450 feet tall, covers two city blocks, and has more than 4 million square feet of office and commercial space. It is still one of the tallest buildings in the world.

The Empire State Building Construction on the Empire State Building began in 1930. The building took only one year and 45 days to build. It is 1,250 feet tall and is currently the tallest building in New York City.

The Space Needle The Space Needle was built in 1962. It is 605 feet tall and has a revolving restaurant at the top. Every year, more than one million people visit the Space Needle. It is the biggest tourist attraction in the Northwest.

U.S. Facts READING

1. If possible, have students look at a map. Ask: *Where have you been in the U.S.? What parts of the U.S. would you like to visit?*

2. Have students look at the title of the reading. Ask: *What is the reading about?* Have students use the title to make predictions about the reading.

3. Preteach any vocabulary words your students may not know, such as *population* and *minority*.

Reading Glossary

minority: people of a different race, ethnic background, or religion from those of the majority of people in a nation

population: all of the people living in a specific area

BEFORE YOU READ

5-10 mins

1. Have students discuss the questions in pairs.

2. Ask for a few volunteers to share their answers with the class.

◀)) Reading ──★

CD 2
TR 24

10-15 mins

1. Have students first read the text silently. Tell them to pay special attention to comparatives and superlatives. Then play the audio and have students read along silently.

2. Check students' comprehension. Ask questions such as: *Which city has the most people?* (New York) *Are there more Hispanics in the U.S. than African-Americans?* (yes, since 2003) *Is Alaska bigger than California?* (yes)

Did You Know?

Have students read the information. Tell them that California's state motto is *Eureka*, which is a Greek word meaning *I have found it*. It is believed that the motto refers to the discovery of gold during the California Gold Rush.

Practice Idea: Listening

To practice listening skills, have students first listen to the audio alone. Ask a few comprehension questions such as: *Is the United States the largest country in the world?* (no, it is the third largest) *What is the tallest building in the United States?* (the Willis Tower). Then have students open their books and read along as they listen to the audio.

Practice Idea: Speaking

Put students in teams and quiz them on their knowledge of some of the regions in the U.S. Ask: *Do you know which states form New England?* (CT, RI, MA, VT, NH, and ME) *Which states are considered the Northeast?* (New England plus NY, NJ, and PA) *Which states are considered the South?* (FL, GE, SC, NC, MD, WV, VA, KY, TN, AK, LA, MS, AL, OK, and TX) *The Midwest and the Great Plains?* (OH, MI, IN, WI, IL, MN, IA, MO, ND, SD, NE, and KS) *The Rocky Mountain States?* (MT, ID, WY, NV, UT, CO, AZ, and NM) *The Southwest?* (CO, NM, UT, AZ, NV, and CA) *The Pacific States* (CA, OR, and WA)

12.1 Comparatives and Superlatives—An Overview

1. Have students cover up grammar chart **12.1** on page 355. Say: *We use the superlative to point out the number-one item in a group of three or more. We use the comparative to compare two items.* Then have students go back to the reading on pages 354–355. Say: *Underline five superlatives and five comparatives.* Ask volunteers to name the adjectives they underlined and circled, and ask them to explain how they identified them as comparative or superlative (e.g., *Third largest*

5-10 mins

country in the world—there are more than three countries in the world.).

2. Have students look at grammar chart **12.1**. Say: *Now compare your work with the chart.*

3. Quickly go over the examples and explanations in the chart.

EXERCISE

ANSWERS: 1. isn't; **2.** larger; **3.** smaller; **4.** Alaska; **5.** Hispanics; **6.** fewer; **7.** California; **8.** isn't

5-10 mins

1. Have students read the direction line. Say: *These facts are based on the reading.* Go over the example in the book.

2. Have students complete Exercise 1 individually. Remind them to review grammar chart **12.1** on page 353 if necessary. Check the answers as a class.

12.2 Comparative and Superlative Forms of Adjectives and Adverbs

10-15 mins

1. Have students cover up grammar chart **12.2** on pages 356 and 357. Write the following adjectives on the board: *tall, fast—easy, happy—frequent, active—important, difficult.* Ask: *What do you notice about each group of adjectives?* If students have difficulty, give them a hint: *Look at the syllables.*

2. Then have students look at grammar chart **12.2**. Say: *Let's look at how we form the comparative and superlative forms. For short adjectives, we usually add -er for the comparative form. For the superlative, we add -est. For longer adjectives, we add* more *before the adjective to form the comparative and* the most *before the adjective to form the superlative.* Go over the examples and explanations for each kind of adjective. Explain that some two-syllable adjectives have two forms.

3. Point out that *-ly* adverbs use *more* and *most*. The last category of adjectives and adverbs is irregular; their forms must be memorized. Explain that except for *good/well* and *bad/badly*, the adjective and adverb are the same.

4. Direct students' attention to the Language Notes. Point out the exceptions. Say: *Even though*

bored *and* tired *are short adjectives, we form the comparative by adding* more *and the superlative, by adding* the most. *Point out the other two-syllable adjectives that have two forms.*

5. Direct students' attention to the rules for spelling short adjectives and adverbs on page 357. Have students cover up the rule side of the chart. Say: *Study these adjectives and adverbs and their superlative and comparative forms. Can you guess the rules?*

6. Have volunteers write the rules on the board. Then have students look at grammar chart **12.2**. Say: *Now compare your work with the chart.* Go over the examples and rules.

EXERCISE 2

ANSWERS: 1. more interesting, most interesting; **2.** younger, youngest; **3.** more beautiful, most beautiful; **4.** better, best; **5.** commoner (OR more common), commonest (OR most common); **6.** thinner, thinnest; **7.** more carefully, most carefully; **8.** prettier, prettiest; **9.** worse, worst; **10.** more famous, most famous; **11.** luckier, luckiest; **12.** simpler (OR more simple), simplest (OR most simple); **13.** higher, highest; **14.** more delicious, most delicious; **15.** farther, farthest; **16.** more foolishly, most foolishly

1. Have students read the direction line. Ask: *What are we going to write in the blanks?* (the comparative and superlative forms of the adjectives) Go over the examples in the book.

    5-10 mins

2. Have students complete Exercise 2 individually. Remind them to review grammar chart **12.2** on pages 356–357 if necessary. Go over the answers as a class.

Practice Idea: Speaking

Have a spelling bee. Make a list of about 40 adjectives and adverbs. Divide the class into Team A and Team B. Give one team member from Team A an adjective or adverb and tell him or her to spell the comparative or superlative form on the board. Do the same with Team B. Then give Team B an adjective or adverb and ask one member to spell the comparative or superlative form, and so on. Make sure that team members take turns.

12.3 Superlative Adjectives

1. Have students look at grammar chart **12.3** on page 358. Say: *When you use the superlative, use the* before *it. It's wrong to say:* New York is biggest city in the U.S. Also, point out that a prepositional phrase is usually at the end of a superlative sentence. Go over the examples. Have students circle the prepositional phrases in each sentence in the grammar chart.

    5-10 mins

2. Explain that we often use *one of* before a superlative. Say: *One of the most popular tourist attractions means that there are others that are just or almost as popular.* Go over the examples.

EXERCISE 3

ANSWERS: 1. The biggest; **2.** The longest; **3.** The highest; **4.** the most popular; **5.** the most expensive; **6.** the most beautiful; **7.** the best; **8.** the tallest; **9.** the worst; **10.** the oldest

1. Have students read the direction line. Ask: *What are we going to write in the blanks?* (the superlative of the adjective and *the*) Go over the example in the book.

    5-10 mins

2. Have students complete Exercise 3 individually. Remind them to review grammar chart **12.3** on page 358 if necessary. Have students compare answers in pairs. Monitor pair work. Give help as needed.

Practice Idea: Writing

Have students write facts about their countries (*e.g., La Paz, Bolivia is the highest capital city in the world. The Andes is the longest mountain range in the world.*). If possible, have students from the same country work in pairs or groups.

EXERCISE 4
Answers will vary.

1. Say: *You're going to write about your family now.* Have students read the direction line. Go over the examples in the book. Have volunteers model the examples.

    10-15 mins

2. Have students complete the exercise individually. Remind them to review grammar charts **12.2** on pages 356–357 and **12.3** on page 358 if necessary. Then have students compare work in pairs. Have a few students share some of their sentences.

EXERCISE 5

Answers will vary.

1. Have students read the direction line. Say: *When you use one of the …, don't forget to use a plural noun.* Go over the examples in the book. Have volunteers model the examples.

2. Have students complete Exercise 5 individually. Remind them to review grammar charts **12.2** on pages 356–357 and **12.3** on page 358 if necessary. Then have students compare answers in pairs or groups.

Practice Idea: Speaking

Do a survey of the class and have a discussion about the items in Exercise 5.

12.4 Word Order with Superlatives

1. Direct students' attention to chart **12.4** on page 360. Tell students to look at the first example. Ask: *Where does the superlative adjective belong?* (before the noun)

2. Have students look at the second example. Ask: *What verb is connecting the subject noun to the superlative + noun?* (be) *How many ways can we write this sentence?* (two) Write a scrambled sentence on the board: *the tallest mountain/ in the world Mount Everest is* Ask students to unscramble the sentence in two ways.

3. Have students look at the next example. Ask: *Where are the superlative adverbs in these two sentences?* (after the verb)

4. Have students look at the fourth row. Ask: *Is the* most *in these sentences an adjective or an adverb?* (an adverb) *Where are the adverbs in these two*

examples? (after the verb) Say: *The most, the least, the best, and the worst come after a verb.* Then have students look at the last row. Ask: *Are the most and the least adjectives or adverbs in these sentences?* (adjectives) *Where are they located in the sentence?* (before the noun)

5. Review all the examples and explanations with the class.

EXERCISE 6

Answers will vary.

1. Have students read the direction line. Say: *In this exercise, we are putting the superlative after the verb. Are the superlatives in these sentences adjectives or adverbs?* (adverbs) Be sure students understand they are to make statements about the members of their family. Go over the examples in the book. Have students model them.

2. Have students complete Exercise 6 individually. Remind them to review grammar charts **12.2** on pages 356–357 and **12.4** on page 360 if necessary. Have students compare answers in pairs. Monitor pair work. Give help as needed.

EXERCISE 7

Answers will vary.

1. Have students read the direction line. Say: *In this exercise, we are putting the superlative before the noun. Are the superlatives in these sentences adjectives or adverbs?* (adjectives) Go over the example in the book. Say: *Whenever possible, give additional information.* Have a volunteer model the example.

2. Have students complete Exercise 7 individually. Remind them to review grammar charts **12.2** on pages 356–357 and **12.4** on page 360 if necessary. Then have students compare answers in pairs. Monitor pair work. Give help as needed.

A Tale of Two Cities READING

1. Have students look at the photos. Ask: *If the names of the cities weren't on these photos, would you know which cities they are? How? Has anyone been to one or*

both of these cities? Do you think they're very different from each other? Which one do you like the most?

2. Have students look at the title of the reading. Ask: *What is the reading about?* Have students use the title and photos to make predictions about the reading. Ask: *Which city do you think has more people? Which city do you think is more expensive to live in? Which do you think is more polluted? More dangerous?*

3. Preteach any vocabulary words your students may not know, such as *ozone* and *climate*.

Reading Glossary

climate: the type of weather that a place or region has
ozone: a poisonous gas found in parts of the earth's upper atmosphere, which is a form of oxygen

BEFORE YOU READ

5-10 mins

1. Have students discuss the questions in pairs.

2. Ask for a few volunteers to share their answers with the class.

Reading —★

CD 2 TR 25

10-15 mins

1. Have students first read the chart and the text silently. Tell them to pay special attention to comparative forms. Then play the audio and have students read along silently.

2. Check students' comprehension. Ask questions such as: *Which city has more people?* (Chicago) *Which city is more expensive?* (San Francisco) *Which city is more polluted?* (Chicago) *Which city is more dangerous?* (Chicago)

Practice Idea: Listening

To practice listening skills, have students first listen to the audio alone. Ask a few comprehension questions such as: *Which city is warmer in the summer?* (Chicago) *Which city has less crime?* (San Francisco). Then have students open their books and read along as they listen to the audio.

12.5 Comparisons —★

10-15 mins

1. Have students look at grammar chart **12.5** on page 363. Go over the examples. Explain that

the comparison is used to compare two items. Point out that *than* is used before the second item of comparison.

2. Say: *If there is no comparison with a second item, omit* than. Write the example from the chart on the board.

3. Say: Much *and a little* can be used in front of a comparative. Go over the examples in the chart.

4. Explain that there are two ways to make comparisons when pronouns are used after *than*: a formal way and an informal way. Say: *In the formal way, you use an auxiliary verb after the subject pronoun. In the informal way, you use an object pronoun and no verb.* Go over the examples.

Presentation Idea

Have students go back to the reading on page 362. Ask: *Is* than *always used?* (no) *When is it used?* (when there are two items being compared in the sentence) *When is it not used?* (when only one item is mentioned in the sentence) Then go over the examples and explanations in grammar chart **12.5**.

EXERCISE 8 —★

ANSWERS: 1. larger; **2.** more dangerous; **3.** less expensive; **4.** worse; **5.** more

5-10 mins

1. Have students read the direction line. Say: *This exercise is based on the facts from the reading.* Go over the example.

2. Have students complete Exercise 8 individually. Remind them to review grammar chart **12.5** on page 363 if necessary. Go over the answers with the class.

EXERCISE 9

Answers will vary.

10-15 mins

1. Say: *Now you're going to make comparisons.* Have students read the direction line. Say: *You can make a comparison with yourself or with two other people.* Go over the examples. Have volunteers model the examples.

2. If necessary, review the meanings of the adjectives. Have students complete the exercise individually. Remind them to review grammar chart **12.5** on page 363 if necessary. Then have students compare answers in pairs. Circulate to give help as needed.

EXERCISE 10
Answers will vary.

1. Have students read the direction line. Have volunteers model the examples. If necessary, review the meanings of the adjectives.

2. Have students complete Exercise 10 individually. Point out that students should start their statements with *In my opinion*. Remind them to review grammar chart **12.5** on page 363 if necessary. Then have students practice telling each other their opinions in pairs. Monitor pair work. Give help as needed.

Practice Idea: Speaking

Do a survey. What does the class think of adults and children? Do they agree? Write the results on the board.

EXERCISE 11
Answers will vary.

1. Have students read the direction line. Say: *You can make comparisons with any city you know.* Go over the examples in the book. Have volunteers model the examples.

2. Have students complete Exercise 11 individually. Remind them to review grammar chart **12.5** on page 363 if necessary. Then have students compare answers in pairs. Monitor pair work. Give help as needed.

12.6 Word Order with Comparisons ≡★

1. Have students cover up grammar chart **12.6** on page 365. Make a matching exercise on the board:

1. *Houses in San Francisco are more expensive than houses in Chicago.*
2. *I want to move to a warmer climate.*
3. *The Hispanic population is growing more quickly than the African-American population.*
4. *It rains more in Chicago.*
5. *San Francisco has more sunshine than Chicago.*

a. Put *more, less, better,* and *worse* after a verb.
b. Put comparative adjectives after the verb *be*.
c. Put *more, less, fewer, better,* and *worse* before a noun.
d. Put comparative adjectives before a noun.
e. Put comparative adverbs after the verb.

Have volunteers match the examples with the explanations on the board.

2. Have students compare their work with grammar chart **12.6**. Go over the examples and explanations.

EXERCISE 12 ≡★
Answers will vary.

1. Say: *We're going to be comparing people we know.* Have students read the direction line. Go over the examples. Have volunteers model the examples.

2. Have students complete Exercise 12 individually. Remind them to review grammar chart **12.6** on page 365 if necessary. Then have them compare their answers in pairs. Monitor pair work. Give help as needed.

EXERCISE 13 ≡★
Answers will vary.

1. Have students read the direction line. Go over the examples in the book. Have volunteers model the examples.

2. Have students complete Exercise 13 individually. Remind them to review grammar chart **12.6** on page 365 if necessary. Then have students compare answers in pairs. Monitor pair work. Give help as needed.

Practice Idea: Writing

Have students write a paragraph comparing two cities in pairs. If possible, have students from the same country or region (South America, for example) compare towns and cities.

EXERCISE 14

Answers will vary.

1. Have students read the direction line. Say: *Look at the words you're going to make comparisons with: are they adverbs or adjectives?* Go over the examples. Ask: *In the example, is the comparison with an adverb or adjective?* (adjective) Point out that students should give reasons for their opinions. Have a volunteer model the example.

2. Have students complete Exercise 14 individually. Remind them to review grammar chart **12.6** on page 365 if necessary. Then have students compare work in pairs. Monitor pair work. Give help as needed.

Practice Idea: Speaking

Have students discuss their opinions in groups. If possible, put students from different countries in groups.

EXERCISE 15

ANSWERS: 1. warmer than; **2.** the biggest; **3.** the farthest; **4.** more crowded than; **5.** more crowded than; **6.** the most crowded; **8.** the most beautiful; **9.** The tallest

1. Say: *In this exercise, you must decide if you're going to use a superlative or a comparative.* Have students read the direction line. Go over the examples in the book.

2. Have students complete Exercise 15 individually. Remind them to review grammar charts **12.1** on page 353, **12.2** on pages 356–357, and **12.3** on page 358 if necessary. Then have them compare answers in pairs. Monitor pair work. Give help as needed. Go over answers as a class.

Practice Idea: Writing

Have students work in pairs to write similar statements about cities in other parts of the world. For more of a challenge, have students from different countries and regions work together.

 ### EXERCISE 16

 CD 2 TR 26

ANSWERS: 1. larger (OR bigger) than; **2.** the tallest; **3.** better; **4.** hottest; **5.** bigger (OR larger); **6.** biggest (OR largest); **7.** sunnier (OR drier); **8.** best (OR most famous); **9.** more expensive; **10.** safer; **11.** more; **12.** the most interesting

1. Have students read the direction line. Explain that this is a conversation between two students Go over the example in the book.

2. Have students complete Exercise 16 individually. Remind them to review grammar charts **12.1** on page 355, **12.2** on pages 356–357, **12.3** on page 358, **12.4** on page 360, **12.5** on page 363, and **12.6** on page 365 if necessary. Then play the audio and check answers as a class.

Practice Idea: Listening

To provide practice with listening skills, have students close their books and listen to the audio. Ask comprehension questions, such as: *What's person A planning to do?* (visit Chicago) *Does person B think Chicago is a beautiful city?* (yes) *What's the second largest city in the U.S.?* (Los Angeles) Then have students open their books and complete Exercise 16.

Practice Idea: Speaking

Have students practice this conversation or create a similar conversation about two other cities in pairs. Then have volunteers role-play all or part of the conversation in front of the class.

Summary of Lesson 12

20-30 mins

1. **Adjectives.** Have students cover up the Summary on page 369. Say: *Write three sentences with* big *and three sentences with* populated. *Write a sentence with* big *as a simple adjective, as a comparative, and as a superlative. Do the same with* populated. Then have students compare their sentences with the ones in the Summary.

    If necessary, have students review:

    12.2 Comparative and Superlative Forms of Adjectives and Adverbs (pp. 356–357)
    12.3 Superlative Adjectives (p. 358)
    12.5 Comparisons (p. 363)

2. **Adverbs** Have students cover up the Summary on page 367. Say: *Write three sentences with* fast *and three sentences with* fluently. *Write a sentence with* fast *as a simple adverb, as a comparative, and as a superlative. Do the same with* fluently. Then have students compare their sentences with the ones in the Summary.

    If necessary, have students review:

    12.2 Comparative and Superlative Forms of Adjectives and Adverbs (pp. 356–357)
    12.5 Comparisons (p. 363)

3. **Word Order** Have students cover up the Summary on page 367. Scramble the four example sentences in the book, and write them on the board. Have students unscramble the sentences and compare them with the ones in the Summary. If necessary, have students review:

    12.6 Word Order with Comparisons (p. 365)

Editing Advice

15-20 mins

Have students close their books. Write the first few sentences without editing marks or corrections on the board. For example: *California is a bigger state.* Ask students to correct each sentence and provide a rule or explanation for each correction. Then have them compare their work with the Editing Advice on pages 369–370.

Editing Quiz

ANSWERS: **1.** one of the biggest cities; **2.** largest; **3.** C; **4.** prettier than; **5.** more interesting than; **6.** C; **7.** my; **8.** the most crowded; **9.** C

10-15 mins

1. Tell students that they are going to put the editing advice into practice. Have students read the direction line. Ask: *Do all the shaded words and phrases have mistakes?* (no) Go over the examples with the class. Then do #1 together.

2. Have students complete the quiz individually. Then have them compare answers with a partner before checking answers as a class.

3. For the items students had difficulties with, have them go back and find the relevant grammar chart and review it. Monitor and give help as necessary.

Lesson 12 Test/Review

30-40 mins

Use the Assessment CD-ROM with Exam*View*®, Online Workbook, and Web site for additional practice, review, and assessment materials.

PART 1

ANSWERS: **1.** I have more problems than you. **2.** I woke up earlier than you. **3.** Paris is the most beautiful city in the world. **4.** C; **5.** You type faster than I do. **6.** C; **7.** Your car is more expensive than my car. **8.** C; **9.** C; **10.** C

1. Part 1 may be used in addition to the Assessment CD-ROM with Exam*View*® as an in-class test to assess student performance. Have students read the direction line. Ask: *Does every sentence have a mistake?* (no) Go over the examples with the class.

2. Have students complete Part 1 individually. Collect for assessment.

3. If necessary, have students review:

    12.4 Word Order with Superlatives (p. 360)
    12.6 Word Order with Comparisons (p. 365)

PART 2

Answers: 1. the highest; **2.** worse than; **3.** the most common (OR the commonest); **4.** more populated than; **5.** the longest; **6.** better than; **7.** the largest; **8.** more quickly than; **9.** better than; **10.** friendlier (OR more friendly than); **11.** more carefully than; **12.** the best; **13.** more fluently than; **14.** more intelligent

1. Part 2 may also be used in addition to the Assessment CD-ROM with Exam*View*® as an in-class test to assess student performance. Have students read the direction line. Go over the examples with the class.

2. Have students complete Part 2 individually. Collect for assessment.

3. If necessary, have students review:

   12.2 Comparative and Superlative Forms of Adjectives and Adverbs (pp. 356–357)

   12.3 Superlative Adjectives (p. 358)

   12.5 Comparisons (p. 363)

Expansion

These expansion activities provide opportunities for students to interact with one another and further develop their speaking and writing skills. Encourage students to use grammar from this lesson whenever possible.

CLASSROOM ACTIVITIES

10-15 mins per activity

1. Have students work individually to complete the information. Then put students in groups to compare.

> ### Practice Idea: Speaking
>
> Do a quick survey to find the class superlatives (e.g., *Sara is the funniest girl in the class. Ahmed is the tallest guy in the class.*).

2. Model some possible comparisons: *In the U.S., women work more outside the home. In the U.S., women have fewer children.* Have students make comparisons in pairs. Then have them share their opinions with the class.

> ### Practice Idea: Speaking
>
> After students discuss men and women in pairs, have a class discussion to compare different cultures.

3. After students have discussed in pairs, ask volunteers to tell the class some of their arguments. Then take a class vote to see what things are the most popular.

TALK ABOUT IT

15-20 mins

Write on the board: *problems in the U.S.* and *living in big cities/small towns.* Elicit ideas for these two topics and write them on the board. Then have students discuss each question in groups. Then have them report back to the class.

WRITE ABOUT IT

20-30 mins

1. Have students read the direction line. Brainstorm some ideas with the class about problems in the world. Write the ideas on the board. Have students complete the writing task individually or in pairs.

2. Have students read the direction line and the model paragraph. With the class, choose one of the topics from the list and have students suggest ideas for comparing, write them on the board. Then begin a paragraph on the board following the model in the book. Then have students write their own comparisons individually. Students can write about one of the topics in the book, or they can write a comparison about another topic that interests them. Encourage them to write a list of ideas before they begin writing.

> ### Practice Idea: Writing
>
> Have students exchange first drafts with a partner. Ask students to help their partners edit their drafts. Refer students to the Editing Advice on pages 369–370.

OUTSIDE ACTIVITY

Have students interview a native speaker of English and get his or her opinion about the superlative of each of the following items. Tell students they will share their findings with the class.

1. good car
2. beautiful actress
3. good president in the last 25 years
4. beautiful city in the U.S.
5. good university in the U.S.
6. popular movie at this time
7. terrible tragedy in American history
8. big problem in the U.S. today
9. popular singer in the U.S.
10. best athlete
11. handsome actor

Have students prepare the questions in writing in class (for example, **1.** good car: *What do you think is the best car?*). Ask students if there are additional topics they would be interested in asking about. Have them add these to the list.

Practice Idea: Writing

Ask students to make a poster of the interview. Hang the posters up in class and let students circulate to look at them.

INTERNET ACTIVITIES

1. Tell students to use the Internet to find a site that compares cities. Tell them to compare any two American cities that interest them. Ask them to print out the information they find on the Internet and to bring it in to class.

2. Tell students to use the Internet to find out about the city where you live. Have them find out:
   a. the name of the mayor
   b. the population
   c. the annual rainfall
   d. the coldest month
   e. interesting places to visit

Have students prepare a brochure for their city with the information they find on the Internet.

Lesson 13

Lesson Overview

GRAMMAR

1. Ask: *What did we study in Lesson 12?* (comparatives and superlatives)

2. *What are we going to study in this lesson?* (auxiliary verbs with *too* and *either*; auxiliary verbs in tag questions) *What are some auxiliary verbs?* (do, does, did) Have students give examples. Write them on the board.

CONTEXT

1. Ask: *What are we going to learn about in this lesson?* (dating and marriage) *How many people here are married? Is being married difficult? Why or why not?*

2. Have students share their knowledge and personal experiences.

> ### Practice Idea: Speaking
>
> Ask students to talk about the differences between dating and marriage. Have students discuss the benefits and drawbacks of both dating and marriage. Is one better than the other?

Dating and Marriage READING

1. Have students look at the photo. Ask: *Are these people married or are they dating? Why do you think so?*

2. Have students look at the title of the reading. Ask: *What is the reading about?* Have students use the title and photo to make predictions about the reading.

3. Preteach any vocabulary words your students may not know, such as *lifestyle* and *lonely*.

Reading Glossary

lifestyle: the manner in which one lives
lonely: alone and feeling sad

BEFORE YOU READ

1. Have students discuss the questions in pairs.

2. Ask for a few volunteers to share their answers with the class.

 5-10 mins

Reading

CD 2
TR 27

10-15 mins

1. Have students first read the text silently. Tell them to pay special attention to auxiliary verbs and *too* and *either*. Then play the audio and have students read along silently.

2. Check students' comprehension. Ask questions such as: *How long after they met did Meg and Don decide to get married?* (one year) *When did they discover they had differences?* (when they started to plan the wedding) *What are some ways they have resolved differences?* (Once a month, they do something with friends; when Don goes on a fishing trip, Meg goes out with her friend.)

> ### Practice Idea: Listening
>
> To practice listening skills, have students first listen to the audio alone. Ask a few comprehension questions such as: *Did Don get together with friends very often when he was dating Meg?* (no) *Do they get to cook very often?* (no, they often bring home carry-out dinners or eat fast food) Then have students open their books and read along as they listen to the audio.

13.1 Auxiliary Verbs with *Too* and *Either*

10-15 mins

1. Have students cover up grammar chart **13.1** on page 377. Write on the board: *be, do, does, did, modals (can, could, will, etc.)*

   Say: *These verbs are all auxiliary verbs.* Have students go back to the reading on page 376. Say: *Go back to the reading and study how these auxiliary verbs are used with* too *and* either. Ask volunteers to give you some examples from the reading (*Meg wanted to get married, and Don did, too. Meg works hard, and Don does, too.*). Explain that auxiliary verbs with *too* and *either* are used to show similarity. Ask: *Why do we use auxiliaries with* too *in these sentences?* (to avoid repeating the same verb phrase)

2. Have students look at grammar chart **13.1**. Say: *Now let's look at the chart.* Go over the examples and explanations in the chart. Point out that *too* is used with affirmative statements and *either* is used with negative statements. Explain that in informal speech we often say *me too* and *me neither.* They're both expressions of agreement. Point out that Americans substitute *do, does, did* for *have,* but the British use *have.*

EXERCISE 1

ANSWERS: 1. does too; **2.** is too; **3.** will too; **4.** was too; **5.** did too

5-10
mins

1. Have students read the direction line. Go over the example in the book. Ask: *What tense are the main verb and the auxiliary verb in?* (present)

2. Have students complete Exercise 1 individually. Remind students that they need to use the same tense as the main verb. Remind them to review grammar chart **13.1** on page 377 if necessary. Check the answers as a class.

EXERCISE 2

ANSWERS: 1. didn't either; **2.** isn't either; **3.** doesn't either; **4.** can't either; **5.** doesn't either

5-10
mins

1. Have students read the direction line. Go over the example in the book. Ask: *What tense are the main verb and the auxiliary verb in?* (present)

2. Have students complete Exercise 2 individually. Remind students that they need to use the same tense as the main verb. Remind them to review grammar chart **13.1** on page 377 if necessary. Go over the answers as a class.

13.2 Auxiliary Verbs with Opposite Statements

5-10
mins

1. Have students go back to the reading on page 376. Say: *Find a sentence where Meg and Don don't agree* (Meg wanted a big wedding, but Don didn't.) *What word shows they have an opposite opinion?* (but)

2. Then have students look at grammar chart **13.2** on page 378. Say: *We can use auxiliary verbs with* but *to show contrast.* Go over the examples and explanations. Point out the position of the comma.

3. Explain that in conversation, we don't usually use *but* when one person says the opposite of another person. Ask students to go through the reading and underline all the statements with *but* and an auxiliary verb.

EXERCISE 3

ANSWERS: 1. doesn't; **2.** does; **3.** doesn't; **4.** didn't; **5.** isn't; **6.** is; **7.** can't

5-10
mins

1. Have students read the direction line. Say: *Don't forget to put the auxiliary verb in the same tense as the main verb.* Go over the example in the book.

2. Have students complete Exercise 3 individually. Remind them to review grammar chart **13.2** on page 378 if necessary. Have students compare answers in pairs. Quickly go over the answers as a class.

EXERCISE 4

Answers will vary.

1. Say: *Now you're going to compare countries.* Have students read the direction line. Go over the examples in the book. Have volunteers model the examples.

2. Have students complete the exercise individually. Remind them to review grammar charts **13.1** on page 377 and **13.2** on page 378 if necessary. Then have students compare work in pairs. Monitor pair work. Give help as needed. Have some students share their answers with the class.

Practice Idea: Writing

Have students write about towns and cities in their countries or regions. If possible, have students from the same country or region work together.

EXERCISE 5

Answers will vary.

1. Have students read the direction line. Go over the example in the book. Have volunteers model #1.

2. Have students complete the chart individually. Remind them to review grammar charts **13.1** on page 377 and **13.2** on page 378 if necessary. Then have them exchange books and write statements about themselves and their partners.

Practice Idea: Speaking

For an extra challenge, have students ask and answer questions (*Do you speak Spanish? Yes, I do.*) instead of exchanging books. Then have students make statements about themselves and their partners.

**CD 2
TR 28**
EXERCISE 6

ANSWERS: 1. does; **2.** doesn't; **3.** does too; **4.** would too; **5.** either; **6.** does

1. Have students read the direction line. Tell them this is a conversation between two friends. Go over the example in the book. Point out the photo of men moving furniture.

2. Have students complete Exercise 6 individually. Remind them to review grammar charts **13.1** on page 377 and **13.2** on page 378 if necessary. Then play the audio and check answers as a class.

Practice Idea: Listening

To provide practice with listening skills, have students close their books and listen to the audio. Ask comprehension questions, such as: *What is person A doing on Saturday?* (moving) *What is person B's brother doing on Saturday?* (working) *Can person B help person A move?* (yes) Then have students open their books and complete Exercise 6.

Practice Idea: Speaking

Have students practice the conversation in pairs. Then ask volunteers to act out the conversation for the class.

13.3 Tag Questions

1. Have students cover up grammar chart **13.3** on page 381. Ask students questions using tags (e.g., *It's cold outside, isn't it? This is a big room, isn't it?*). Ask: *Does anyone know what those little questions I'm putting on the end are called?* (tag questions) Say: *We use tag questions to ask if a statement is correct or if a listener agrees with you.*

2. Have students look at grammar chart **13.3**. Go over the examples and explanations. Point out that the verb in the tag question is in the same tense as the main verb.

Saturday with Meg and Don READING

1. Have students look at the photo. Say: *Compare this photo to the photo on page 376. What is different? What might they be talking about?*

2. Have students look at the title of the reading. Ask: *What is the reading about?* Have students make predictions.

3. Preteach any vocabulary words your students may not know.

BEFORE YOU READ

5-10 mins

1. Have students discuss the questions in pairs.

2. Ask for a few volunteers to share their answers with the class.

Reading

CD 2
TR 29

10-15 mins

1. Have students first read the text silently. Tell them to pay special attention to tag questions. Then play the audio and have students read along silently.

2. Check students' comprehension. Ask questions such as: *Why doesn't Don want to go to the movies?* (He's tired.) *What kind of activities do they do on the weekends?* (They usually do chores such as cleaning and shopping. They don't do anything fun.) *Is Meg happy?* (Yes, but she wants to spend more "quality time" with Don.)

Practice Idea: Listening

To practice listening skills, have students first listen to the audio alone. Ask a few comprehension questions such as: *Does Meg want to see a movie?* (yes) *Why don't Don and Meg eat the fish Don catches?* (because they don't have time to cook). Then have students open their books and read along as they listen to the audio.

13.4 Auxiliary Verbs in Tag Questions

10-15 mins

1. Have students cover up grammar chart **13.4** on pages 382–383. Tell students to look at the reading on pages 381–382. Say: *Underline*

negative tag questions and circle affirmative tag questions. Ask: *How do you form the tag question after an affirmative statement?* (auxiliary verb + *not* + subject pronoun) *How do you form the tag question after a negative statement?* (auxiliary verb + subject pronoun) Point out that a comma separates the statement and tag question.

2. Write the following sentences from the grammar chart on the board: *There isn't a lot of free time, is there? This is a typical marriage, isn't it? These are normal problems, aren't they?*

   Say: *Study these sentences. What does each sentence begin with? How is each tag question formed?* Elicit the answers: *If the sentence begins with* there is *or* there are, *what do we use in the tag?* (*there*) *If the sentence begins with* this *or* that, *what do we use in the tag?* (*it*) *If the sentence begins with* these *or* those, *what do we use in the tag?* (*they*)

3. Have students look at grammar chart **13.4**. Go through the examples and explanations. On the board, review how to make contractions in negative tag questions.

4. Explain that *Am I not?* is very formal. For more informal occasions, use *Aren't I?*

EXERCISE 7

ANSWERS: 1. aren't you? **2.** can't you? **3.** won't we? **4.** shouldn't we? **5.** isn't there? **6.** wouldn't you? **7.** isn't it? **8.** aren't I? (OR am I not?)

5-10 mins

1. Have students read the direction line. Go over the example in the book. Ask: *If the main clause is affirmative, what tense will the tag question be in?* (negative)

2. Have students complete Exercise 7 individually. Remind them to review grammar chart **13.4** on pages 382–383 if necessary. Go over the answers as a class.

EXERCISE 8 =★

ANSWERS: 1. are you? **2.** can she? **3.** should we? **4.** were you? **5.** are there? **6.** is it?

5-10 mins

1. Have students read the direction line. Go over the example in the book. Ask: *If the main clause is negative, what tense will the tag question be in?* (affirmative)

2. Have students complete Exercise 8 individually. Remind them to review grammar chart **13.4** on pages 382–383 if necessary. Then have students compare answers in pairs. Monitor pair work. Give help as needed.

EXERCISE 9

ANSWERS: **1.** doesn't it? **2.** don't you? **3.** didn't you? **4.** don't you? **5.** didn't they? **6.** didn't we?

5-10 mins

1. Have students read the direction line. Ask: *If the main verb is not a modal or the verb* be, *what auxiliary verb do we use in the tag?* (do/ did) Go over the example.

2. Have students complete Exercise 9 individually. Remind them to review grammar chart **13.4** on pages 382–383 if necessary. Then have students compare answers in pairs. Circulate to give help as needed.

EXERCISE 10

ANSWERS: **1.** does she? **2.** did he? **3.** did you? **4.** do we? **5.** do I? **6.** does she?

5-10 mins

1. Have students read the direction line. Go over the example. Remind students that the statements are negative. Ask: *If the main verb is negative, what will the auxiliary verb be?* (affirmative)

2. Have students complete Exercise 10 individually. Remind them to review grammar chart **13.4** on pages 382–383 if necessary. Then have students compare answers in pairs. Monitor pair work. Give help as needed.

EXERCISE 11

CD 2
TR 30

ANSWERS: **1.** weren't we? **2.** didn't we? **3.** didn't she? **4.** isn't it? **5.** didn't you? **6.** didn't you? **7.** didn't she? **8.** didn't you?

10-15 mins

1. Have students read the direction line. Say: *Remember, the auxiliary verb should be in the same tense as the main verb and if the main verb is negative, the auxiliary verb should be affirmative.* Explain that this is a conversation between two acquaintances, Bob and Sam,

and that Sam can't remember where he met Bob. Go over the example in the book.

2. Have students complete Exercise 11 individually. Remind them to review grammar chart **13.4** on pages 382–383 if necessary. Then play the audio and check answers as a class.

Practice Idea: Listening

To provide practice with listening skills, have students close their books and listen to the audio. Ask comprehension questions, such as: *Does Sam remember Bob's name?* (no) *Does he remember Bob's face?* (yes) *Did they meet in math class?* (no) Then have students open their books and complete Exercise 11.

Practice Idea: Speaking

Have students practice the conversation in pairs. Ask volunteers to role-play all or part of the conversation in front of the class.

EXERCISE 12

ANSWERS: **1.** can't you? **2.** aren't there? **3.** do you? **4.** won't they?

10-15 mins

1. Have students read the direction line. Explain that in this conversation, a mother is talking to her daughter. Go over the example.

2. Have students complete Exercise 12 individually. Remind them to review grammar chart **13.4** on pages 382–383 if necessary. Then check answers as a class.

Practice Idea: Speaking

Have students practice the conversation in pairs. Ask volunteers to role-play all or part of the conversation in front of the class.

13.5 Answering a Tag Question

5-10 mins

1. Have students cover up the explanations side of grammar chart **13.5** on page 386. Say: *Study the tag questions and the short answers. Do you see any patterns?* Have students try to figure out the patterns.

2. Have students look at grammar chart **13.5**. Have them look at the explanations. Go over all the examples. Explain that answering *no* or *yes* to tag questions can get a little confusing even for native speakers. Often a second sentence is needed to clarify a response.

EXERCISE 13

ANSWERS: 1. I'm not., Person B isn't married. **2.** I don't., Person B doesn't like this city. **3.** I do., Person B has a watch. **4.** I don't., Person B doesn't speak Russian. **5.** I can't., Person B can't drive. **6.** it isn't., Person B doesn't agree with this statement. **7.** I do., Person B works on Saturday.

10-15 mins

1. Have students read the direction line. Say: *First complete the short answers on the left side. Then work with a partner to decide the meaning of the short answer.* Go over the example.

2. Have students complete Exercise 13. Remind them to review grammar chart **13.5** on page 386 if necessary. Go over answers with the class. Then have students take turns asking and answering the questions.

Practice Idea: Speaking

Have students clarify their answers with another sentence. For example: *You don't have a car, do you? Yes, I do. I have a minivan.*

EXERCISE 14

ANSWERS: 1. aren't you? **2.** don't you? **3.** did you? **4.** don't you? **5.** do you? **6.** won't you? **7.** will you? **8.** didn't you? **9.** don't you? **10.** does she (OR he)? **11.** can't you? **12.** is it? **13.** wasn't there? **14.** do you? **15.** aren't I (OR am I not)?

10-15 mins

1. Have students read the direction line. Say: *If your answer is negative, then add the correct information.* Go over the examples. Have students model the examples.

2. Have students complete the tag questions individually. Remind them to review grammar chart **13.5** on page 386 if necessary. Then have students ask and answer questions in pairs. Monitor pair work. Give help as needed.

Practice Idea: Speaking

Have students create five more statements with tag questions to ask their partners. Then have students take turns asking and answering their new questions.

EXERCISE 15

ANSWERS: 1. No, I don't; **2.** don't they? **3.** No, they don't; **4.** is it? **5.** No, it isn't; **6.** don't you? **7.** Yes, I do; **8.** are they? **9.** Yes, they are; **10.** didn't you? **11.** No, I didn't; **12.** are you? **13.** No, I'm not

10-15 mins

1. Say: *In this conversation, you will be writing tag questions and giving short answers.* Have students read the direction line. Go over the example in the book.

2. Have students complete Exercise 15 individually. Remind them to review grammar chart **13.5** on page 386 if necessary. Then check answers as a class.

Practice Idea: Speaking

Have students practice the conversation in pairs. Then ask volunteers to act out the conversation for the class.

CD 2 TR 31
EXERCISE 16

ANSWERS: 1. Yes; **2.** is; **3.** aren't I (OR am I not); **4.** yes; **5.** are; **6.** aren't you; **7.** I'm not; **8.** wasn't it; **9.** do you; **10.** No; **11.** don't; **12.** are you;

13. No, we aren't (OR No, I'm not); **14.** isn't it; **15.** Yes; **16.** is; **17.** is it; **18.** didn't you; **19.** Yes; **20.** did; **21.** aren't there; **22.** wasn't I

10-15 mins

1. Say: *This conversation is between Meg, the woman from the reading, and her best friend, Lydia.* Have students read the direction line. Go over the example in the book.

2. Have students complete Exercise 16 individually. Remind them to review grammar chart **13.5** on page 386 if necessary. Then play the audio and check answers as a class.

Practice Idea: Listening

To provide practice with listening skills, have students close their books and listen to the audio. Ask comprehension questions, such as: *Where's Don?* (at home) *What's he doing?* (watching TV) *Who is Peter?* (Lydia's new boyfriend) Then have students open their books and complete Exercise 16 on page 388.

Practice Idea: Speaking

Have students practice the conversation in pairs. Then ask volunteers to act out the conversation for the class.

Summary of Lesson 13

20-30 mins

1. **Use auxiliary verbs to avoid repetition of the same verb phrase.** Have students cover the chart in the Summary on page 390. On the board, create an exercise from the Summary chart. Have students fill in the blanks.

   Affirmative + too

   Meg has a job, and Don _____.

   Meg is busy, and Don _____.

   Negative + either

   Meg doesn't work on Saturdays, and Don _____.

   Meg can't find free time, and Don _____.

Negative

Meg finished college, but Don _____.

Don likes fishing, but Meg _____.

Affirmative

Don doesn't like movies, but Meg _____.

Don didn't want a big wedding, but Meg _____.

Then have students compare their answers with the Summary. If necessary, have students review:

- **13.1** Auxiliary Verbs with *Too* and *Either* (p. 377)
- **13.2** Auxiliary Verbs with Opposite Statements (p. 378)

2. **Use auxiliary verbs in tag questions.** Have students cover the chart in the Summary. On the board, create an exercise from the Summary chart. Have students fill in the blanks.

   Negative Tag

   You're busy now, _____?

   We have a hard life, _____?

   There are a lot of things to do, _____?

   Affirmative Tag

   You don't like fishing, _____?

   I can't go fishing alone, _____?

   We never have time together, _____?

   Then have students compare their answers with the Summary. If necessary, have students review:

   - **13.3** Tag Questions (p. 381)
   - **13.4** Auxiliary Verbs in Tag Questions (pp. 382–383)
   - **13.5** Answering a Tag Question (p. 386)

Editing Advice

10-15 mins

Have students close their books. Write the first few sentences without editing marks or corrections on the board. For example:

1. *My brother has a new house, and I too.*
   John didn't take the test, and I either.

Ask students to correct each sentence and provide a rule or explanation for each correction. This activity can be done individually, in pairs, or as a class. After students have corrected each sentence, tell them to turn to page 391. Say: *Now compare your work with the Editing Advice in the book.*

Editing Quiz

ANSWERS: 1. do; **2.** don't; **3.** C; **4.** do we; **5.** No; **6.** isn't; **7.** is; **8.** C; **9.** don't either; **10.** did too; **11.** C

10-15 mins

1. Tell students they are going to put the editing advice into practice. Have students read the direction line. Ask: *Do all the shaded words and phrases have mistakes?* (no) Go over the examples with the class. Then do #1 together.

2. Have students complete the quiz individually. Then have them compare answers with a partner before checking answers as a class.

3. For the items students had difficulties with, have them go back and find the relevant grammar chart and review it. Monitor and give help as necessary.

Lesson 13 Test/Review

30-40 mins

Use the Assessment CD-ROM with Exam*View®*, Online Workbook, and Web site for additional practice, review, and assessment materials.

PART 1

ANSWERS: 1. do too; **2.** don't; **3.** does; **4.** don't; **5.** does too; **6.** doesn't either; **7.** would; **8.** did too

1. Part 1 may be used in addition to the Assessment CD-ROM with Exam*View®* as an in-class test to assess student performance. Have students read the direction line. Point out that this is a conversation between two students who are meeting for the first time. Go over the examples with the class. Say: *Remember, not every sentence needs* too *or* either.

2. Have students complete Part 1 individually. Collect for assessment.

3. If necessary, have students review:
   13.1 Auxiliary Verbs with *Too* and *Either* (p. 377)
   13.2 Auxiliary Verbs with Opposite Statements (p. 378)

PART 2

ANSWERS: 1. isn't she? **2.** does she? **3.** won't we? **4.** don't we? **5.** can we? **6.** aren't you? **7.** is it? **8.** shouldn't I? **9.** do you?

1. Part 2 may be used in addition to the Assessment CD-ROM with Exam*View®* as an in-class test to assess student performance. Have students read the direction line. Point out that in this conversation a new student is trying to find out information about the school and class. Go over the example with the class.

2. Have students complete Part 2 individually. Collect for assessment.

3. If necessary, have students review:
   13.3 Tag Questions (p. 381)
   13.4 Auxiliary Verbs in Tag Questions (pp. 382–383)
   13.5 Answering a Tag Question (p. 386)

Expansion

These expansion activities provide opportunities for students to interact with one another and further develop their speaking and writing skills. Encourage students to use grammar from this lesson whenever possible.

CLASSROOM ACTIVITIES

10-15 mins per activity

1. Have students work individually to complete the information. Then put students in pairs to take turns asking and answering questions.

2. Model the activity. Have a student call out the first statement. Then stand up and make a statement as if the statement were true for you.

3. Tell students to find a partner they don't know very well. Have volunteers tell the class something new they learned about their partners.

4. Have students work with a partner to write six to ten statements with tag questions on what they think they know about the U.S. and Americans. Respond to the questions in front of the class.

TALK ABOUT IT

15-20 mins

Write on the board: *What makes a good marriage?* Write students' ideas on the board. Then have students discuss each question in pairs. Then have them report back to the class.

WRITE ABOUT IT

20-30 mins

Have students read the direction line and the model paragraph. Have them help you choose two things from the list to compare. Have them brainstorm ideas for the comparison and write them on the board. Then have them help you begin a paragraph on the board. Have students write their own comparisons individually. Students can choose any of the topics in the book, or they can write a comparison about another topic that interests them. Encourage students to brainstorm a list of ideas for comparing before they begin writing. Collect for assessment and/or have students present their paragraphs to the class.

Practice Idea: Writing

Have students exchange first drafts with a partner. Ask students to help their partners edit their drafts. Refer students to the Editing Advice on page 391.

INTERNET ACTIVITY

Tell students to find a Web site that gives marriage, dating, or relationship advice. Have them bring an article to class and discuss the advice in groups. Then have groups report to the class.

Lesson 14

Lesson Overview

GRAMMAR

1. Ask: *What did we study in Lesson 13?* (auxiliary verbs with *too* and *either*; auxiliary verbs in tag questions)

2. *What are we going to study in this lesson?* (all the verb tenses) *Do you remember all the tenses we've learned?* (simple present tense, present continuous tense, future tense, simple past tense) Have students give examples. Write them on the board.

CONTEXT

1. Ask: *What are we going to learn about in this lesson?* (Washington interns) *How many people here have ever worked as an intern? Where?*

2. Have students share their knowledge and personal experiences.

Presentation Idea

The topic for this lesson can be enhanced with the following ideas:

1. Advertisements seeking Washington interns
2. Articles about being an intern
3. Ask students to talk about government internships in their countries. Does this type of work exist in their countries? Are they paid or voluntary positions?

Context Note

There are three branches of the U.S. government: the executive (the president), the legislative (Congress), and the judicial (the Supreme Court). The first Supreme Court was assembled in 1790. The principal role of the Supreme Court is to act as the final authority on the U.S. Constitution. U.S. justices are appointed for life. There have only been 16 chief justices in American history. Compare that with more than 40 U.S. presidents!

Washington Interns READING

1. Have students look at the title of the reading. Ask: *What is the reading about?* Have students make predictions about the reading.

2. Preteach any vocabulary words your students may not know, such as *gain* and *manage*.

Reading Glossary

gain: to obtain, acquire
manage: to run something, be in charge of something

BEFORE YOU READ

 5-10 mins

1. Have students discuss the questions in pairs.
2. Ask for a few volunteers to share their answers with the class.

 Reading ≡★

 CD 2 TR 32

10-15 mins

1. Have students first read the text silently. Tell them to pay special attention to verb tenses. Then play the audio and have students read along silently.

2. Check students' comprehension. Ask questions such as: *Do interns get paid?* (no) *Why is it a good idea for Lena to intern at the Supreme Court?* (She's going to law school next year.) *How did she feel at first?* (lost and lonely) *What else is she doing?* (taking classes at Georgetown University) *Who does she share an apartment with?* (Nicole. She works at the Department of Education.) *What is something she doesn't like about her job?* (wearing formal clothes) *How did she pay for her work clothes?* (She used her parents' credit card.)

Practice Idea: Listening

To practice listening skills, have students first listen to the audio alone. Ask a few comprehension questions such as: *Where is Lena working as an intern?* (the Supreme Court) *How does Lena meet people?* (through her classes and her job) *Is Lena making any money?* (no). Then have students open their books and read along as they listen to the audio.

14.1 Verbs =

10-15 mins

1. Have students cover up grammar chart **14.1** on pages 402–403. Write on the board:

   simple present tense
   present continuous tense
   future tense
   simple past tense
   be
   modals
   infinitives
   imperatives

   Say: *Find two examples for each in the reading.* Have volunteers write example sentences under each category on the board.

2. Have students look at grammar chart **14.1**. Go over the examples and explanations in the chart.

EXERCISE 1 =★

ANSWERS: 1. 'm working; **2.** 'm gaining; **3.** go; **4.** 'll have; **5.** apply; **6.** will look; **7.** felt; **8.** didn't know; **9.** changed; **10.** meet (OR 'm meeting); **11.** take (OR 'm taking); **12.** are; **13.** 'm learning; **14.** is increasing; **15.** have; **16.** is (OR 's); **17.** works; **18.** become; **19.** have; **20.** shop; **21.** make; **22.** 'm learning; **23.** 'm becoming; **24.** have; **25.** go; **26.** have; **27.** go; **28.** have; **29.** wear; **30.** look; **31.** didn't have; **32.** arrived; **33.** went; **34.** spent; **35.** don't mind; **36.** put; **37.** know; **38.** 'm not making; **39.** worry; **40.** won't spend; **41.** get; **42.** 'll tell; **43.** know; **44.** write; **45.** don't have

15-20 mins

1. Have students read the direction line. Go over the example in the book. Say: *This exercise is based on the reading on pages 398–399. Check your work after you complete the exercise.*

2. Have students complete Exercise 1 individually. Then, in pairs, have students check their answers against the reading on pages 398–399.

3. As students check their answers, circulate around the room to see if there are any common trouble spots. Review those points with the whole class.

14.2 Statements and Questions =★

20-30 mins

1. Have students close their books and work in pairs to write statements and questions using the tenses and verbs in the chart. For the simple present tense, write the following on the board:

   simple present tense (live/wear)

   Say: *Write the following for the simple present tense:*

   1. *an affirmative statement*
   2. *a negative statement*
   3. *a question*
   4. *a short answer*
   5. *a wh- question*
   6. *a negative question*
   7. *a subject question*

   Tell students to write seven sentences with the *-s* form and seven sentences with the base form. Say: *Use the verbs in parentheses.* Ask a volunteer to give an example of an *-s* form and a base form in a sentence. Monitor pair work. Give help as needed.

2. For the present continuous tense, write on the board:

   present continuous tense (plan/take)

   Tell students to use one of the verbs in parentheses to write the seven sentence types using *is*, and the other verb to write another seven sentences using *are*.

3. For the future tense, write on the board:

   future tense (go/buy)

   Tell students to use one of the verbs in parentheses to write the seven sentence types using *will*, and the other verb to write another seven sentences using *be going to*.

4. For the simple past tense, write on the board: *simple past tense (use/buy)*

Tell students to write the seven sentence types using *use* (regular verb), and another seven sentences using *buy* (irregular verb).

5. For the verb *be*, have students write the seven sentence types using the simple present form of *be*, and another seven sentences using the simple past form of *be*.

6. For the modals, write on the board: *modals (can/should)*. Tell students to write the seven sentence types using *can*, and another seven sentences using *should*.

7. Then have students look at grammar chart **14.2** on pages 405–406. Say: *Check your work against the chart*. Go over the examples and explanations. Find out where students had difficulty and provide a more thorough review of that grammar point.

EXERCISE 2

ANSWERS: **1.** isn't getting; **2.** didn't buy; **3.** doesn't write; **4.** won't finish; **5.** isn't going to return; **6.** can't wear; **7.** must not look

5-10 mins

1. Have students read the direction line. Tell students that this exercise is about Lena. Go over the example in the book.

2. Have students complete Exercise 2 individually. Then have students check answers in pairs. Monitor pair work. Give help as needed.

3. As students check their answers in pairs, circulate around the room to see if there are any common trouble spots. Review those points with the whole class.

EXERCISE 3 ★

ANSWERS: **1.** Do interns have to take classes? **2.** Do they (OR interns) live in dorms? **3.** Are they busy? **4.** Will they receive college credit? **5.** Can Lena wear jeans to work? **6.** Is she learning how to cook? **7.** Did she know anyone when she arrived in Washington? **8.** Does she work at the Supreme Court? **9.** Did she buy some new clothes?

10-15 mins

1. Have students read the direction line. Go over the examples in the book. Ask: *What kind of questions do we write here?* (yes/no questions)

2. Have students complete Exercise 3 individually. Then have students check answers in pairs. Monitor pair work. Give help as needed.

3. As students check their answers in pairs, circulate around the room to see if there are any common trouble spots. Review those points with the whole class.

Practice Idea: Speaking

Have students practice asking and answering questions from Exercise 3 in pairs.

EXERCISE 4

ANSWERS: **1.** will she go home? **2.** doesn't her mother remember the roommate's name? **3.** can't Lena (OR she) go home for a weekend? **4.** does Lena (OR she) have? **5.** is she learning? **6.** doesn't she have time to write letters? **7.** did she go to Virginia? **8.** does Nicole (OR she) come; **9.** didn't Lena (OR she) cook (before this summer)? **10.** went to Virginia? **11.** will the internship (OR it) help Lena (in the future)? **12.** is she working? **13.** did she feel lonely? **14.** can't she wear jeans to work? **15.** must she take? **16.** is she going to get? **17.** should she call her parents (OR them)?

15-20 mins

1. Have students read the direction line. Point out that they are writing *wh-* questions. Go over the example in the book.

2. Have students complete Exercise 4 individually. Then have students check answers in pairs. Monitor pair work. Give help as needed.

3. As students check their answers in pairs, circulate around the room to see if there are any common trouble spots. Review those points with the whole class.

<table>
<tr><td>

Practice Idea: Speaking

Have students practice asking and answering questions from Exercise 4 in pairs.

 EXERCISE 5

CD 2
TR 33

ANSWERS: 1. hear; **2.** never call; **3.** don't have; **4.** don't you have; **5.** went; **6.** drove; **7.** used; **8.** Are you getting; **9.** cooks; **10.** 'm learning; **11.** cook; **12.** Are you; **13.** cooked; **14.** hated; **15.** cook; **16.** invite; **17.** 's; **18.** told; **19.** Don't you remember; **20.** remember; **21.** comes; **22.** is your job; **23.** Do you like; **24.** 'm learning; **25.** Will this internship help; **26.** Do you have; **27.** spent; **28.** gave; **29.** can use; **30.** miss; **31.** Can you come; **32.** 'll pay; **33.** have; **34.** Will you call; **35.** have; **36.** 'll call; **37.** have; **38.** 'll call

15-20 mins

1. Have students read the direction line. Explain that this is a phone conversation between Lena and her mother. Lena is calling from Washington. Go over the example in the book.

2. Have students complete Exercise 5 individually. Then have students compare answers in small groups. Play the audio and check answers as a class.

3. Review any common trouble spots with the whole class.

Practice Idea: Listening

To provide practice with listening skills, have students close their books and listen to the audio. Repeat the audio as needed. Ask comprehension questions, such as: *Why is Lena's mother happy?* (because Lena called) *Does Lena write often?* (no) *Why doesn't Lena have time?* (She has to work, go to classes, and participate in activities all day.) Then have students open their books and complete Exercise 5.

</td><td>

Practice Idea: Speaking

Have students practice the conversation in pairs. Then ask volunteers to act out the conversation for the class.

Editing Advice

 Have students close their books. Write the first few sentences without editing marks or corrections on the board. For example:

15-20 mins

1. *Where does work your brother?*

   Why you can't find a job?

   How old your brother is?

Ask students to correct each sentence and provide a rule or explanation for each correction. This activity can be done individually, in pairs, or as a class. After students have corrected each sentence, tell them to turn to pages 411–413. Say: *Now compare your work with the Editing Advice in the book.*

Editing Quiz

ANSWERS: 1. don't live; **2.** don't you; **3.** C; **4.** used; **5.** found; **6.** moved; **7.** did you move; **8.** C; **9.** have (OR had); **10.** didn't realize; **11.** I'm lonely; **12.** calls; **13.** C; **14.** I know; **15.** C; **16.** C; **17.** does your family live; **18.** They're; **19.** want to visit; **20.** save; **21.** C; **22.** have; **23.** I'll have; **24.** will they stay; **25.** can stay; **26.** dad is still working; **27.** C; **28.** C; **29.** to talk; **30.** C; **31.** does a phone card cost; **32.** costs; **33.** C; **34.** prefer to save

 1. Tell students they are going to put the editing advice into practice. Have students read the direction line. Ask: *Do all the shaded words and phrases have mistakes?* (no) Go over the examples with the class. Then do #1 together.

10-15 mins

2. Have students complete the quiz individually. Then have them compare answers with a partner before checking answers as a class.

3. Have students find and review the relevant grammar chart for items they had difficulties with. Monitor and give help as necessary.

</td></tr>
</table>

Lesson 14 Test/Review

60-80 mins Use the Assessment CD-ROM with Exam*View*®, Online Workbook, and Web site for additional practice, review, and assessment materials.

PART 1

ANSWERS: 1. decided to move; **2.** to leave; **3.** wanted to come; **4.** lived; **5.** came; **6.** didn't find (OR couldn't find); **7.** found; **8.** want to find; **9.** 'll get ('m going to get); **10.** speak; **11.** 'm saving; **12.** have; **13.** 'll begin to take; **14.** will be (OR are going to be); **15.** graduate; **16.** 'm taking; **17.** studied; **18.** can't understand; **19.** speak; **20.** don't understand; **21.** laugh; **22.** don't understand; **23.** to learn; **24.** stay; **25.** know; **26.** should practice; **27.** was; **28.** lived; **29.** have; **30.** am; **31.** to get; **32.** to earn; **33.** save

1. Part 1 may be used in addition to the Assessment CD-ROM with Exam*View*® as an in-class test to assess student performance. Have students read the direction line. Ask: *What do you write on the line?* (the correct tense or form of the verb in parentheses) Go over the example with the class.

2. Have students complete Part 1 individually. Collect for assessment.

3. If necessary, have students review Lesson 14.

PART 2

ANSWERS: 1. didn't study; **2.** doesn't want to work; **3.** isn't going to study; **4.** isn't taking; **5.** isn't saving; **6.** don't know; **7.** shouldn't; **8.** can't understand

1. Part 2 may also be used in addition to the Assessment CD-ROM with Exam*View*® as an in-class test to assess student performance. Have students read the direction line. Ask: *Which form of the underlined words do you write?* (the negative) Go over the example with the class.

2. Have students complete Part 2 individually. Collect for assessment.

3. If necessary, have students review Lesson 14.

PART 3

ANSWERS: 1. Will he study accounting? No, he won't. **2.** Do Indians understand him? Yes, they do. **3.** Is he studying American English? Yes, he is. **4.** Does he live with his family? No, he doesn't. **5.** Can he understand American English (well)? No, he can't. **6.** Is it hard to live in another country? Yes, it is. **7.** Does he want to get married next year? No, he doesn't. **8.** Did he live with his grandparents in India? Yes, he did.

1. Part 3 may also be used in addition to the Assessment CD-ROM with Exam*View*® as an in-class test to assess student performance. Have students read the direction line. Ask: *What do you write on the line?* (a yes/no question and a short answer) Go over the example with the class.

2. Have students complete Part 3 individually. Collect for assessment.

3. If necessary, have students review Lesson 14.

PART 4

ANSWERS: 1. Why is he saving his money? **2.** When is he going to get married? **3.** Who laughs at him? **4.** Why is he lonely? **5.** Why aren't his parents (OR they) in the U.S.? **6.** Why didn't he find a job at first? **7.** When will he graduate from the university? **8.** Why did he come to the U.S. alone? **9.** Why don't his coworkers (OR they) understand his accent? **10.** When did he live in a big house?

1. Part 4 may also be used in addition to the Assessment CD-ROM with Exam*View*® as an in-class test to assess student performance. Have students read the direction line. Ask: *What do you write on the line?* (a wh- question) *Do you write an answer?* (no) Go over the example with the class.

2. Have students complete Part 4 individually. Collect for assessment.

3. If necessary, have students review Lesson 14.

Expansion

These expansion activities provide opportunities for students to interact with one another and further develop their speaking and writing skills. Encourage students to use grammar from this lesson whenever possible.

CLASSROOM ACTIVITIES

10-15 mins per activity

1. Have students interview each other in the class. If everyone or nearly everyone in your class is from the same country, have them interview people from outside the class. Have students write out the questions before the interview if necessary.

2. Have students fill out the charts individually with sentences about themselves. Then put students in pairs to compare charts.

TALK ABOUT IT

15-20 mins

Write on the board: *getting a job.* Elicit ideas about what you need to do, or have, to get a job. Write the students' ideas on the board. Then have students discuss each question in pairs or groups. Have them report back to the class.

WRITE ABOUT IT

20-30 mins

Have students read the direction line and the model paragraph. Have them help you begin a paragraph about yourself on the board. Then have students write their own paragraphs individually. Collect for assessment and/or have students present their paragraphs to a group.

Practice Idea: Writing

Have students exchange first drafts with a partner. Ask students to help their partners edit their drafts. Refer students to the Editing Advice on pages 411–413.

OUTSIDE ACTIVITY

Tell students they are going to interview a native speaker of English at this school. Tell them they will practice the simple present, the present continuous, the future, and the simple past tenses. Give them the following list and have them use these prompts for their questions. Explain that the words in parentheses are for follow-up questions after a *yes/no* question. Go over the example and #1 with them to help them form the questions correctly.

EXAMPLE

you have a car (what kind)

A: Do you have a car?
B: Yes, I do.
A: What kind of car do you have?
B: I have a Honda.

1. you / study another language now (what language)
2. you / live alone (who ... with)
3. your family / live in this city
4. you / like this city (why / why not)
5. you / go to high school in this city (where)
6. what / your major
7. you / graduate soon (when)
8. what / you do / after / you / graduate
9. you / like to travel (when ... your last vacation) (where ... go)
10. you / own a computer (what kind) (when ... buy it)
11. you / eat in a restaurant / last week (where)
12. you / buy something new / in the near future (what)
13. you / do something interesting / last weekend (what ... do)
14. you / plan to do something interesting / next weekend (what ... do)

Have students report something interesting to the class about the person they interview. Ask students to make a poster of their interview with the native speaker. If possible, have students include a picture of the person interviewed.

INTERNET ACTIVITY

Tell students to use a search engine and look up "Washington internship" on the Internet. Have them find out what some students say about their experience as an intern. Have students discuss any interesting information they found on Web sites in groups. Then have groups report to the class.